THE RUSSIAN
CONSTITUTIONAL EXPERIMENT

Soviet and East European Studies

Editorial Board

Soviet and East European Studies

BOOKS IN THIS SERIES

THE RUSSIAN
CONSTITUTIONAL EXPERIMENT
Government and Duma, 1907-1914

GEOFFREY A. HOSKING
Department of History, University of Essex

CAMBRIDGE
AT THE UNIVERSITY PRESS
1973

Published by the Syndics of the Cambridge University Press
Bentley House, 200 Euston Road, London NW1 2DB
American Branch: 32 East 57th Street, New York, N.Y. 10022

Library of Congress Catalogue Card Number: 72-871181

ISBN: 0 521 20041 5

Printed in Great Britain
at Aberdeen University Press
Aberdeen

Contents

Acknowledgement

The author gratefully acknowledges permission from the editors of the *Slavonic & East European Review* to reproduce material originally contained in his article 'Stolypin and the Octobrist Party', published in vol 47 (1969), pp 137-60.

Preface

Revolutions are precipitated as much by the old regime as by the revolutionaries, a fact which Lenin himself was not slow to appreciate. In the analysis of a revolutionary situation he considered the 'crisis of the élites' (*krizis verkhov*) as important as the unity and determination of the masses. This book grew out of reflection on the 'crisis of the élites' which came to a head in Russia in February 1917, when the monarchy was deserted by all the élites of the old society, the landowners, the army officers, the industrialists, and the politicians of the Duma. Scarcely twelve years before, Nicholas II had granted a constitution to appease the moderates, and less than ten years before had altered the electoral law to assure the government a loyal parliament with which to undertake reform. Yet these efforts were in vain: not only the revolutionaries, but also the normally loyal and moderate elements of society, turned on him in the midst of war and overthrew him and his government.

Most general histories of Russia pay a good deal of attention to the brief and meteoric career of the first two Dumas. Yet the more I read on the subject, the more it seemed to me that these first two Dumas, dominated by the radicals and revolutionaries, were not a serious test of the constitutional system introduced in 1905-6. The vital assembly, as it seemed to me, was the Third Duma, tailor-made by a new electoral law and genuinely anxious to work with the government for constructive change. It was in this house that the government had a genuine chance to achieve a stable working relationship with moderate public opinion. This book is an attempt to trace the course of that relationship, and to explain why it failed (as I believe it did) even before the outbreak of the First World War. The problem is an important one, since, if what I maintain is true, then there are really no grounds for supposing that the Tsarist system could ever have made a constitutional order work or could have achieved the peaceful modernisation of Russia.

The question that I have tackled, then, is a fairly ambitious one.

But my approach is quite narrow: it is strictly focussed on the relationship between the government and the Duma majority parties. I have little to say about the socialist parties, and not too much even about the Kadets: that is because they were not usually important to this relationship. Likewise, I have not dealt with most of the legislation debated in the Duma, or the questions raised there, confining myself to those issues which affected substantially the relations between the government and the house.

The system of transliteration I have adopted corresponds closely to that regularly used by the *Slavic Review*. I have tried in the text to avoid awkwardnesses such as 'yi', 'ii' and apostrophes in the middle of words, which to the eye of the English reader are disturbing. On the other hand, in the footnotes and bibliography I have given the form most likely to be found by the user of a library catalogue. I hope this compromise will be acceptable and convenient. Dates throughout are in Old Style, except as noted in Chapter 8.

I owe thanks to many people for the progress of this investigation from its original conception through the stage of doctoral thesis to that of published book. Dr N. E. Andreyev provided much-needed advice and encouragement in the early stages of the work. Professor E. D. Chermensky, of Moscow University, and Dr A. Ya. Avrekh, of the U.S.S.R. Institute of History, both helped to guide me through the complexities of Soviet archival sources. The staffs of the Central State Archive of the October Revolution in Moscow, and of the Central State Historical Archive in Leningrad, afforded me their expert assistance. Professor Leopold Haimson read over both the thesis and the typescript of the present book, and offered invaluable comments, as well as the benefit of his wider research into the social problems of the period. The Department of Education and Science, the British Council and the University of Essex have all at various times financed research time and study trips. Lastly, my wife, Anne, bore cheerfully most of the burdens of a long summer and autumn while this final text was being prepared.

Needless to say, I alone am responsible for all errors of fact and judgment.

G. A. H.

February 1972

Abbreviations

ASEER	*American Slavonic and East European Review*
GDSO	*Gosudarstvennaya Duma, Stenograficheskie Otchety*
GM	*Golos Moskvy*
GSSO	*Gosudarstvennyi Sovet, Stenograficheskie Otchety*
Ist. SSSR	*Istoriya SSSR*
Ist. Zap.	*Istoricheskie Zapiski*
JGO	*Jahrbücher für Geschichte Osteuropas*
JMH	*Journal of Modern History*
KA	*Krasnyi Arkhiv*
L	Leningrad
M	Moscow
NV	*Novoe Vremya*
PSZ	*Polnoe Sobranie Zakonov*
SEER	*Slavonic and East European Review*
SPB	St Petersburg
SR	*Slavic Review*
TsGAOR	*Tsentral'nyi Gosudarstvennyi Arkhiv Oktyabr'skoi Revolyutsii*
TsGIAL	*Tsentral'nyi Gosudarstvennyi Istoricheskii Arkhiv v Leningrade*
Vop. Ist.	*Voprosy Istorii*

1

The ambiguous constitution

The Russian constitutional experiment has to be viewed against the background of centuries of autocracy. Nowhere in the world at the beginning of the twentieth century, save only perhaps Imperial China, had autocracy still such a mystique. Autocracy was the force which from the nucleus of the Muscovite duchy had united the lands of Russia, and had since defended them against both internal rebellion and foreign incursion. Furthermore, Russia had always lacked the social and political institutions in defence of which constitutionalism, in the sense of a permanent legal curb on state power, was born in Western Europe. It has often been remarked that Russia never experienced the European Renaissance. Even more serious, perhaps, in her history there was no high Middle Ages, the period when Europe west of the Elbe gave birth to parliaments, provincial estates, municipalities, universities and independent law courts, institutions which formed an integral part of medieval society, yet also pointed beyond it, to modern civil society. Russia lacked the institution of Roman law, which postulated an absolute individual right of property, and also laid the basis for the notion of natural law as an indispensable ground for political sovereignty. Above all, perhaps, Russia lacked the Catholic church, independent of the state, sometimes in conflict with it, and bearing witness to a world of laws and obligations higher than those of the state.

Thus in Russia the state was always the dominant social institution, and the only alternative to this domination was usually held to be anarchy and dissolution. The autocracy created and sustained all other social institutions (in the eighteenth century it even managed to make the church a department of the bureaucracy): privilege and status came to men not by virtue of inherited standing or signal achievement, but through service to the state. In the nineteenth century, contrary to the situation in both Western and Central Europe, autocracy was, if anything, reinforced. Nicholas I,

Alexander III and Nicholas II explicitly endorsed it as the guarantee of Russia's physical strength and moral probity against the false glamour of Western Europe. Alexander II modified the structure considerably, but in the end he paid for his audacity at the hands of the revolutionaries. His son and grandson understandably concluded that it was dangerous to be a reforming Tsar, and began their reigns by reaffirming the exclusive rectitude of autocracy.

Of course, autocracy did not mean that the Emperor decided everything for himself. He delegated most of his authority, and always consulted his leading advisers and officials. But what was not generally accepted was that he should consult the social groups or local elements that would be affected by any proposed measure. In part, this was because of the weakness of the internal organisation of the various groups of Russian society. Only the nobility (*dvoryanstvo*) had a stable tradition of local organisation, and even they rarely concerned themselves with political issues on a national scale. Alexander II, however, had changed this situation through the reforms with which he tried to remodel Russian society after the disaster of the Crimean War. He created zemstvos and municipal councils, local government bodies elected by the people, which required teachers, doctors, agronomists, lawyers and other professional men to staff them. He created law courts on a European pattern, which needed barristers and other legal officials. He passed army reforms which created a new, properly trained professional officer class. His educational reforms gave new freedoms to the universities and widened the network of secondary schools. In all these changes, undertaken for the advancement of Russian society and the maintenance of the Empire's position as one of the Great Powers of Europe, the autocracy was helping to create and disseminate throughout the country a new class of professional men, educated in Western modes of thought and fascinated by the political life of Britain, France and the United States. A culture which had hitherto been concentrated largely in St Petersburg and Moscow, and in the nobility, now began to take roots throughout the provinces, and in other social classes.

These were the processes which heralded the end of the general acceptance of autocracy in Russia. But other changes helped to prepare for the upheaval in which autocracy was actually overthrown. The growth of rural population in the second half of the nineteenth century was aggravated by an official fiscal policy which might have been purposely designed to prevent the improvement of agricultural methods or the emigration of land-hungry peasants to the towns or overseas. It gave rise to a perpetual danger of famine and to rural discontent which broke out into active rebellion in 1902 in the provinces of Poltava and Kharkov, and thereafter in other areas of the country. The huge industrial growth of the 1880s and 1890s led to the concentration of an unsettled working class in the big cities, aided the dissemination of revolutionary socialist propaganda, and provoked national as well as class warfare among the variegated peoples of the Empire.

In fact, what happened in 1905 was a sign, not of the ' decline ' of Tsarist Russia, but of its energetic expansion into new fields. The trouble is, the ways in which Russian society developed were often mutually conflicting. The 1905 revolution was a kind of explosion. Social discontent burst out in a variety of diverse and unco-ordinated forms. Sedate professional men passed subversive resolutions, factory workers went on strike and formed revolutionary assemblies, peasants seized crops and animals, burned hayricks and manor-houses, sailors mutinied against their officers, students used university lecture halls for wild and noisy political meetings. The whole country seethed with a multitude of dissatisfactions, and nobody, either in the government or in the revolutionary movement, could gain an overall view or knew what was likely to happen next.

It is not surprising, then, that the constitutional monarchy which emerged from this turmoil carried within itself the marks of the complex and violent conflict of which it was born. The new state structure was created at a time when the fortunes of government and revolutionaries swung unpredictably from day to day, and it absorbed the uncertainties, the compromises and semi-retractions attendant upon its birth. Since the time of Nicholas I, and especially in the reigns of Alexander III and Nicholas II, the words ' autocracy ' and ' constitution ' had become an obsession. Nicholas II spoke of ' groundless dreams ' and Pobedonostsev warned of the fatal demoralising influence of the Western European ' talking-shops ', while the zemstvos, and increasingly the associations of professional men, urged that a ' roof be put on the edifice ', in other words, that the elective principle applied in local government be extended to the central government by the creation of a parliament. So powerful was this obsession that it may be said to have diverted the attention of both sides from growing social problems and from demands which the masses, from lack of organisation, were unable to articulate.

The government's gravest weakness in 1905 was that it did not have the reliable support of any section of public opinion. The nobility was divided, and men of conservative views were only gradually seeing the need to organise. The moderate non-revolutionaries, in the Union of Liberation and the zemstvo constitutionalist movement, were as much against the government as the workers or peasants seemed to be.

It was from this need to end the alienation of even moderate elements of public opinion that the constitution grew. In so far as any one man was its author, that man was Witte. Svyatopolk-Mirsky, Minister of the Interior in the autumn of 1904, had (with Witte's help) seen and expressed the need for social reform;[1] and his successor, Bulygin, had drawn up plans for a purely consultative parliament, elected on a fairly limited suffrage.[2] But it was Witte who, in the paralysing crisis of the general strike of October 1905, grasped the essential factor in the government's danger, and expressed it to Nicholas in a forceful memorandum:

The collisions with the police and army, the bombs, the strikes, the events in the Caucasus, the disorders in the institutes of learning, the agrarian upheavals, and so on, are important not so much in themselves as by virtue of their impact on the mature and balanced strata of society, who do not take serious action against them. Extreme political views exist always and everywhere. Excesses can cause the state great

[1] In the Ukaz of 12 December 1904, published on the advice of Svyatopolk-Mirsky, then Minister of the Interior, the Emperor promised reform in the fields of local government, justice, the welfare of the factory workers, emergency legislation, religious toleration, the nationalities question and press censorship. The English text is in S. Harcave, *First Blood: the Russian Revolution of 1905,* London 1965, pp 282-5. Witte, as Chairman of the Committee of Ministers, participated in the drafting of Svyatopolk-Mirsky's proposals: see T. H. von Laue, 'Count Witte and the Russian Revolution of 1905 ', *ASEER,* vol 17 (1958), p 29.

[2] Legislation of 6 August 1905, drawn up under the Minister of the Interior, Bulygin, provided for a consultative parliament 'to provide preliminary consideration and discussion of legislative proposals ', to be elected on a limited franchise which would exclude most non-Russians and many less wealthy townsfolk (F. I. Kalinychev, *Gosudarstvennaya Duma v Rossii: Dokumenty i Materialy,* M 1957, pp 30-54).

damage: but it is not on the extremists that the existence and integrity of the state depend. As long as the government has support in the broad strata of society, a peaceful solution to the crisis is still possible. That indispensable support is slipping away from the government. The law of 6 August has scarcely affected the attitude of society. It came too late, and was not accompanied by the change in the governmental system which the proclaimed reform directly entails. Since the 18 February[3] events, on the one hand, and the whirlpool of revolutionary thought, on the other, have carried the ideals of society much further. One cannot close one's eyes to this.[4]

' The government ', he asserted, ' has no choice: it must boldy and openly take over the leadership of the liberation movement.[5] The idea of civil liberty does not in any way threaten the state's existence. On the contrary, consistently applied in legislation and in life, it guarantees the state's existence in the most certain way, binding the citizens consciously – with a genuine bond.'[6]

In this private memorandum (though not in his subsequent published report) Witte challenged the long-held taboos of autocratic Russia by proposing that the Emperor should openly and explicitly grant a constitution:

This word should not cause panic and be prohibited. The government should openly and sincerely strive for the good of the state, and not for the preservation of one or another of its forms. If it is shown that the good of the state lies in a constitution – then the autocratic monarch, whose interests cannot be separated from his people's welfare, will without doubt take that path.[7]

As Witte saw it, the government's most urgent task was to gain the support and co-operation of those moderate elements of public opinion which still regarded the government with such suspicion.

[3] The date when the Tsar had published a rescript to Bulygin instructing him to submit proposals for the establishment of a State Duma.
[4] Witte's memorandum to the Tsar of 9 October 1905, *KA*, vol 11, p. 53.
[5] The liberation movement, centred around the émigré journal *Osvobozh-denie* (Liberation), was an organisation of zemstvo deputies and professional men calling for a constitution.   [6] *KA*, vol 11, p 56.
[7] ibid, p 57. According to the Soviet historian E. D. Chermenskii, Witte had been in touch with the radical liberals, then on the point of forming the Constitutional Democratic party, and had taken much of his memorandum from a draft by the lawyer V. D. Kuz'min-Karavaev (E. D. Chermenskii, 'Russkaya Burzhuaziya osen'yu 1905g ', *Vop. Ist.*, 1966, no 6, p 63).

To win that social backing, he recommended that Bulygin's parliamentary proposals be much extended. The new Duma should be given full legislative powers, including that of vetoing all legislation of which it disapproved; its franchise should be broadened to include all or most inhabitants of the Empire; and the government should guarantee the civil liberties of all subjects. To Witte these were the indispensable prerequisites of social support, and he told the Emperor that the alternative to them was a military dictatorship.

No less important a change was that which Witte proposed in the field of governmental organisation. If the public was going to irrupt into the field of legislative authority, then the Ministers needed to join together in a more cohesive body. Witte wanted the establishment of a Council of Ministers, or cabinet, with a formally appointed President, who would both in theory and in practice be a Prime Minister. In the past, except in the crisis periods of 1861 and 1880-1, there had never been a regularly working cabinet with a first Minister at its head. The Emperor chose his own ministers, received their reports privately, and only summoned them together in committee informally and for the settlement of individual issues. Consequently, especially in the 1890s and early 1900s, the conduct of government often suffered from the unco-ordinated and sometimes even mutually antagonistic policies of different ministries.[8] In the crisis of 1905 Witte (and others) argued vehemently that a properly organised cabinet was needed to co-ordinate the struggle against the revolutionary movement and to plan the large-scale reforms demanded by the emergency. Some top officials disapproved of the idea: the new Prime Minister, they maintained, would become a kind of Grand Vizier, and would encroach on the prerogatives of the Emperor. They insinuated that Witte was trying to make himself into a dictator, or was even building himself up to become the President of a future Russian Republic.[9]

[8] N. P. Eroshkin, *Ocherki Istorii Gosudarstvennykh Uchrezhdenii Dorevolyutsionnoi Rossii*, 2nd, revised edition, M 1968, pp 154, 205-6; E. Amburger, *Geschichte der Behördenorganisation Russlands von Peter dem Grossen bis 1917*, Leiden 1966, pp 125-6; V. I. Gurko, *Features and Figures of the Past: Government and Opinion in the Reign of Nicholas II*, Stanford 1939, pp 31-2.

[9] Among those who objected to the idea of a Prime Minister were Ignat'yev, Lobko and Stishinsky (*TsGIAL*, f 1276 (Council of Ministers), dd 1-2; K. N. Mironenko, 'Sovet Ministrov po Ukazu 19-ogo oktyabrya 1905g', *Uchenye Zapiski Leningradskogo Gosudarstvennogo Universiteta*

Witte's proposal envisaged a Council of Ministers which would settle its differences internally: Ministers would be bound by decisions once taken there. Ministers who did not accept those decisions would have to resign. The President of the Council would further be responsible for nominating new Ministers to the Emperor.[10] In effect, then, the Emperor would lose a lot of his influence over ministerial appointment and decision-making, and would take a large step towards what might be termed the British model of monarchy. Nicholas accepted Witte's proposal and, as expected, appointed Witte the first chairman of the new body.

In spite of the clarity and firmness of his arguments, Witte was not wholly unambivalent about the changes he was proposing. He had been a lifelong believer in autocracy, and remained one at heart; but he had no respect for Nicholas II as an autocrat, and felt that because of the Emperor's own mistakes, the country had been plunged into a revolution which made the continuation of autocracy impossible. He took a certain malicious pleasure in Nicholas's discomfiture, and Nicholas retained the suspicion that Witte was somehow tricking him.

Nicholas himself, of course, has gone down to history as a weak and vacillating figure, a good family man, but not fit to occupy the throne of the Tsar of all the Russias. This is partly, but not wholly, just. Part of the explanation for Nicholas's changes of policy and for his hesitations lies in objective circumstances, which were indeed both difficult and confused. The whole of his upbringing and education had inculcated in him the sense of being alone answerable to God for the conduct of affairs in the Empire entrusted to his charge. Others might advise him or execute his commands, but he alone, he felt, was *responsible* in the eyes of God. Hence he tended to regard the establishment of a Duma, or of a Council of Ministers as being on his part a dereliction of duty. His wife reinforced these scruples by constantly reminding him that he was to pass on his autocratic powers unimpaired to his son and heir. And in any case, was not

---

(Seriya Yuridicheskikh Nauk), vol 1 (1948), pp 354-6; ibid, pp 357-8; *Dnevnik A.A. Polovrtseva, KA,* vol 4, p 76). Such insinuations were later used against both Stolypin and Kokovtsev: they were powerful arguments in an era of transition from autocracy to constitutionalism, especially when the Emperor was as divided in his own mind as was Nicholas II.
[10] *KA*, vol 4, p 65.

a ' constitution' something foreign, characteristic of the decadent money-grubbing, libertarian West? Courtiers and, later, monarchist political parties did not fail to exploit these questionings of his conscience.

When Witte put before him the choice between a constitution and a military dictatorship, Nicholas consulted the Grand Duke Nikolai Nikolaievich (who might have headed such as dictatorship) and the Governor-General of St Petersburg, D. F. Trepov. Both independently warned him that repressive measures could not be relied upon to restore order, and Trepov remarked that, as the Prussian example showed, constitutions could be useful for maintaining order and authority.[11]

So Nicholas adopted Witte's advice. But he resolved that, if he were to take the agonising decision to renounce his autocratic powers, he would do so in a public gesture of magnanimity, in a Manifesto which might reconcile his troubled subjects and pacify his realm. Witte had simply wanted his memorandum of 9 October confirmed, fearing that a public Manifesto would arouse exaggerated hopes and fears. Nicholas, however, issued his Manifesto, on 17 October 1905. He was disappointed if he hoped for quick results: only ten days later he wrote to his mother: ' It is strange that such a clever man [Witte] should be wrong in his forecast of an early pacification.' The Manifesto did indeed introduce a new era in Russia, but it could not and did not simply end the revolution. Indeed, its immediate effect was to increase public disorder. Though Nicholas was a man sorely buffeted by events, he always tried to convince himself of the correctness and indeed profound significance of every step he had taken as Emperor. For that reason, after 17 October his instincts were in painful conflict over the Manifesto he had himself signed. He wanted to believe that what he had granted he could also take away. This was to be a major leitmotiv in Russia's constitutional politics.

The Manifesto of 17 October announced the Emperor's resolution to establish a unified government, and also (i) to grant the full range of civil freedoms, (ii) to broaden the Duma electoral law,

<hr/>

[11] Memorandum of N. I. Vuich, secretary to the Committee of Ministers, *KA,* vol 11, p 66; *The Letters of Tsar Nicholas and Empress Marie* (ed E. J. Bing), London 1937, pp 177-8; ' Vsepoddanneishaya Zapiska D. F. Trepova ', *Byloe,* no 14 (1919), pp 110-11; S. Yu. Vitte, *Vospominaniya,* M 1960 edition, vol 3, pp 10-47.

and (iii) to make it an unalterable rule that no law should take effect without the Duma's consent, and that the people's representatives should participate in verifying the legality of the acts of government officials.[12]

Whilst it made these promises, the Manifesto did not indicate how they would be carried out, nor did it give them legislative effect. The promise to widen the franchise was fulfilled in the electoral law of 11 December 1905, which, though it retained certain restrictions and continued the system of indirect voting, did give peasants, workers, poorer urban dwellers, and non-Russian nationalities considerable representation in the Duma.[13] Witte at this time was capable of believing (though he did not consistently) that the peasants would prove reliable bearers of the Russian state idea. Special conferences also took place in the months after October 1905 to draft the statutes of the new Duma, of the reformed State Council (which was to be the upper house of the new legislature), and the Fundamental Laws.

The Emperor's ambivalence (and Witte's inconsistencies) expressed themselves very clearly at these conferences. The most delicate discussion was that on the nature of the supreme power, as it would be defined in the Fundamental Laws. During the conference at Tsarskoe Selo in April 1906, the Emperor received numerous telegrams from monarchist organisations all over the country urging him to stand firm and not to have the word ' autocratic ' expunged from the Fundamental Laws.[14] These appeals touched a chord in his heart, and he expatiated at length on his dilemma:

I have not ceased to ponder this question ever since I first looked at the draft of the new Fundamental Laws. For a whole month I have kept the draft by me, and have continued to think constantly about the question even after the President of the Council of Ministers reported to me on the altered draft. All that time I have been tormented by the question, have I the right before my ancestors to change the confines of the power which I inherited from them? The struggle continues within me. I have not yet come to a final conclusion. . . . The act of 17 October I granted quite consciously, and I have firmly resolved to carry it through to fulfilment. But I am not convinced that

[12] *Letters of Tsar Nicholas and Empress Marie,* p 191.
[13] The full text, in English, is in Harcave, *First Blood,* pp 195-6.
[14] N. S. Tagantsev, *Perezhitoe,* Petrograd 1919, p 86.

it is necessary in doing that to renounce my autocratic rights, and to change the definition of the Supreme Power which has stood in Article 1 of the Fundamental Laws for 109 years. It is my conviction that for many reasons it is extremely dangerous to change that article and to accept its reformulation . . .

I know that if Article 1 remains unchanged, that will cause discontent and criticisms. But one must consider from what quarter the reproaches will come. They will, of course, come from the so-called educated element, the proletariat, and the third *soslovie*. But I am convinced that 80 per cent of the Russian people will be with me, will give me support, and will be grateful to me for such a decision.[16]

He wanted, in fact, to have both autocracy and the October Manifesto. On this occasion, however, even Akimov, the Minister of Justice, a man of stern conservative views, insisted that the Emperor had bound himself by the October Manifesto to limit his powers: ' I am not a supporter of freedoms granted to the people. But on 17 October Your Highness voluntarily placed limits on your legislative power; it remains in your power only to veto resolutions of the Duma and State Council of which you disapprove. Where legislative power does not belong fully to the Emperor, there monarchy is limited.[16]

A compromise was reached. The word ' autocratic ' was retained, but the accompanying epithet, ' unlimited ', was removed. Now, although in the fifteenth century the word ' autocratic ' had meant no more than ' sovereign ', in the sense of owing no allegiance to any outside power, legal opinion seemed to concur that it could not be held in the twentieth century to carry this meaning.[17] Thus the Fundamental Laws were ambiguous in defining the powers of the head of state.

Nor was this the only ambiguity the Fundamental Laws contained. The articles concerning command of the armed forces and emergency legislation were also to cause problems, because they likewise raised issues which were bound to be sensitive in the transition from autocratic to constitutional politics.

In the case of the armed forces, one of the problems was that, while the Emperor retained supreme command of them, their

[15] *Byloe*, 1917, no 4, pp 192-3.   [16] ibid, pp 206-7.
[17] See the discussions in N. I. Lazarevskii, *Russkoe Gosudarstvennoe Pravo*, SPB 1913, vol 1, pp 197-203; P. Chasles, *Le Parlement Russe*, Paris 1910, pp 148-58; O. Palme, *Die Russische Verfassung*, Berlin 1910, pp 95-7.

organisation often required new expenditure which had to be approved by the legislative chambers. And while Article 14 gave the Emperor power to order ' anything concerning the organisation of the armed forces and the defence of the Russian state ', Article 96 attempted a closer definition of his powers, deferring to him, in consultation with the War and Admiralty Councils, legislative authority in the combat (*stroevoi*), technical and supply spheres of military life, as well as the power to issue decrees and instructions in so far as they did not affect the general legislation of the Empire and did not require fresh expenditure. In either of the latter eventualities, they had to come before the Duma and State Council as well. The mixture of rather precise definitions of the Emperor's military powers with all-inclusive general statements was to cause confusion later on.

Article 87, concerning emergency legislation, was not in itself ambiguous, and was a necessary part of the Fundamental Laws, but offered the means by which autocracy might be reasserted against a recalcitrant legislature. It gave the Council of Ministers the right, if an emergency arose when the chambers were not sitting, to put before the Emperor laws for immediate enactment. Such measures were not to concern the Fundamental Laws, the Statutes of the Duma or the State Council (or the electoral laws which were part of them), and they were to become invalid if not brought before the legislature within two months of its resuming sittings or if rejected by the Duma or State Council. The government was in practice frequently to use this article for legislation it was not sure the chambers would accept.[18]

The position of the State Council also occasioned some confusion and resentment. The October Manifesto did not mention it (though the accompanying memorandum did), and it seems to have been widely assumed by the public that it would simply be abolished and that the Duma alone would share the Emperor's legislative responsibilities. The promulgation, on 20 February 1906, of revised Statutes for the State Council came as a surprise to the public, and was widely interpreted as evidence of new reactionary determination on the part of the government.[19] What was most repugnant to liberal opinion was that the State Council should receive the full status

[18] Kalinychev, *Gosudarstvennaya Duma v Rossii*, pp 141-7.
[19] P. N. Milyukov, *Vospominaniya (1859-1917)*, New York 1955, vol 1, pp 362-3.

of an upper chamber, enjoying equal legislative rights with the Duma. In actual fact, this point had been closely discussed at the conference. Kutler (then Minister of Agriculture[20]) had proposed that if the State Council reject a bill which had passed the Duma, the bill should be returned to the Duma, and on passing that house again by a two-thirds majority be submitted straight to the Emperor for confirmation. The proposal was turned down on the grounds that it would detract from the legislative status of the State Council and place the Emperor in the invidious position of having to adjudicate between the two chambers. In keeping with its new functions, the reformed State Council was to consist at least half of members elected by the zemstvos, nobility and other established institutions of the Empire; the other half was to be appointed by the crown. It was expressly seen as a conservative institution, representing the continuity of the state system in an era of rapid change. And indeed, it was in practice destined to be a powerful bastion for those who wished to prevent such change.[21]

Overall, then, there were important ambiguities and loopholes in the Fundamental Laws and the other legislation which defined the new state system. These were significant less for themselves than as a symptom of uncertainty about the location of power. In seeking, through new state institutions, the support and co-operation of educated society, the government was beginning the transition from autocracy to the more complicated politics of constitutionalism. In such a transition period uncertainty about the location of authority is inevitable; but when the transition is also a period of explosive social conflict, disputes about the nature of authority are dangerous and deeply challenging to the beliefs and allegiances of all political groups involved.

Thus, even independently of express ambiguities, the October Manifesto and its accompanying legislation held different meanings for the different people concerned with their operation. And these difficulties were to obstruct the main aim which Witte had set before the government in pressing for the adoption of a constitution:

---

[20] I use this term throughout as a convenient and substantially correct abbreviation of the Russian title Chief Administrator of Land-Organisation and Agriculture.

[21] Kalinychev, *Gosudarstvennaya Duma v Rossii*, pp 105-14; Chasles, *Le Parlement Russe*, pp 108-34.

co-operation with moderate opinion in the country. The story of this attempted co-operation is largely the story of the 3rd June system. But, before turning to it, it remains to consider why the government failed to achieve anything in this direction with the first two Dumas.

2

The foundations of the 3rd June system

The liberals and the first two Dumas

What was this 'moderate public opinion', these 'mature and balanced strata of society', with which Witte hoped to work? And what forces did they represent?

With the granting of the October Manifesto, the Russian liberals were in a triumphant yet bewildered mood. Their old centres of agitation, the zemstvo congresses, the Union of Liberation, the Union of Unions, had at one and the same time achieved a kind of victory and also rendered themselves obsolete. New formations were taking their place, political parties, the first ever to operate in Russia outside the world of conspiracy.

Even as the general strike of October 1905 was at its height, the first of these parties, the Constitutional Democrats (universally known, for short, as the Kadets[1]) was holding its foundation congress. The delegates represented the majority both of the professional and of the zemstvo-constitutionalist movements. The new party demanded a national legislative assembly, elected by universal, equal, direct and secret suffrage,[2] to which the government would be responsible; in their speeches, many members actually called for a Constituent Assembly, but this provocative term was kept out of the congress resolution.[3] Among the other reforms demanded were the proper legislative guarantee of all civil rights, the compulsory expropriation, with compensation, of private land necessary to ease land-hunger, and the restoration of constitutional autonomy to Poland and Finland.[4] The October Manifesto was published right in the middle of the congress, but after initial

---

[1] At their Second Congress, in January 1906, they tried to democratise their image by giving themselves the name of '*Partiya Narodnoi Svobody*' (Party of the People's Freedom). But the new title never caught on: they were always constitutionalists rather than democrats. And the convenient term 'Kadets' stuck.   [2] The so-called 'four-tail' formula.

[3] E. D. Chermenskii, *Burzhuaziya i Tsarizm v Pervoi Russkoi Revolyutsii*, 2nd, revised edition, M 1970, p 158.

[4] V. V. Vodovozov, *Sbornik Programm Politicheskikh Partii v Rossii*, SPB 1905-6, vol 1, pp 40-9.

rejoicing a sceptical mood prevailed. Milyukov, widely regarded as the leading figure in the new party, proclaimed 'Nothing has changed, the struggle continues ',[5] and the party issued a declaration reaffirming its devotion to the principle that a Constituent Assembly (the word was directly used here), elected by all the people, would decide on the new state system. The declaration also demanded an amnesty for all ' so-called political and religious offences '.[6]

Nevertheless, in the longer term, the fact that the October Manifesto had been issued, together with the perils represented by the St Petersburg Soviet and the Moscow December uprising, did prove a sobering force. In January 1906, at its second congress, the party dropped the demand for a Constituent Assembly, and simply stated ' Russia should be a constitutional and parliamentary monarchy.'[7] The Kadet party, in other words, was at its inception both steaming along under the impetus of what George Fischer, following Schumpeter, has called ' the radicalism of impotence ',[8] and yet also trying to change gear and assume the more moderate pose dictated by the possibility of political responsibility. This duality was to persist until a cold douche was administered by the deafening silence following the Vyborg Appeal.[9] It made the Kadets prickly and unreliable negotiators in the early months of the constitutional era. Ambivalence, in fact, dogged the political parties no less than the autocracy.

The moderate wing of Russian liberal opinion was slower in forming itself into an organised party. Its core consisted of those members of the zemstvo congress movement who had not felt able to follow their nimbler colleagues in the heady summer of 1905, and who were now in October completely satisfied by the Emperor's concessions. Their first public statement was an appeal issued on 10 November 1905. It called upon those who ' reject both stagnation and revolution upheavals ' to ' rally together round the principles proclaimed in the Manifesto of 17 October ', and ' to co-operate

[5] According to V. A. Maklakov, *Vlast' i Obshchestvennost' na Zakate Staroi Rossii*, Paris 1936, vol 3, p 431; Milyukov, in his recollections of the occasion, transcribes his words in less dramatic form, but the purport is the same (Milyukov, *Vospominaniya*, vol 1, p 311).

[6] Vodovozov, *Sbornik Programm Politicheskikh Partii*, vol 1, pp 49-54.

[7] ibid, vol 3, p 11.

[8] G. Fischer, *Russian Liberalism: from Gentry to Intelligentsia*, Cambridge, Mass., 1958, p 202.   [9] see below, p 21.

with the government in its path of salutary reforms aimed at a complete reconstruction of every branch of the state and social structure of Russia '.[10] Among the leading signatories were A. I. Guchkov, D. N. Shipov, Count P. A. Geiden and M. A. Stakhovich. Central Committees were set up in St Petersburg and Moscow, and in the following months individuals and groups who favoured a constitutional monarchical state structure, or who were repelled by the radicalism of the Kadets, came together to form the Union of 17 October. Its founding congress met in Moscow in February 1906. Its main differences from the Kadets were (i) that it unequivocally supported the notion of the constitutional monarchy and the Duma as already laid down in the October Manifesto, and rejected the idea of a Constituent Assembly, (ii) that it envisaged compulsory expropriation of private land only ' in cases of state necessity ', and (iii) that it valued the ' unity and indivisibility of the Russian state ' higher than autonomy for Poland or Finland.'[11]

Clearly the embryonic Octobrists were more to Witte's liking than the Kadets. Yet the efforts he made immediately after the October Manifesto to draw them into the government were not successful. One reason for this was that they themselves considered public opinion to be behind the Kadets. When Witte offered Shipov a ministerial portfolio, the latter replied that he belonged to the minority in the zemstvo movement and therefore could not promise to have public opinion on his side: he advised Witte to turn to the majority group in the movement.[12] Witte thereupon addressed himself to the bureau of the zemstvo congress movement, which referred him to the Kadets F. A. Golovin, F. F. Kokoshkin and Prince G. E. Lvov: these, in the spirit of extremism of the first Kadet congress, demanded the declaration of a political amnesty and the convening of a Constituent Assembly as conditions for participation in the government. Witte, of course, could not agree to any such demands.[13] So he tried his luck again with the moderate leaders Shipov, Guchkov, M. A. Stakhovich and Prince E. N. Trubetskoi. In his memoirs, Witte states that he was unsuccessful on this occasion because of his insistence on appointing P. N. Durnovo as Minister of the Interior: the four found him unacceptable as a

[10] Vodovozov, *Sbornik Programm Politicheskikh Partiĭ*, vol 2, pp 43-4.
[11] ibid, pp 42-55.
[12] D. N. Shipov, *Vospominaniya i Dumy o Perezhitom*, 1918, p 335.
[13] ibid, pp 338-9; Milyukov, *Vospominaniya*, vol 1, pp 320-1.

prospective colleague.[14] However, the letters of Stakhovich, Shipov
and rubetskoi to Witte, preserved in the Leningrad archives, give
a rather different picture. All three emphasised their agreement with
Witte's basic programme, but claimed that they could do more to
help him by remaining outside the government. Shipov maintained
that only a broad alliance of all elements in the zemstvo movement,
including its left wing, could ensure social support for the government during the transition to the new political system. Trubetskoi,
then still a Kadet, felt himself bound by the declarations of his party;
but his lack of confidence in them is demonstrated by his advice to
Witte not to ally his government too closely with any particular
party.[15] Even Milyukov, in a private conversation with Witte at
this time, advised him to begin by forming his ministry from the
bureaucracy, and then to gain the confidence of the public by
granting a full constitution – a copy of the Belgian or Bulgarian
constitution, if necessary.[16]

In general, the October Manifesto had suddenly plunged the
emergent political parties from the world of dreams into the world
of reality and responsibility. Once there, they started back before
the age-old abyss which had separated government and society, held
on to their dreams and did not venture to discredit themselves by
too close an association with the government. Nor was enthusiasm
on the government's side overwhelming: Nicholas was writing to
his mother commenting disapprovingly on Witte's ' habit of getting
in touch with certain extremists '.[17] Both sides retreated from one
another in disappointment and suspicion.

So Witte took all his Ministers from the bureaucracy. Preparing
for work with the new legislative institutions, his government drew
up a wide programme of social reforms. The central issue was the
peasant question. As a memorandum of the Council of Ministers,
of 24 January 1906, noted:

Among the major political and socio-economic problems posed by
Russian life, one unquestionably has paramount significance: that is

---

[14] Durnovo had a scandal in his past: he had once organised a fire in the
residence of the Spanish ambassador in order to take possession of some
letters belonging to a former mistress. He was also known as a man of
determined disposition and a convinced and efficient policeman.

[15] *TsGIAL*, f 1276, op 1, d 33, pp 1, 2, 6.

[16] Vitte, *Vospominaniya*, vol 3, pp 106-10.

[17] *Letters of Tsar Nicholas and Empress Marie,* ed Bing, p 191.

the peasant question. The whole legal structure of local life, and likewise the economic future of Russia depend to a greater or lesser extent on the successful solution of the peasant question in its two aspects, (i) legal and (ii) economic.[18]

Witte's social reform programme was not submitted to the Emperor till the day of his resignation, 23 April 1906. It developed the proposals of Svyatopolk-Mirsky and to a large extent determined the reform programme of Stolypin. It began with the proposal to end the peasant's 'estate segregation' (*soslovnaya obosoblennost*) and to give him full legal equality with all other citizens of the Empire, including the full right to own private property in land. This was the key reform, and it entailed far-reaching changes in other aspects of local life, though without the compulsory expropriation of privately held land which the Kadets and the socialists wanted and which for a time in 1905 seemed virtually unavoidable. The peasant, Witte argued, had to be given the right to leave the commune, claiming as his personal property the allotment land he held under communal tenure. The peasant's separate 'estate' institutions had to be abolished, in particular the cantonal (*volost*) administration and the cantonal court, to be replaced by local institutions open to and serving all groups of the population. The cantonal administrative bodies were to be replaced by zemstvos at the level of the canton, and the cantonal courts by Justices of the Peace; zemstvos and Justices would be elected by all classes of the population. Both these local reforms would satisfy long-held liberal aspirations. A rational programme of land organisation was envisaged, with the guidance of the Peasant Land Bank and local land committees. Other reforms to which Witte's programme gave prominence were factory laws, the establishment of a workers' insurance scheme, and the introduction of income and inheritance taxes.[19]

Witte was not, however, present to put his programme before the First Duma when it opened in April 1906. He was dismissed four days before that event. During his six months as premier he had become a bitter and unbalanced man as a result of his own inner conflicts and of his failure to find stable support from any side. It

---

[18] *TsGIAL*, f 1276, op 2, d 4, p 12. The peasant question will be examined in detail later in Chapter 3; for the moment, I shall confine myself to presenting as much of it as is necessary to understand the conflicts in the First and Second Dumas.   [19] ibid, pp 209-20.

may be, as von Laue suggests,[20] that he was no longer fit to bear the responsibility of leading the government. All the same, his successor, Goremykin, was plainly out of place in the innovating role of a semi-constitutional premier. He had for most of 1905 been an opponent of the growing bureaucratic consensus for allowing, and indeed encouraging, the peasant commune to break up; he was devoted to the old autocracy; and he had no programme of his own.[21]

The Kadets on the other hand, who had done extremely well in the elections to the First Duma, had a clear programme, and one that flatly disagreed with Witte's in a number of fields. Allying themselves with the large Labour (Trudovik) group, the Kadets drew up and passed through the Duma an Address to the Throne which demanded a ministry responsible to the Duma and enjoying its confidence, a general political amnesty, abolition of the death penalty, the ' four-tail ' formula for elections to the Duma, abolition of the State Council, legislative guarantee of full civil liberties, and the cumpulsory expropriation of some private lands in order to relieve land-hunger.[22] The last point was the most important, and the text of the Address was quite unequivocal:

The greater part of the population of the country, the toiling peasantry, awaits with impatience the satisfaction of its urgent need for land, and the First Russian State Duma would not be fulfilling its duty if it did not draw up a law for the satisfaction of that vital need by requisitioning to that end state, appanage, cabinet and monastery lands, and by the compulsory expropriation of privately owned lands.[23]

Goremykin called the Duma's demands in general ' inadmissible ', and declared on the agrarian question:

The state cannot recognise the right to property in land for some whilst depriving others of that right. Nor can the state deny at all the right

[20] *ASEER*, vol 17 (1958), p 44.
[21] M. S. Simonova, 'Agrarnaya Politika Samoderzhaviya v 1905g ', *Ist. Zap.*, vol 81, pp 199-215. *TsGIAL*, f 1276, op 2, d 4 contains the documents concerning the government's overall reform programme. There are numerous items for the periods of Witte's and subsequently Stolypin's premierships, but *not a single one* for Goremykin's period in office.
[22] N. I. Astrov (ed), *Zakonodatel'nye Proekty i Predlozheniya Partii Narodnoi Svobody, 1905-7gg*, SPB 1907, pp 370-4; A. A. Mukhanov and V. D. Nabokov (eds), *Pervaya Gosudarstvennaya Duma*, SPB 1907, vol 3, pp 37-53. The Trudoviki were Populist socialists who did not accept the Socialist Revolutionaries' boycott of the Duma.
[23] *GDSO*, I, vol 1, pp 239-41.

of private property in land without simultaneously denying the right
to all other kinds of property. The principle of the inalienability and
inviolability of property is throughout the world and at all stages of
the development of civil life the keystone of the people's welfare and of
social development, the foundation of the state's being, without which
the very existence of the state would be unthinkable.

In rejecting the Duma's proposals, Goremykin outlined a programme corresponding entirely with that which had been prepared by Witte's government and was to be taken over by Stolypin's.[24]

This head-on collision between government and Duma over fundamentals made the political situation extremely difficult. Goremykin
did not even present alternative food for thought, as Witte might
have done, and Stolypin later did, by putting some or all of the
government's reform programme before the Duma, in the hope of
provoking business-like discussion on less abstract issues. What the
government did do, however, in rather a mysterious and round-
about fashion, was to begin tentative negotiations with the Kadets
over the possibility of the formation of a ministry composed at least
partly of members of that party. There seem to have been two sets
of negotiations, one, probably unofficial, between D. F. Trepov and
Milyukov, the other, authorised by the Emperor, between Stolypin
and Izvolsky on the one hand and various Kadets (plus Shipov) on
the other. Goremykin did not take part in either. Trepov was
angling for a purely Kadet ministry (possibly in the hope that it
would be a sensational failure, and the whole Duma experiment
could then be abandoned with the appearance of right on the Emperor's side); Stolypin and Izvolsky envisaged a coalition ministry
composed partly of Kadets and partly of members of the existing
cabinet. At one or two points the wires got crossed, but the main
reason for the failure of both attempts was that the Kadets felt they
had the public behind them and could afford to go all out for what
they really believed in – a parliamentary monarchy on the British
model, and a radical solution to the land problem. Rather than
accept this, the government decided to risk the consequences of
dissolving the Duma.[25]

[24] ibid, pp 321-4.
[25] R. L. Tuck, 'Paul Milyukov and Negotiations for a Duma Ministry,
    1906 ', *ASEER*, vol 10 (1951), pp 117-29. The consequences might have
    been serious, for all anyone knew. Indeed there is some evidence that

On 20 June it invited a showdown by issuing a public declaration, warning the peasants against the Duma's promises of land, and repeating Goremykin's assertion that compulsory expropriation of private land was out of the question in a state which had any respect for property.[26] The Duma responded in kind on 6 July with an Appeal to the People, dissociating itself totally from the government's declaration and promising the people a law which would take away private land for the benefit of the land-hungry.[27] On 9 July the Duma was dissolved, and Goremykin was replaced as Prime Minister by Stolypin. Kadet and Labour members of the Duma reassembled at Vyborg, across the frontier in Finland. There they issued another Appeal to the People, calling on then to refuse to pay taxes or give military service. But they seem hardly to have been surprised when nobody took any notice of it. This was the last flash of the ' radicalism of impotence '.

The appointment of Stolypin was an imaginative one, and something of a new departure. Stolypin both was and was not a bureaucrat. He was, in that his experience immediately prior to taking over the Ministry of the Interior had been as governor of the notoriously rebellious Saratov province; he was not, in that he had spent most of

the government had been sounding Austria-Hungary on the possibility of the latter's intervention to help suppress peasant risings in the Ukraine – a kind of 1849 in reverse. In the semi-official newspaper *Rossiya* of 5 July 1906 appears a report that the German government had sounded Austria-Hungary on her attitude to the Russian revolution. There follows this enigmatic statement: ' Fully realising the significance which the Russian revolutionary movement in general, and the agrarian revolutionary movement in particular, has for the internal life of a friendly power bordering on Russia, ruling spheres in Vienna also admit that, in certain circumstances, active intervention of that power in the internal affairs of Russia, for the suppression or containment of that movement, might be desirable and useful.' The report emphasised that this would not be done without the express wish of the Russian government. This ' inspired ' article must be considered a warning to the public before dissolution. If there were indeed approaches to the Austro-Hungarian government, they must have been unofficial, probably through the State Controller, P. Kh. Schvanebakh, who was a close contact of the Austro-Hungarian ambassador in St Petersburg, Aerenthal. (See H. Heilbronner, 'Aerenthal in Defence of the Russian Autocracy ', *JGO*, vol 17 (1969), pp 380-96.)

[26] *GDSO*, I, vol 2, pp 1953-4.   [27] ibid, pp 1955-6.

his life as a landowner and Marshal of the Nobility[28] in the western provinces (where, however, Marshals of the Nobility were appointed by the government, not elected). He had come from his years there with strong convictions about the future of Russia, which were mainly based on his experiences of the agrarian and national problems. The western provinces (Lithuania, Belorussia and the Right-Bank Ukraine) were an area where both the hereditary (*podvornoe*) form of peasant commune and individual farming, on the *khutor* or *otrub*, were much commoner than in central Russia. In that sense they were a model for the policy of loosening the ties of the commune which had by the spring of 1906 become generally agreed in the government. Stolypin had always taken a particular interest in the peasant smallholding economy: as a founder member of the Kovno Agricultural Society, and as chairman of the Grodno provincial committee on the needs of agriculture, he had had ample occasion to observe the development of private farming and to encourage improvements in agricultural technique. And when he moved to Saratov, he reported that the dissolution of the commune and the easing of credit for smallholders would do much there as well to neutralise the threat of revolution in the province.[29] But the western provinces had another peculiar feature which helped to mould Stolypin's outlook on politics: this was the cohabitation of a number of nationalities in the area. For in the centuries during and after the Mongol domination in the heartlands of Russia, the Western Ukraine and Belorussia had been ruled by the Poles and Lithuanians. These influences had never entirely disappeared: for one thing they had given the Russian peasantry of the region a language and culture distinct from that of Great Russia, and they had left a large number of Poles and Lithuanians living in the region. The Poles were landowners, the Lithuanians peasants and townsfolk. In addition, there was a large Jewish population in the towns. The Russian landowners and administrators of the region were therefore very conscious of representing a nation, a language, a culture and a religion which were not universally accepted and had to some extent to be consciously implanted. Stolypin's 'Russianness' had an assertive and étatiste quality which came from his

[28] The Marshal of the Nobility (*predvoditel' dvoryanstva*) was the head of the local association of nobles in each province or district. In all but the western provinces (where the government was suspicious of the Polish *szlachta*) he was elected by his peers.   [29] *KA*, vol 17, pp 83-7.

roots in the western provinces. Not that this nationalism was entirely exclusive: one of Stolypin's early initiatives in government was a project for easing the disabilities of the Jews (the Emperor rejected it, following the 'voice of conscience ').[30] Indeed, his nationalism was closely allied to his concept of the social changes needed in the region: in his view, the establishment of a strong class of Russian smallholding peasantry would create a bulwark both for the new state system (the sturdy conservative peasantry of France was always before his eyes), and for the Russian nationality.[31]

Neither in his agrarian nor in his national ideals did Stolypin agree with the Kadets who had dominated the First Duma. That was why he was very pleased to see it dissolved, and had probably never been very serious about the negotiations for a ministry to include Kadets.[32] But his appointment did represent the triumph of that stream in the bureaucracy which accepted and wished to work with the Duma: less schizophrenically than Witte, he believed that the Duma would strengthen the monarchy in Russia. He was dubious about its electoral law, and he was less than doctrinaire in his observation of constitutional niceties, but he did see the Duma as a symbol of the co-operation between government and society which was necessary both for the repression of revolution and for fruitful reform.

Both repression and reform were important to him. A few days after coming to power, he sent a circular to all provincial governors ordering the relentless suppression of revolutionary activities, but at the same time insisting that:

The struggle is being waged not against society, but against the enemies of society. Therefore indiscriminate repression cannot be approved.

[30] Gurko, *Features and Figures of the Past*, pp 504-6; *KA*, vol 5, p 105.
[31] For an account of Stolypin's early life and his convictions, see especially A. S. Izgoev, *P. A. Stolypin*, M 1912, pp 5-24; N. A. Savickij, ' P. A. Stolypine ', *Le Monde Slave*, November 1933, pp 227-63. The best general appraisal of Stolypin as a statesman is A. Levin, ' Peter Arkad'evich Stolypin: a Political Re-appraisal ', *JMH*, vol 37 (1965), pp 445-63.
[32] Milyukov subsequently wrote: ' From the first words of my conversation with Stolypin I realised that he was talking to me, not in order to probe the essentials of the problem, but merely in order to carry out formally a duty which had been laid on him and at the same time to reinforce his own opinion of a Kadet ministry.' P. N. Milyukov, *Tri Popytki: k Istorii Russkogo Lzhekonstitutsionalizma*, Paris 1921, p 33.

Unconsidered and illegal actions, which generate resentment rather than pacification, are intolerable. The Emperor's intentions are unchanging. The government is therefore firmly resolved to expedite the legislative annulment or amendment of laws which are outdated or no longer fulfil their function. The old order will be renewed. In the meantime order must be fully preserved. In this matter you must take your own initiative and responsibility, for it lies with you.

A firm, strong government, acting as indicated above, will undoubtedly find support in the best part of society.[33]

A third, and last, attempt to draw ' the best part of society ' into the government did not, however, succeed. Stolypin held a number of conversations in mid-July 1906 with Shipov, Guchkov, Count P. A. Geiden, Prince G. E. Lvov, N. N. Lvov and A. F. Koni. He was prepared to make available a limited number of portfolios to them. They put to him the conditions they considered indispensable to the moderate liberals (to the right of the Kadets) at the time: a programme to ease land-hunger including ' in case of necessity ' compulsory expropriation of private land, suspension of the death penalty till the Duma could meet again, an amnesty for crimes committed in the liberation movement and not involving life or property, annulment of the operation of emergency decrees, and the immediate legislative fulfilment of the civil liberties promised in the October Manifesto. This was the most moderate set of demands which the government had yet met in its various attempts to draw members of the political parties into co-operation, but like the previous ones it was unacceptable. The Emperor remained suspicious of ' groups of people with some programme or other '.[34]

So the government carried on by itself. On 12 August the ' Maximalist ' wing of the Socialist Revolutionary party made an attempt on Stolypin's life, as a result of which his villa on Aptekarsky Ostrov, in the north of St Petersburg, was wrecked and large numbers of people, most of whom were waiting to see the Premier, were killed or wounded. Stolypin himself remained unhurt, but his son and daughter were seriously injured. The government replied with the Ukaz of 19 August, which gave Governors-General the right, where commission of a crime of revolutionary violence was ' so evident as not to require investigation ', to waive preliminary investigation and

---

[33] *TsGIAL*, f 1276, op 1, d 34, p 59.
[34] *TsGAOR*, f 601, op 1, d 1125, pp 59-60; Shipov, *Vospominaniya*, pp 461-84; A. F. Koni, *Sobranie Sochinenii*, vol 2, Moscow 1966, pp 360-76.

normal court procedure, and bring the accused before a military
field court, carrying out the sentence (usually death) immediately
after the verdict. This was an extremely harsh law for a country
which had a tradition of abhorrence to the death penalty; it renewed
the hostility and sense of moral outrage felt by the public, and of
course provoked Lev Tolstoy's famous pamphlet 'I cannot be
Silent' (written in May 1908).

At the same time Stolypin published his programme of promised
reforms, developing that which Witte had put before the Tsar on
the eve of his dismissal. And he began during the autumn to pass
items in the government's agrarian reform programme under Article
87, without waiting for the Duma. As Alfred Levin has commented,
'he expected co-operation from individuals and parliament, while
insisting on his own measures for reform '.[35]

In fact, the period between the First and Second Duma shows
both the strengths and the weaknesses of Stolypin as a statesman
for the new era. He was certainly a man of courage, eloquence and
personal integrity. He possessed a certain political vision, and even
if he took over his legislative programme from others, he assumed
personal responsibility for carrying it through, and he saw very
clearly the need for closer co-operation with the public in doing so.
Yet his staunch, unswerving character, which well fitted his role as
the suppressor of revolution and as leader of the government in a
period of crisis, was less suited to the actual task of bringing government and political parties into a closer relationship. He was a poor
judge of men,[36] and was thus not adept at handling the weapons
which have to constitute a major part of the armoury of the constitutional statesman, those of persuasion, manoeuvre and compromise.
His control over his own officials was uncertain, and in spite of fine,
resolute circulars, there is not much evidence that he actually took
action against arbitrary officials.[37] He was particularly ill-suited to
deal with a kind of political pressure which became stronger in proportion to his success in achieving his first aim of suppressing revolution: the intrigues of those whose interests were most directly
threatened by the new state system. These were the former ministers,

---

[35] Levin, ' Peter Arkad'evich Stolypin: a Re-appraisal ', p 455.
[36] This is a characteristic noted by several observers: e.g. S. I. Shidlovskii,
    Vospominaniya, Berlin n.d., vol 1, p 187; Gurko, *Features and Figures
    of the Past*, p 461.
[37] Levin, ' Peter Arkad'evich Stolypin: a Re-appraisal ', p 452.

high officials and members of the palace staff, who had flourished on the right of personal private report to the unlimited autocrat, and now found their influence severely curtailed by the Duma and the Council of Ministers; and also many of the landowners, who found that the government was inclined to give their interests second place to those of the peasantry, and to diminish their influence in local government and justice. To skilful political opposition of this type, Stolypin would react, as we shall later see, either by abject retreat or by exaggeratedly violent action. His instincts were those of the Russian étatiste tradition, and in facing the problems posed by centres of power outside immediate governmental control (such as must be characteristic of a pluralist society), he did not show the competence and courage which he manifested in the face of revolution.

Much of this can be discerned in his relationship to the Second Duma. He wanted it to meet, but only if it would do the things he intended it to do. Already on 15 July 1906 he had written to the Emperor that it had been a mistake to admit so many peasants to the Duma and proposed to remedy the situation by ' energetic government pressure on the course of the elections '.[38] This indeed he did, but the results were not those he had hoped for. The right wing of the Duma was strengthened by the election of 54 Octobrists, 10 declared Rights and 50 ' non-party ' deputies of centre or right-wing persuasion. But the left wing was strengthened even more, with 65 Social Democrats, 37 Socialist Revolutionaries, 16 Popular Socialists and 104 deputies of the Labour group, whilst the Kadets, cut down to 98 seats, held the balance along with the Polish Kolo.[39]

The main point at issue, once again, was the agrarian question. This time, however, the government had made its intentions quite clear by issuing its new agrarian legislation under Article 87. This fait accompli placed the Kadets in a dilemma: they could not ignore the Ukazes; yet to accept them would, they felt, discredit the party in the eyes of the peasants and the socialists, whilst to reject them would lead straight to a second dissolution of the Duma. And anyway, did the Kadets not have their own land programme? What they in fact did, in accordance with their new determination to ' save the Duma '[40] at all costs, was to try to avoid a debate on the govern-

[38] From the personal fund of Nicholas II in *TsGAOR*, quoted in Chermenskii, *Burzhuaziya i Tsarizm*, p 338.
[39] A. Levin, *The Second Duma*, 2nd ed, Hamden, Connecticut, 1966, pp 66-9.
[40] Milyukov, *Vospominaniya*, vol 1, p 425.

ment's legislation, and instead to draw up a new agrarian bill softening the more intransigent features of their declared programme The socialist parties, however, were not to be thus won over: they all had land programmes which involved, in one form or another, the abolition of private property in land, and the creation of a land fund to be administered and equitably distributed among the land-hungry population by democratically elected (local or central) government bodies. The new Kadet bill differed considerably from this: it did not recommend the *abolition* of private property, but merely the expropriation of excess private land in areas of land shortage; it insisted on the payment of compensation, partly at the peasants' expense, to expropriated landowners; and it envisaged local land committees in which existing landowners and officials would have considerable influence. These proposals (extremely modest when compared with the land reforms in, for example, parts of Eastern Europe after the First World War) the Kadets defended from the tribune of the Duma and in the agrarian committee.[41]

Stolypin, in reply, was not totally intransigent. He rejected in general the principle of compulsory expropriation of private land, but accepted it where it was necessary to eliminate strips or facilitate access to water or pasture; and he also accepted the notion of a ' land fund ', provided it was organised through the Peasant Land Bank. His acceptance was in words, not in substance; but still, the political battle was partly about words. Some Kadets saw in this the possibility of a compromise, but others wanted the party to reject unequivocally the government's Article 87 legislation. In the fraction's deliberations on the subject, one peasant member, Odnokozov, complained that the peasants' needs were being forgotten in the political manoeuvring, and threatened to quit the party.[42] In the end, deeply split, the fraction resolved to try to get the Duma to avoid passing any motion at all on the government's agrarian policy, but if the majority of the Duma insisted on such a motion, then to support one which would simply entrust the Duma agrarian committee with drafting a legislative bill on the whole question.[43] Meanwhile the agrarian committee had in fact been working on such a

[41] Levin, *The Second Duma*, pp 165-94.

[42] *TsGAOR*, f 523, op 1, d 1, p 109.

[43] Protocols of Kadet fraction meetings of 10, 12, 14, 21, 25 May 1907: *TsGAOR*, f 523, op 1, d 1, pp 97-110.

bill, and by 30 May the main lines of it had become clear: it demanded compulsory expropriation and the establishment of a land fund, and it also had begun to demand the annulment of the government's Article 87 laws. In short, there was little sign here that the Duma was moving towards compromise with the government, however much some of the Kadets might want to.

On another major issue, too, the government failed to reach agreement with the Kadets and the socialist parties. This was the problem of political terror. The Kadets and the socialists wanted the abrogation of the Ukaz of 19 August, while the government and the right wing of the Duma wanted the Duma to declare its condemnation of revolutionary terror. Again, there was an attempt at a compromise; Stolypin allowed the Ukaz to lapse without renewal, and in private conversation with Milyukov he offered to legalise the Kadet party if the Duma would openly condemn terror. When Milyukov replied that he could not decide this for his party, Stolypin suggested instead that Milyukov should write an article in the Kadet newspaper *Rech* condemning revolutionary assassinations. Milyukov agreed to do this, but only on condition that the other party leaders approved. The veteran Petrunkevich, however, admonished him: ' You will ruin your reputation and drag the whole party with you . . . Better to sacrifice the party than to disgrace it.'[44] The article remained unwritten. On such issues, there was still no bridging the gap between the government and the majority in the Duma.

Sources of support in society

If the constitutional experiment was to be continued at all, it would have to be with a different kind of Duma. That, by May 1907, was clear to all members of the government. And, if the electoral law was to be changed, it would have to be done by coup d'état, since the Duma could not be expected to approve such a change.[45]

Such direct violence on the new constitution would be extremely unadvisable unless the benefits were obvious and assured. The question therefore arises: what allies did the government expect to find in a differently elected Duma?

[44] Milyukov, *Vospominaniya*, vol 1, pp 430-1.
[45] Under Article 87 of the Fundamental Laws, one of the areas *not* open to emergency legislation was the Statutes of the Duma, which included its electoral law.

One powerful and growing source of grass-roots support was beginning to come from an area where one might at first not expect it. This was from the zemstvo assemblies. After all, for forty years the governmental bureaucracy had been waging a war of attrition against the zemstvos. And had not the zemstvos, with their Western-educated nobles and their 'third element' of busy conscience-stricken professional radicals repeating more soberly the 'going to the people' of an earlier generation, taken a leading part in the campaign of banquets and political resolutions which led to the 1905 revolution?

But of course the very intensity of the upheavals of that year had profoundly affected the mood in the local zemstvos. The zemstvo congresses which met continually throughout 1905 were self-avowedly political and did not directly represent the local zemstvos, where opinion was, from the beginning, more cautious. In the provincial and district towns of Russia, potentially violent mobs seemed much nearer and organised protection much further away than in the capitals.[46] After the October Manifesto, local zemstvos, where they were not even further to the right, supported the Guchkov–Shipov current of opinion, accepting the Manifesto as an adequate basis for the new state system. And after the dissolution of the First Duma, most provincial and district zemstvos voted to exclude signatories of the Vyborg Appeal. Some even began to appeal for a restriction of the electoral law of 11 December 1905, and to cut expenditure on the kind of projects, educational, statistical, agronomic, with which representatives of the 'third element' were associated, and to dismiss some of their professional salaried staff.[47] In the zemstvo elections which took place during late 1906 and early 1907, the Octobrists and the right wing substantially increased their representation at the expense of the Kadets and Progressists.[48] The political allegiance of the chairmen elected by the zemstvo assemblies in 1907 was as follows (figures for 1905 in brackets):

---

[46] B. B. Veselovskii, 'Dvizhenie Zemlevladel'tsev', in *Obshchestvennoe Dvizhenie v Rossii v Nachale XX veka*, ed L. Martov, P. Maslov and A. Potresov, SPB 1909-11, vol 2, pt 2, pp 1-17.

[47] Veselovskii, 'Dvizhenie Zemlevladel'tsev', pp 18-20; see also the same author's *Istoriya Zemstva za sorok let*, SPB 1909, vol 4, pp 37-8, 42-4.

[48] The Progressists was the name given to small groups, such as the Party of Peaceful Renewal, which lay between the Kadets and the Octobrists.

Kadets	1	(15)
Progressists	3	(6)
Octobrists	19	(13)
Rights	11	(0)

Many zemstvos (at least half the total number) sent telegrams to Stolypin after the Socialist Revolutionary attempt on his life, congratulating him on his recovery and promising to support his government in its repression of revolutionary terror and in the fulfilment of the October Manifesto and of the reforms necessary to the economy.[49]

Both Witte and Stolypin closely followed the evolution in zemstvo opinion, and had provincial governors submit reports on the trend of local feeling as expressed in zemstvo elections and resolutions; these reports were collated for the Emperor's benefit.[50] The potential value of the zemstvos to Stolypin was enormous: they were bodies with practical administrative experience, they were a sounding board for local opinion (Stolypin was fond of contrasting the inbred cosmopolitan pessimism of the capital with the healthy organic patriotism of provincial Russia), and they could provide an abundant reserve of deputies to be elected to the Duma – if the electoral law were changed.

No less important to the government was the support of the nobles' associations, who of course shared a good proportion of their membership with the zemstvo assemblies. But if the growing conservatism of the zemstvos coincided with the disappearance of their central congress, exactly the opposite was the case with the nobles' associations. The pressures on nobles were the same as those on local zemstvo deputies. Even where violence had not actually been applied, most of them had had to fear for their properties: A. N. Naumov, Marshal of the Nobility of Samara province, returning to his Golovkino estate in February 1906, found the local peasants preparing, after the October Manifesto, 'to settle accounts with their landlords, divide up their land " justly ", and assume freedom to fell trees, make hay, hunt, fish and pasture cattle on the landlord's estates'. A terrorist centre in the nearby village of Rozhdest-

---

[49] Veselovskii, *Istoriya Zemstva*, vol 4, pp 49-52, 58.
[50] These reports are collected in *TsGIAL*, f 1288 (Ministry of the Interior, Zemskii Otdel), op 2, d 76.

venno added emphasis to these intentions.[51] Furthermore, to the nobles' horror, this pressure appeared to come not only from the peasants, for in the winter of 1905-6 the government was preparing a weighty voice for those peasants in the Duma, and, horror of horrors, was considering a proposal (that of Kutler[52]) which would take away some nobles' land to give to them.

It was in the midst of the growing anxiety about this last scheme that P. N. Trubetskoi, Marshal of the Nobility of Moscow province, called a congress of provincial Marshals of the Nobility for 7-11 January 1906. Many nobles had felt for some time that the nobility as a whole was reacting too weakly to the threats which both the revolutionary movement and the government posed to their vital interests. According to Naumov, he and Prince V. M. Volkonsky, of Tambov province, took the initiative in persuading Trubetskoi that something must be done to organise the nobles; privately, also, they felt that the two leading nobles, Trubetskoi and Gudovich, Marshal of the Nobility of St Petersburg province, were too much under the influence of the constitutionalists, and that it was time to rally the nobles as a conservative, stabilising force.[53]

The Moscow congress of January 1906 discussed mainly the two burning issues of the day, the general disorder in the Empire and the land problem. The government it warned, had proclaimed freedoms in the October Manifesto, but had not defined their extent, nor had it yet convened the promised Duma. This had led to a state of uncertainty in the country at large, which the revolutionaries were exploiting. The government must clearly demonstrate its authority throughout the Empire, and must call the Duma to begin serious legislative work. As far as the land question was concerned, the congress made the vital recommendation (not universally accepted in Witte's government at the time) that its solution must rest on the ' inviolability of private property ' (the very principle called in question by Kutler's proposal), although in exceptional circumstances, compulsory expropriation of small areas of land might be made for the sake of proper land-organisation. The easing of the land problem should be undertaken by facilitating the transfer of land through the Peasant Land Bank, by organising resettlement and a more rational land tenure, and by allowing the peasant to

[51] A. N. Naumov, *Iz Utselevshikh Vospominanii*, New York 1954-5, vol 2, pp 73, 96.   [52] see Chapter 3 below.
[53] Naumov, *Iz Utselevshikh Vospominanii*, vol 2, pp 45-6.

leave the commune and set up his own smallholding.[54] In fact they put forward exactly the proposals that Stolypin was later to make to the second Duma. This clear warning that the nobles were not prepared to acquiesce in a land reform requiring confiscation and redistribution of part of their estates was very important to a government looking for reliable social support. The Emperor wrote on his copy of the resolution: ' To be examined in the Council of Ministers '.[55]

Following the January session, some busy organisational work was done, particularly by those nobles who wanted to outflank the far from negligible liberal-constitutional wing in many nobles' assemblies. They set about preparing a congress of delegates from the nobles' associations all over the country. At first Trubetskoi chaired this preparatory group: his aim was to continue the long tradition of constitutional agitation by the nobility, going back to the celebrated Tver address of 1862. But he was later replaced by N. F. Kasatkin-Rostovsky, from Kursk, where the provincial zemstvo and the nobles' association were notoriously reactionary.[56] The aim of this group was not so much to gather a congress which would speak for the nobles all over Russia, as to set up a strong conservative pressure group at the centre of things, with some kind of nation-wide organisation behind it. For this reason, the key body in the nobles' new organisation was its Permanent Council, to which the organisation's charter delegated strong executive powers. Not all local associations acquiesced in this policy; six provincial associations boycotted the congress, while nine others failed to send representatives. So that the congress initially represented only twenty-nine provinces, and even at that a number of delegates, both at the first and third congresses, objected to the concentration of power in the Permanent Council and to its intention of interceding with the government not only on questions directly concerning the nobles, but on general political questions as well. Answering these criticisms, the Chairman of the Council, Count A. A. Bobrinsky,

[54] *TsGAOR*, f 434, op 1, d 1/303, pp 8-22.
[55] *TsGIAL*, f 1276, op 2, d 2, p 1: the marginal note is dated 27 January 1906.
[56] I. D. Vaisberg, ' Sovet Ob''edinennogo Dvoryanstva, i ego Vliyanie na Politiku Samoderzhaviya, 1906-14gg ', Candidate's dissertation, M 1956, p 87. The correct title of the nobles' national organisation was the Congress of Delegates of the Nobles' Associations: it is usually known as the United Nobility, and I shall give it this title, even if it is a slightly misleading one.

depicted the nobles as a besieged minority, whose salvation was for the good of the state as a whole:

It is suggested we turn the congresses and the Council into a preparatory bureau, which . . . would be limited to the clerical drafting of reports for the consideration of the nobles' associations . . . The house is burning, the roof is in flames. *Hannibal est ante portas.* And you suggest we wait a bit and talk things over! No, the time for red tape has passed . . . To deprive the congress and the Council of the United Nobility of any right of initiative would be to nullify the work we have started . . . In the Council, in its constant activity, energetic and when necessary resolute, lies the salvation of the nobility.[57]

This concept, though contested, was accepted by the congresses. The Council set up offices in St Petersburg, and maintained constant contact with the government, and even with the Emperor. The nobles' social position, their connections, and their closeness to the palace hierarchy, the government, the right wing Duma parties and the State Council gave them a uniquely favourable position for agitation and influence.

As far as their programme was concerned, Stolypin's field courts Ukaz and his agrarian legislation did much to satisfy them, and at their Second and Third Congresses (November 1906 and May 1907) they concentrated their attention on the Duma electoral law. Kasatkin-Rostovsky complained of the nobility being crowded out of the Duma by ' publicans and lackeys ' and maintained that if the British parliament adopted the Duma electoral law for their Empire, then a hundred English deputies at Westminster would be confronted by ' 350 Indians, 150 Somalis and Canadians '. Count D. A. Olsufyev declared that with a more restrictive electoral law the nobility could play the same role in the new Russia as in England or Poland, where they were the bearers of the ' religious, national and political idea '. They should take their place as the rallying point for a bloc of right-wing parties ' including the party of 17 October, which after A. I. Guchkov's speech[58] and the resignation from it of D. N. Shipov, has become a party of state order.'[59]

The Third Congress's resolution called for mixed *soslovno-gruppovye* elections to the Duma, that is, election by historical

[57] *Trudy 3-ego S[ll]ezda Upolnomochennykh Dvoryanskikh Obshchestv*, SPB 1907, p 68; Vaisberg, ' Sovet Ob[ll]edinennogo Dvoryanstva ', pp 83-100.
[58] Published on 27 August 1906; see below, p 39.
[59] *Trudy 3-ego*, pp 21, 29-33.

estates (*sosloviya*), where these still existed, or by natural groups or classes of the population, ' as these are created by everyday life '. It recommended that the electoral assembly of each province should be divided into four curiae, peasants (who should have no more deputies in the house than other groups), small landowners, large landowners, and representatives of the towns ' in such a way that after elections in each group have taken place the remaining vacant seats should be filled by deputies elected by the general mass of electors '.[60]

As we shall see, the Government incorporated some of these ideas into the new electoral law which followed the dissolution of the Second Duma. The support of the United Nobility was very welcome to the government at this time, when it was still struggling with revolutionaries and with a hostile Duma. But the circumstances of the formation of the United Nobility had given it a ' siege mentality ' and delivered it to domination by a centralising and conservative element, dedicated to a narrow defence of class interest. This later made the United Nobility and its numerous connections more difficult for the government to handle when it came to carrying out the promised reform programme.

A third group existed to which the government, perhaps somewhat more equivocally, could look for social support. This was in the vague, ill-defined area of the monarchist political parties. The fact that men of monarchist political opinion organised themselves into parties at all is, like the formation of a nobles' pressure group, an indication of the extent to which Russian politics had changed in 1905. The legitimate authority of autocratic monarchy had previously been self-evident, and political parties had been by definition subversive. But the events of 1905, and in particular the Manifesto of 17 October, had ended such certainties. The autocratic Monarch had, at any rate in appearance, divested himself of his autocratic authority; and those who still believed that autocracy was right for Russia had henceforth to form themselves into the kind of political organisations which should have been anathema to their own beliefs. They also had to agitate in favour of a policy opposed to that which the Monarch to whom they were loyal now appeared to be pursuing. So there were contradictions implicit in their very existence. But such contradictions were not necessarily fatal. Indeed, as we have

[60] ibid, pp 78-9.

seen, they were reflected in the Emperor's own dilemmas and inner struggles. And the agitation of the monarchists played a considerable part in the final inclusion of the word 'autocratic' in the Fundamental Laws' definition of the Monarch's power.[61] The monarchist parties, and in particular the most important of them, the Union of the Russian People, grew out of earlier attempts to organise conservative opinion. As early as 1900, a so-called 'Russian Assembly' had been set up in St Petersburg, with the aim of conducting cultural and educational activities to combat the growing cosmopolitan and oppositional spirit of educated society. It was not a political party as such, and its membership remained limited almost entirely to senior clergymen and officials, with a sprinkling of newspaper editors, university lecturers and lawyers.[62] The groups formed in 1905 were of a different nature, and deliberately set out to attract mass support. Many of them arose in provincial towns in the disorders of the spring and summer of that year. Bearing names such as 'National Union', 'Patriotic League', 'Legion for Struggle with Sedition', 'Autocracy and Church', 'For Tsar and Order', they issued pamphlets and held meetings at which they called for support for the Tsar, the church and the Russian people against the revolutionary attempts of Jews, intellectuals, liberals and socialists. Sometimes they formed armed bands to attack students or Jews, and even whole Jewish quarters, especially in the days following the October Manifesto, when the general strike and the Emperor's response to it occasioned widespread confusion and resentment. These were the bands known as the Black Hundreds.[63] Often they were organised, or at least tolerated, by local police officials, desperately anxious for support against a revolutionary movement which threatened to overwhelm their limited resources while the government wavered in indecision and gave no clear leadership. In their membership, these bands came mostly from the *meshchanstvo*, the minor officials, shopkeepers, traders, schoolteachers, artisans and lower ranks of the clergy – those, in fact, who felt most isolated and helpless, threatened by peasant

[61] see above, p 10.
[62] H. Rogger, 'The Formation of the Russian Right, 1900-1906', *California Slavic Studies*, vol 3 (1964), pp 69-72.
[63] Rogger, 'Formation of the Russian Right'; V. Levitskii, 'Pravye Partii', in *Obshchestvennoe Dvizhenie*, ed Martov, Maslov and Potresov, vol 2, pp 370-6.

violence, by proletarian organisation and by revolutionary ideas. Monarchist propaganda proclaimed to them that they were the 'real' nation, hitherto disunited, which must now band together to face the national crisis under the banner of the Tsar, who was awaiting their help.

A first attempt to give coherence and a nation-wide organisation to these outbursts was that of V. A. Gringmut, publisher and editor of the newspaper *Moskovskie Vedomosti*, who in March 1905 founded the so-called Monarchist Party. Its ideology envisaged a complete return to the pre-1905 past of an autocratic Tsar ruling through a strong bureaucracy, and this extreme conservatism proved to be a handicap, especially after the October Manifesto. No right-wing party could be successful which did not make some concessions to the constitutional era and to the existence of a parliament. Perhaps for similar reasons, another party, the Union of Russian Men (Soyuz Russkikh Lyudei), also formed in March 1905, likewise failed to extend its membership very far into the provinces. Its version of good, conservative Russia went back further into the past, and borrowed from the Slavophile view of pre-Petrine Muscovy. Although this golden age had included a parliament of sorts, the Zemsky Sobor, summoned and appointed by the Tsar, the programme of the Union of Russian Men also failed to catch on.[64]

Much the most successful of the monarchist parties was the Union of the Russian People (Soyuz Russkogo Naroda). It came to the scene relatively late, in autumn 1905; but in this it did perhaps have the advantage of being able to take account of the October Manifesto in its programme and frame its proposals accordingly. Its principal organiser was a doctor of unknown antecedents, A. I. Dubrovin, whilst much of its finance was contributed by a wealthy woman publisher, E. A. Poluboyarinova.[65] The U.R.P., though not without hesitations, took the position that the October Manifesto should properly be regarded not as a constitution, but as a reinforcement of autocracy; the new Duma would enable the Emperor more effec-

[64] Rogger, 'Formation of the Russian Right', pp 76-84.
[65] Gurko, *Features and Figures of the Past*, pp 435-6 actually insinuates a shadier origin for the Union's money, stating that Mme Poluboyarinova was proprietress of a large 'establishment' on the Voskresensky Quay in St Petersburg which gave her some trouble with the police. I have not seen this confirmed elsewhere.

tively to unite with his people in the struggle against socialism and international Jewry. As we have seen, Nicholas himself would have liked to believe that something of this sort was true; he was very pleased by the appearance of the Union, and in December 1905 even went so far as to accept the party's insignia from a delegation. A particular forte of the Union was the organisation of campaigns of telegrams from loyal subjects: as already noted, the Tsarskoe Selo conference of April 1906 was influenced by such a campaign to retain the word ' autocratic ' in the Fundamental Laws, and a similar campaign urging the Emperor to dissolve the Second Duma certainly sharpened the Emperor's impatience to do so.

In other respects, too, the U.R.P.'s programme was acceptable to the government, for example on the necessity of legislation to improve the conditions of factory workers and on the need to provide additional land for peasants without infringing on private property. And, like the government, they accepted, with some reluctance, the representative principle, but wanted to see the relatively broad suffrage of 11 December 1905 brought within narrower limits.[66] Furthermore, though they doubtless exaggerated their membership figures, they did offer the government some prospect of mass support for these policies.

Nevertheless, none of the monarchist parties, not even the U.R.P., was an entirely satisfactory ally. One reason for this was their unimpressive electoral performance. In the elections to the First Duma only one candidate of clearly monarchist persuasion was returned; with government pressure on their side, they did somewhat better in the Second Duma, but at no time did they look capable of attracting the nation-wide mass support that they had hoped for from the loyal sons of Russia.

Another reason why the government regarded the monarchists with reserve was the disrepute into which their political methods brought them in the eyes of moderate public opinion. The Union of the Russian People, at least, had armed terrorist bands. Their opposition to the First Duma was not contained within the limits of the always correct, if determined, hostility of the United Nobility: it extended to the murder of two Kadet deputies, Iollos and Gertsenstein, and to an attempt on the life of Witte.[67] Furthermore, their

---

[66] Rogger, ' Formation of the Russian Right '; see also his article, ' Was there a Russian Fascism?', *JMH*, vol 36 (1964), pp 407-8.

[67] Levitskii, ' Pravye Partii ', pp 437-41, 450-3.

organisation was never strong, and they were inclined to petty wrangles and splits, sometimes over principles, sometimes over personalities. For these reasons, the subsidies which Stolypin's government initially gave them were gradually whittled down.[68]

In some respects, the plight of the monarchist parties reflected the ambiguous and as yet embryonic nature of Russia's constitutionalism. Hans Rogger has argued that in a more fully developed parliamentary system, their call for order, social discipline and national greatness, as well as their search for a mass base, might have been more successful. As it was, they could not operate independently, but had to rely both for their moral authority and for some of their funds on a discredited autocracy.[69] For its own part, the government, finding them morally dubious and electorally ineffectual, reaped the benefits neither of whole-hearted support for their activities, nor of firm dissociation from them. One of the consequences of this equivocation, as we shall see, was that the right wing of the Duma, though it was to be strengthened in numbers by a new electoral law, never had the benefit of coherent party organisation.

Political support: the Octobrists

Long before the Second Duma even met, then, the government was assured of support from most of the zemstvo assemblies, from the United Nobility, and from the monarchist parties, for a policy of dissolving that Duma, restricting the electoral law and passing an agrarian reform based on the inviolability of private property. But if the new Duma were to be a reliable ally, it needed at its centre an

[68] S. E. Kryzhanovskii, *Vospominaniya, iz Bumag S. E. Kryzhanovskogo, poslednego Gosudarstvennogo Sekretarya Rossiiskoi Imperii,* Berlin n.d., pp 152-9; testimony of N. E. Markov, in *Padenie Tsarskogo Rezhima,* Moscow-Leningrad 1925-7, vol 6, pp 179-83; V. N. Kokovtsev, *Iz Moego Proshlogo,* Paris 1933, vol 2, pp 111-12. In her testimony to the Provisional Government's Investigatory Commission, Mme Poluboyarinova stated, as the U.R.P.'s treasurer, that Stolypin's initial subsidy, offered soon after the S.R. attempt on his life, was about 150,000 rubles, but that later on no official subsidies were given, at any rate to Dubrovin's wing of the movement, which was formed after a split in 1908. Markov's wing, being more conciliatory towards the Duma, evidently continued to receive a subsidy, if on a more modest scale. See A. Chernovskii and V. P. Viktorov (eds), *Soyuz Russkogo Naroda,* Moscow-Leningrad 1929, p 38.

[69] Rogger, ' Formation of the Russian Right ', pp 93-4.

electorally attractive and well-organised political party, prepared to give the government consistent support.

Witte's and Stolypin's early contacts with the leaders of the Union of 17 October had not hitherto justified hopes that that party would prove to be such an ally. But in the summer of 1906 a split took place in the Octobrist leadership which moved the majority of the party in the direction of compromise with the government, and enabled the party to act as a focus for the loyal elements in the zemstvos and among the nobility.

The split took place over an interview Guchkov gave to the conservative newspaper *Novoe Vremya*, published on 27 August 1906. The surprising point about this interview was that Guchkov accepted not only the reform programme which Stolypin's government had then just published, but also the military field court Ukaz of 19 August. He called the field courts a ' sad necessity ' and added: ' In our troubled system we need a firm and decisive governmental policy. The government's indication of decisive measures in the struggle against revolution gives hope that those who want to work peacefully will find in this government a firm authority, able to defend our new political freedom.'

This endorsement of Stolypin's harshest repressive enactment was a sharp departure from the aloof stance which leaders of public opinion had hitherto taken. And it brought an immediate rebuttal from Shipov, whose moral authority, dating from the long, hard years of the zemstvo constitutional movement, was immense. He wrote to the Central Committee of the Octobrist Union, and announced that he felt compelled to leave the party. He declared it intolerable that the Octobrists should ally themselves unreservedly with Stolypin's government:

The ministry of P.A. Stolypin is the ministry of the Duma's dissolution, a ministry created by the conflict between an outmoded bureaucratic regime and the people's representatives. For that reason the policy of the present cabinet can only be reactionary, and this is shown every day by numerous instances of administrative caprice. Although the ministerial declaration states that the government is struggling not against society, but only against the enemies of society, it evidently considers all those who do not approve of the government's activities the enemies of society. The path of increased repression is inevitable for the present ministry and has already led it to the widespread use of military field courts. At the present time the most horrifying fact of our social life is the progressive degradation of moral consciousness; without a moral rebirth the country cannot escape from the condition in which we are living now. It is not military field courts which can renew the moral purpose of our Russian land – this measure can only aggravate the process of demoralisation and barbarism in society.[70]

Shipov's letter was a reaffirmation of the traditional moral stance of the Russian intelligentsia against the disavowal of it implicit in Guchkov's acceptance of the most brutal and lawless sides of the government's policy. And as Shipov's letter shows, the dilemmas of constitutional liberalism in this period of violent transition were no less complicated and in many ways more agonising than those of autocracy.

After some hesitation, the Central Committee reiterated the Octobrists Union's dedication to the ' peaceful renewal ' of Russia, but also backed Guchkov by stating that his recent declaration had not departed from this principle. Nevertheless, the small Party of Peaceful Renewal, which had hitherto worked with the Octobrist Union and had considered entering it, now broke all organisational ties with it. Shipov jointed it, along with several leading Octobrists, including S. I. Chetverikov, P. P. Ryabushinsky and A. S. Vishnyakov.[71]

On 5 November 1906 Guchkov made a further statement describing the Octobrists' political outlook after these withdrawals. With the left-wing parties they shared, he said, dedication to the constitution inaugurated by the October Manifesto, with the right-wing parties love for the Russian nation and the Empire; at the same time they rejected the flirtation with revolution still indulged in by the left, but equally rejected the right's view that Russia was still an autocratic state.

The Octobrists also brought their agrarian programme completely into line with the government's. When the government issued its principal agrarian Ukaz of 9 November 1906, the Octobrist Central Committee renounced its own previous land programme, which had

---

[70] Shipov, *Vospominaniya*, pp 495-8.
[71] ibid, loc cit; F. Dan and N. Cherevanin, ' Soyuz 17 oktyabrya ', from *Obshchestvennoe Dvizhenie*, ed Martov, Maslov and Potresov, vol 2, pp 198-204; E. D. Chermenskii, *Burzhuaziya i Tsarizm v Revolyutsiyu 1905-7gg*, M 1939, pp 316-17; V. Ya. Laverychev, *Po tu Storonu Barrikad: iz Istorii Bor'by Moskovskoi Burzhuazii s Revolyutsiei*, M 1967, pp 50-1.

envisaged minimal compulsory expropriation of private land, and announced its full support for that of the government.[72]

The electoral law of 3 June 1907

In this way, even before the Second Duma met, Stolypin's government had in mind an alternative political line-up, with the Octobrists acting as the nucleus of a right–centre alliance which would represent the aspirations of the Russians, the nobles, the zemstvo men and the monarchists. This available alternative did not, as we have seen, lead him to bypass the Second Duma entirely, but he was moderately precipitate in bringing its deliberations to a close. The occasion he chose was the discovery of contacts between some Social Democratic deputies and soldiers in army units stationed in St Petersburg. Such contacts, though technically treasonable, were fairly common, but Stolypin decided to exploit this particular case in the capital as a political weapon to destroy the Second Duma. The meetings were being held in the home of a Social Democrat deputy, Ozol, and Stolypin, acting through a police agent, devised a police raid on Ozol's apartment so as to discover deputies, soldiers and incriminating documents all together in one place. The raid, however, was mistimed, and neither soldiers nor documents were found. Stolypin therefore had to use a copy of the vital document supplied by his informer as a basis on which to announce to the Duma the unmasking of a conspiracy, and to demand that the Duma suspend the parliamentary immunity of all members of the Social Democratic fraction, so that a full investigation could be effected. This the Duma refused to do, replying that it would only suspend the immunity of those deputies against whom a prima facie case could be made out, and setting up a committee to examine the matter further. Stolypin thereupon dissolved it,[73] on 3 June 1907.

He immediately passed the new electoral law which his assistant Minister of the Interior, Kryzhanovsky, had long been preparing for him. As this law formed the basis of parliamentary representation in the years of Russia's most serious constitutional experiment, it requires close examination. Out of three versions drafted by Kryzhanovsky, the Council of Ministers chose the one which most

---

[72] Dan and Cherevanin, ' Soyuz 17 oktyabrya ', pp 204-5.
[73] Levin, *The Second Duma*, pp 307-49; see also his article ' The Shornikova Affair ', in *SEER*, vol 21 (1943), pp 1-18. I use the Russian term ' fraction ' throughout to denote the parliamentary caucus of a political party.

closely corresponded to the electoral law which the United Nobility had recommended at its Third Congress.[74] Its main aim was, without totally excluding the rest of the population, to give the dominant voice in the coming Duma to the Great Russians, the landowners and the wealthier urban elements who formed the strength of the nobility and of the zemstvo assemblies. In some ways this marked a return to an earlier concept of constitutionalism, ignoring the upheavals and the democratic experiments of 1905. As the legal historian V. Leontowitsch observes:

The limitation of the suffrage marked the return to the constitutional idea which had its roots in the zemstvo world, that is, to the predominant constitutional ideas of the 1860s and 1880s, and in many respects of a later period too. The electoral law of 11 December 1905 was in fact an attempt to bypass the zemstvo stage (as one could call it) of Russia's constitutional regime and to construct the constitution on a broader, more democratic basis. Now it had become apparent that this attempt had failed.[75]

The law of 3 June can in some respects be seen as a logical outcome of the October Manifesto, for the effect of that Manifesto had been to split the opposition movement by making concessions to the more moderate part of it and trying to enlist its support. The electoral law of 11 December 1905 (although foreshadowed in the Manifesto) had been inconsistent with that policy in that it gave too powerful a voice to the peasant masses. As Stolypin noted during the Second Duma, 'At the moment the elections are under the control of the peasantry: the rights of control must be given to someone else.'[76] The aim of the new law was to transfer that control to other classes, and above all the landowners.

The most important single provision of the new law was therefore that which increased the representation of the private landowners in the provincial (*guberniya*) electoral assemblies (which actually elected the deputies to the Duma) from, on average, 34 to 51 per cent, while peasant representation fell from 43 to 22 per cent.[77] All landowners

[74] See above, p 33; Kryzhanovskii, *Vospominaniya*, Berlin n.d., pp 108-13.
[75] V. Leontowitsch, *Geschichte des Liberalismus in Russland*, Frankfurt-am-Main 1958, p 410.
[76] A. L. Sidorov (ed), ' Interesnaya Nakhodka (the testimony of Kokov-tsev to the Provisional Government Investigatory Committee)', *Vop. Ist.*, 1964, no 4, pp 97-8.
[77] Chasles, *Le Parlement Russe*, p 93. The number of electors (*vyborsh-*

holding a full electoral qualification (*tsenz*) in terms of the amount of land they owned had the automatic right to participate in the district (*uyezd*) electoral assemblies; those whose holdings were less than the qualification laid down for the area held preliminary meetings at which they chose a number of representatives to the district assembly corresponding to the total of electoral qualifications they held in common.[78] This dominance of the private landowners was strengthened by the further stipulation that, in the provincial electoral assemblies, the deputy from each *soslovny* curia should be chosen not by his colleagues in that curia, but by the whole assembly.[79] This ensured that the landowners, given a minimal degree of organisation, could usually pick for the Duma whoever suited them best from any curia, not merely their own. The division of the urban curia into two parts, a richer and a poorer one, provided an opportunity in provinces with a large urban population for the landowners to combine with the wealthier urban electors to support the candidature of a moderate rather than a radical.[80] It was this alliance that was to ensure a strong Octobrist and right-wing nucleus in the new Duma.

Workers' representation was cut by nearly half in almost all the provinces where they were represented at all. They also suffered from the fact that direct urban elections to the Duma, of which there had been 26, were cut to 7 (St Petersburg, Moscow, Odessa, Kiev, Riga, plus the two Polish towns of Warsaw and Lodz). The workers, who had been a perceptible force in the urban assemblies, were lost among the rural voters of the provincial electoral assemblies.[81]

The law also increased Great Russian representation in the Duma at the expense of all other nationalities. The Poles were severely hit: representation from the Congress Kingdom was reduced from 33 to 14 deputies. From Siberia, which had been very oppositional in its political complexion in the first two Dumas, the number of

chiki) from each *soslovie* is laid down separately for each province in the appendix to Article 8 of the law: *PSZ*, 3rd Series, no 29242. Landowners had an absolute majority in 27 of the 51 provinces of European Russia.   [78] *PSZ*, loc cit, Article 28.   [79] ibid, Article 123.

[80] ibid, Articles 6, 32, 33; the first urban curia, though numerically much smaller, was usually entitled to a slightly higher number of *vyborshchiki* in the provincial electoral assembly (appendix to Article 8).

[81] ibid, Articles 90-5; V. V. Vorovskii, 'Pered Tret'ei Dumoi', *Sochineniya*, M 1933, vol 3, pp 262-72.

deputies was reduced from 44 to 15, and in the Caucasus from 29 to 10. Central Asia lost its representation altogether.[82]

Finally, the Minister of the Interior was given the right to divide all electoral assemblies at district, town or cantonal level by territory, by nationality or by property values, as he saw fit, and thus to carry out such gerrymandering as would benefit candidates he wished to promote.[83]

The government's own view of the new law is probably best summed up in the subsequent judgment of its principal author, Kryzhanovsky, who described its aim as being

to tear the State Duma from the hands of the revolutionaries, to assimilate it to the historical institutions, to bring it into the state system . . . To try, on the basis of the new law, to distil from Russia's chaos those elements in which there lived a feeling for the Russian state system, and from them to create the Duma as an organ for the re-education of society.[84]

The Soviet historian A. Ya. Avrekh has tried to show that Kryzhanovsky almost completely predetermined the make-up of the Third Duma by his law, and that he was aiming to create 'two majorities', an Octobrist–Right majority to support the agrarian reform and reactionary and nationalist policies and an Octobrist–Left majority to pass liberal reforms when required.[85] This is an ingenious theory, and corresponds roughly to the actual situation in the Third Duma (though not in the Fourth, elected on the same law). But there is no direct evidence that the government had in mind anything so precise. And there were so many imponderables that it is difficult to believe that the government could intend to do anything more specific than create a moderate conservative majority relying mainly on the landowners. Before and during the elections, party labels in the centre and right remained imprecise: during the campaign most candidates vaguely described themselves as 'Right' or 'Moderate', and did not choose a party label until they got into

---

[82] Chasles, *Le Parlement Russe*, pp 66-8; A. Leroy-Beaulieu, 'La Russie devant la Troisième Douma', *La Revue des Deux Mondes*, vol 41 (1907), pp 383-6.   [83] *PSZ*, 3rd Series, no 29242, Articles 30, 35, 38.

[84] Kryzhanovskii, *Vospominaniya*, pp 115, 117.

[85] See, for example, his article 'Tret'eiyunskaya Monarkhiya i Obrazovanie Tret'edumskogo Pomeshchich'e-Burzhuaznogo Bloka', *Vestnik Moskovskogo Gosudarstvennogo Universiteta* (Istoriko-Filosofskaya Seriya), 1956, no 1, pp 28, 45.

the Duma and met their associates. The size of the Octobrist fraction in the new Duma was especially unpredictable, and many of the indeterminates of the centre and right were to be drawn into it when the Duma met.

The fairest historical judgment on the law of 3 June is probably that of Alfred Levin, that Stolypin

wished to revise the terms of representation in a way that would ensure a preponderance of trustworthy elements in the Duma while still permitting most major segments of public opinion to be represented. To accomplish this purpose a majority was to be assigned to those segments of the population on which the premier might depend for a co-operative, 'efficient' effort in realising his reform programme and holding the line against precipitate change in the constitution or in social and economic legislation. The new law would create an artificial majority for conservative, rightist and Russian as against oppositional, revolutionary and non-Russian electoral districts; for large property owners of country and town as against smaller propertied, small-income and labour brackets; and for Great Russians as against 'aliens' in any given district.[86]

The Octobrists, who were to be the chief beneficiaries of the new law, issued a statement on the day of its publication, recognising that the law had been promulgated contrary to the Fundamental Laws (which they held to be Russia's constitution), but calling this a ' regrettable necessity '.[87]

Elections to the Third Duma

The elections to the Third Duma, held in September and October 1907, fully justified the government's hopes. An analysis of the returns at the district and provincial stages of the elections shows that the concentration of landowners and wealthy town dwellers in the provincial assemblies had a considerable influence on the results. The electors (*vyborshchiki*) chosen in the district assemblies to take part at the provincial level were of the following political affiliation:[88]

[86] A. Levin, 'The Russian Voter in the Elections to the Third Duma', *SR*, vol 21 (1962), p 660.   [87] *GM*, 7 June 1907.

[88] *Rech'*, 3 October 1907, collating its own sources with the figures of the St Petersburg Telegraph Agency. The 'Popular Socialists' called themselves the Labour group (Trudoviki) in the Duma itself.

Opposition		Pro-government		Others	
Socialists	521	Moderates	319	Non-party	533
Popular Socialists	374	Octobrists	572	Not known	151
Kadets	526	Rights	1,744		—
Progressists	516		———		684
	———		2,635		
	1,937				

Here, among the electors whose political affiliations could be determined, the opposition had 41.5 per cent of the representation. It may furthermore be surmised that many of those who disclaimed affiliation to any party or opinion were oppositional in sentiment, but were anxious not to jeopardise their chances at a later stage by disclosing it. Among the deputies elected to the Duma from the provincial assemblies, however, the opposition was much less well represented. The preliminary returns gave the following figures:[89]

Opposition		Pro-government	
Social Democrats	19	Octobrists and Moderates	98
Popular Socialists	15	Rights	175
Kadets	47		—
Progressists	30		273
	—	Non-Party 16	
	111		

The opposition's share had fallen to 28.9 per cent. These returns do not, of course, reflect precisely the later breakdowns of the Duma in fractions. The Octobrists, in particular, were to be much stronger than these figures suggest.

When one examines the political composition of the Third Duma, regional factors are the decisive ones, so strong was the influence of the provincial electoral assembly as a filter. The opposition was returned almost entirely from certain areas, namely those where noble landownership was weak or nonexistent, and the provincial assembly was dominated by other social groups. These were the large, ' direct-vote ' towns, Siberia, the Caucasus, the Cossack areas, the Urals, the north-eastern provinces of European Russia, and, to a lesser extent, the lower Volga basin, where the Populist tradition was especially strong. The exceptions to this pattern are remarkably

[89] *Rech'*, 22 October 1907.

few. On the other hand, the Octobrists and ' Rights ' of various com-
plexions nearly all came from the heartlands of Russia, the south, the
Ukraine and Belorussia, and from the Baltic provinces. Indeed, they
virtually monopolised the representation of those areas: evidently
here the landowning and upper urban majority in the provincial
assemblies were able to manipulate the elections as they wished. In
Belorussia and the Right-Bank Ukraine even the Octobrists could
scarcely secure a single seat for themselves, yielding them all to the
men who later formed the Right, Moderate Right and Nationalist
fractions. Such was the case in Bessarabia, Volynia, Podolya, Mogilev, Minsk (one Octobrist out of 9 deputies), and Kiev (3 Octobrists
out of 13 deputies, and not one from the city of Kiev, which was
shared between the Rights and the Kadets).[90]

An analysis of the social and occupational composition of the
newly elected Duma confirms that the Octobrists were strongly
landowning and zemstvo in their background. Of 150 members
officially constituting the Octobrist fraction in the first session
(1907-8), no less than 89 (59.3 per cent) called themselves noble
landowners. This was a much higher proportion than for any other
fraction (Rights 15 out of 48 – 31.25 per cent, Moderate Rights and
Nationalists 32 out of 89 – 36 per cent, Kadets 14 out of 53 – 26.4 per
cent, Progressists 9 out of 27 – 33.3 per cent). Forty members of the
Octobrist fraction (26.7 per cent) reported present or former service
as deputies or employees in zemstvos or municipal councils. Again
this was a higher proportion than in any other fraction: of the
Rights, 9 out of 48 reported such service (18.8 per cent), of the
Nationalists and Moderate Rights only 7 out of 89 (7.9 per cent).
By contrast, the deputies of the Rights, Nationalists and Moderate
Rights tended to serve or have served in peasant institutions, government offices, the army or the church. Not even the Kadets (11 out
of 53 – 20.8 per cent) or the Progressists (5 out of 27 – 18 per cent)
could match the Octobrists' record of zemstvo service.[91]

[90] This analysis is derived from information in M. Boiovich, *Chleny Gosudarstvennoi Dumy: Portrety i Biografii, 3-ii Sozyv (1907-12gg)*, M 1908,
and from the index to the Third Duma Stenographic Report, First
Session, pp 51-311. For this index, deputies filled in questionnaires on
themselves. See also C. J. Smith, ' The Russian Third State Duma: an
Analytical Profile ', *Russian Review*, vol 17 (1958), pp 201-10.

[91] The figures are drawn from the index to the Third Duma Stenographic
Report, First Session, pp 51-311.

The Octobrists were, then, as the government evidently wished the nucleus of the Duma majority to be, a strongly noble, landowning and zemstvo party. Many Soviet historians have also regarded them as a party of the commercial and industrial bourgeoisie. It is true that the proportion of their members recording commercial, financial or industrial activity (23 – 15.3 per cent) was higher than for any other fraction; but this was a relatively small section of the party, and one recent Soviet historian has even stated: ' In reality the bourgeois portion of the Duma fraction of Octobrists was very small.'[92] We are less likely to be misled if we regard the commercial and industrial bourgeoisie as being swamped by other groups in the Octobrist fraction, and therefore lacking adequate representation in the Duma, at any rate until the Progressists reactivated themselves on a new basis in 1912.

One further feature of the Octobrist fraction's membership is worth emphasising. This was the relatively high proportion of its leadership which practised a regular urban profession. Of the Duma fraction bureau of 19, 13 did so:

Alexeyenko	Professor of economics at Kharkov University
Anrep	Professor of forensic medicine at Kharkov and St Petersburg
Bennigsen	Official in the Ministry of Agriculture
Glebov	—
Golitsyn	President of the administration of the Russian Society of Vintners
Grimm	—
Guchkov	Banker and director of family firm
Kamensky	Publicist and writer
Kapustin	Professor of medicine at Kazan University
Karyakin	Owner of a bakery in Kazan and of a factory in Kurland
Lerkhe	Chief Inspector of the State Bank
Lyuts	Assistant Procurator of the Odessa circuit court
Meyendorf	Privat-dozent in law at St Petersburg University
Rodzyanko	—
Savich	—

[92] Avrekh, ' Tret'eiyunskaya Monarkhiya ', p 61.

Shidlovsky   —
Skoropadsky   —
Klyuzhev (sec.) School inspector in Samara
Neklyudov (sec.) Official in the Ministry of Finance.

Most of these men were also landowners. Nevertheless, their regular professional activity gave them an outlook somewhat different (and usually more left wing) than most of the rank and file members of the fraction, whose activities, beyond the care of their land, were typically those of zemstvo deputy, land commandant, Marshal of the Nobility or Justice of the Peace, usually rural and non-specialised occupations. When internal strains made themselves felt in the fraction from 1909 onwards, these occupational differences may have been important in inclining much of the leadership towards the left wing. Of the 14 members recorded in the annual Duma index as having left the fraction in a rightward direction (i.e. to join the Nationalists or form the Right Octobrists) between the second and third sessions, only two, Kazansky (an inspector of church seminaries) and Polovtsev (director of the St Petersburg Telegraph Agency) were recorded as exercising a regular urban profession. The other twelve were priests, retired officers or landowners. This contrasts strongly with the profile of the fraction leadership given above, but approximates closely to the occupational composition of the Rights, Moderate Rights and Nationalists, who had relatively few urban professional men in their ranks.

If the Octobrist fraction was less homogeneous than some of the others, and was in due course to be subject to internal splits, this was partly a result of the way in which it was put together at the beginning of the new Duma's first session. As we have seen above, preliminary election returns suggested that there would be no more than 98 Octobrists in the house. However, as deputies arrived in St Petersburg, a bit bemused at their new-found political importance, and not quite sure what their electoral mandate was or how they were going to fulfil it, Guchkov invited so-called ' Moderates ' and ' Rights ' to attend the early Octobrist fraction meetings. He gave the fraction the name of ' Union of 17 October and Adherents ', and enrolled many of the drifters. In this way its size was increased by more than half, at the expense of its cohesion.[93]

[93] Shidlovskii, *Vospominaniya*, vol 1, pp 202-3; *GDSO*, iii, 1-aya Sessiya, *Ukazatel'*.

In his autobiographical notes, Guchkov recounts that he also, after discussion with Stolypin, helped in the formation of a Moderate Right fraction, headed by P. N. Balashov, a member of one of the wealthiest landowning families in the Empire, and consisting of those so-called ' Rights ' who were not eager to be associated with the Union of the Russian People or its more flamboyant representatives in the Duma, such as N. E. Markov and V. M. Purishkevich.[94] A small Nationalist fraction (of 26 members) was also formed: it pursued the same political course as the Moderate Rights, and amalgamated with them in 1909.[95] Together, the Octobrists, Moderate Rights and Nationalists had an absolute majority (287 out of 443 seats): this was the majority which the law of 3 June 1907 had been designed to produce.

Inside his own fraction, Guchkov tried to gain agreement on political aims and a precise reform programme, but here he was to be hampered by the size and variety of the body he himself had created. The Central Committee of the Octobrist Union had drawn up a memorandum to act as the fraction's programme in the Third Duma, and submitted it to the fraction as it began to form itself in the last days of October 1907. The memorandum started by outlining the main aims of the Octobrists in the Third Duma:

1. The basic task of the parliamentary fraction of the Union of 17 October is to create in the Duma a constitutional centre, not aiming to seize governmental power, but at the same time determined to defend the rights of the people's representative assembly within the limits laid down for it in the Fundamental Laws. The creation of such a centre party is, in the fraction's opinion, an essential precondition for the Duma to avail itself fully of its rights in legislation and in the supervision of the activity of the authorities appointed by the Emperor.
2. For the successful fulfilment of this task [the creation of a constitutional centre], the fraction considers it necessary first of all to single out from the overall programme of the Union of 17 October those

94 ' Iz Vospominanii A. I. Guchkova ', *Poslednie Novosti*, 16 August 1936. It appears that during the elections to the Third Duma, Guchkov had, at Stolypin's suggestion, even tried to come to some arrangement with the Moscow branch of the U.R.P. and for that purpose had met its chairman, Archpriest Vostorgov, at the home of the mayor of Moscow, A. A. Reinbot. Testimony of Reinbot, in *Padenie Tsarskogo Rezhima*, vol 4, p 123.
95 P. N. Milyukov, ' Politicheskie Partii v Gosudarstvennoi Dume za 5 let ', *Ezhegodnik Gazety Rech¹*, 1912, p 77; see below, Chapter 4.

guiding principles which underlie the Union's whole activity, or which should be taken up as a first priority for practical reasons. Agreement on these questions would probably lead to the creation of a homogeneous Duma majority, capable of achieving the task before us: to give the government powerful support when the bills it tables coincide with the wishes of the Duma centre, and to use to the full the Duma's powers.[96]

These opening paragraphs bear the imprint of Guchkov's aims from August 1906: to create a strong Duma centre majority as a support for the government, especially in social reform, and to use the Duma's rights to the full. The remainder of the memorandum details the reforms which this centre, in co-operation with the government, should take up. It noted that the Duma had no initiative in amending its own statutes, but recommended a widening of the Duma's budget and interpellation rights; the electoral law should not be changed again before reforms had been passed and the country pacified. The reforms it recommended were:

(i) legislative guarantee of personal inviolability, freedom of press, speech and association;

(ii) reform of the laws concerning emergency rule;

(iii) reform of local government at all levels, to allow greater participation of the population as a whole – though the leading role of the landowning nobility was to be safeguarded: ' it should not be forgotten that it is necessary to ensure an appropriate role in local government to that section of the population which is most experienced in the conduct of public affairs, which is most closely tied to the region, and which makes the greatest material contribution to the local budget ';

(iv) reform of judicial organs to give them greater freedom from administrative interference;

(v) equalisation of the peasant with all other citizens before the law; freedom for him to leave the commune; help for him to establish his own holding and to improve the level of his agriculture; no compulsory expropriation of privately owned land;

(vi) urgent improvement of the conditions of life of the factory worker;

(vii) the development of education, especially the universal introduction of primary education;

[96] *TsGAOR*, f 115, op 2, d 34, p 1.

(viii) reduction of indirect taxes on consumer goods, and introduction of income tax;

(ix) measures for controlling public drunkenness.[97]

This was almost identical with the Witte–Stolypin reform programme of 1906. All the same, and in spite of the urging of the Central Committee, the fraction refused to be bound by it. At early meetings of the fraction, warnings were voiced that the attempt to push through such a detailed and wide-ranging programme of reforms would only cause dissensions within the fraction. On 29 October 1907, the fraction voted merely to 'take cognisance of' the Central Committee's programme, not to be bound by it.[98] Thereafter, they did not return to the question of a binding programme, for which members would be required to vote in the house, and the fraction flourished on what was 'understood' rather than 'spelt out'. As a result of not having an agreed programme in the Third Duma, the Octobrists lacked both vigour and discipline in their approach to reform; they tended to drift, while Guchkov, as his colleague Shidlovsky complains in his memoirs, went off on his own hobby-horse, military questions.[99]

For similar reasons, fraction discipline was left loose. The fraction passed a set of rules stipulating that no fraction decision bound its members' vote unless compulsory voting was specifically ordered, in which case at least 60 members had to attend the meeting taking this decision, and at least three-quarters of those present had to vote for it; even in such cases abstention was to be permitted.[100] This contrasted strongly with Kadet practice, which was that any fraction decision created a presumption of compulsory voting, and even abstention was frowned upon. In the long run, Guchkov was to find this vagueness of programme, organisation and discipline extremely irksome.

If he did not succeed in forming his own fraction into a unified body, Guchkov was even less in a position to impose his concepts on the Duma as a whole. He had hoped, in the manner of the Kadets in the First Duma, to get the Duma to accept an Address to the Throne embodying his view of the new constitution. He hoped to circumnavigate its ambiguities and avoid overt provocation by using

[97] ibid, pp 1-5.
[98] ibid, op 1, d 19, pp 139-40.
[99] Shidlovskii, *Vospominaniya*, vol 1, p 204.
[100] *TsGAOR*, f 115, op 2, d 34, p 31.

neither the word 'autocratic' nor the word 'constitution'. The Octobrist fraction accepted a text in this form, and cautiously voted that the list of speakers for the debate on the Address should be kept as short as possible.[101]

Addressing the house in its opening debate, Guchkov performed a delicate balancing act, insisting on the constitutional nature of the new state system, while proposing a text which did not insist on it:

We know that estimations of what has been granted to us differ. I belong to a political party for which it is clear that the Manifesto of 17 October constituted the Monarch's voluntary abnegation of unlimited powers. We saw the Fundamental Laws as an exact fulfilment of the promises given in the Manifesto; for us it is uncontestable that the state reform carried out by our Monarch was the establishment of a constitutional system in our country, but all the same we do not consider it our right to impose our interpretation on everybody.[102]

In the second part of his speech he argued that the constitution did not weaken, but on the contrary strengthened the Monarch's power:

We constitutionalists do not see the establishment of a constitutional monarchy in our country as in any way diminishing the Tsar's authority. On the contrary, in the reformed state system we see that authority taking on a new glory, we see a great future open out before it . . . We know that the Emperor, seeking support in the people's representative body, will thereby become free, free from the court camarilla and the barrier of the bureaucracy. We regard this act as the emancipation of the Tsar, and will not be backward in proving to you that we are loyal and devoted servants of our constitutional Monarch, just as our ancestors served the unlimited Autocrats.

In the name of this ideal he rejected the 'parliamentarism' of the Kadets, and of the First and Second Dumas: 'The Tsar did not emancipate himself from the *chinovniki* and the courtiers simply in order to hand over his authority, his sacred halo, the great spiritual power pertaining to the Tsar's title, to be bandied around by political parties and their Central Committees.'

He called on the Duma to accept the proposed Address unanimously, and thus to demonstrate the unity of its feeling.[103] But no

---

[101] *GDSO* III, 1, pt 1, col 136; *TsGAOR*, f 115, op 1, d 19, p 48.
[102] *GDSO* III, 1, pt 1, col 137.   [103] ibid, cols 138-9; col 140.

sooner had he sat down than Bishop Mitrofan of Gomel drily proposed on behalf of the Right fraction the addition of the words ' and Autocrat of all Russia ' to the text.[104] On the other side, Milyukov formally agreed on behalf of the Kadets to support Guchkov's text, but reproached him bitterly with not using the word ' constitution ': ' I believe that if you now let pass the great honour that has befallen you of at least calling by its real name that which so many generations have aspired to, then you will commit a crime before those who have sent you here.'[105]

Far from unanimity, it was very difficult to find any kind of majority for Guchkov's text. Eventually, however, Balashov agreed on behalf of the Moderate Rights to an address omitting the word ' autocratic ' in order to avoid ' unnecessary and, in our view, undesirable arguments '. This was the text which was duly passed by the house. The vote was unanimous, but the Rights abstained, and when the result was announced, N. E. Markov leapt to his feet and shouted ' Hooray for the Autocrat of all Russia '; he and his colleagues later presented their own independent address to the Emperor and were, apparently, graciously received. To the other parties, Nicholas returned the rather cool reply: ' I am ready to accept the sentiments expressed; I await your constructive work.'[106]

Nor was Stolypin's government at one with the Octobrists on the nature of the new state system. Though Stolypin started from the common ground that the Monarch's authority had been strengthened by the establishment of the Duma, he went on to insist on the autocratic nature of that authority: ' The historic Auocratic Power and free Will of the Monarch are the most valuable heritage of the Russian state system (stormy applause from the Right) . . . and are destined, in times of upheaval and peril for the state, to save Russia and guide her on the path of order and historical truth.'[107]

The Duma could not come to any agreed position on the ministerial declaration. The formulae proposed by each fraction were rejected in turn.[108]

The very nature of the constitution embodied in the October Manifesto and the Fundamental Laws gave rise to these opposing interpretations. As the elderly courtier General A. A. Kireyev noted in his diary on 16 November, ' the Octobrists, supported by the

[104] ibid, cols 140-1.   [105] ibid, col 158.   [106] ibid, cols 141-9.
[107] *GDSO* III, 1, pt 1, cols 311-12.   [108] *GDSO* III, 1, pt 1, cols 570-4.

Kadets, have tried to show that we have a *Constitution*, while the Monarchists have argued that we have *Autocracy*. The tragedy of it all is that both sides can point to irrefutable evidence: declarations of the Tsar Himself, his Manifestos.'[109]

However, differences on the fundamentals of the system did not necessarily exclude co-operation for limited purposes, especially when there was so much to induce the government and the divided Duma majority to work together: fear both of social revolution and of a return to the pre-1905 system. For some time both sides were prepared to go out of their way to be accommodating and to co-operate with one another, as, for example, over the agrarian reform. Nevertheless, the differences and divisions were in the long run to reassert themselves.

[109] *GDSO, Gosudarstvennaya Biblioteka imeni V. I. Lenina,* Rukopisnyi Otdel, f 126 (diary of General A. A. Kireev), d 4, p 250.

3

The peasant problem

Finding a solution for the agrarian problem was the greatest challenge which faced the new state institutions after 1905. Not only did the peasants form the majority of the Russian population, but their condition acted as the most considerable brake both on economic growth and on socio-political reform.

The root of the problem was that, though the Emancipation of 1861 had released the peasants from personal bondage, it had relieved scarcely any of their other hardships; and these had then, to boot, been aggravated by an unprecedented growth in population. The peasants had been given land, but often less than they had been accustomed to work; moreover what they were given was burdened with a redemption debt repayable to the state over nearly half a century. In order to ensure, for rather narrowly conceived fiscal reasons, that the peasants *would* pay off this redemption debt, they were fixed to their allotted land and permitted to hold it only as part of a village commune. The commune was then jointly responsible for redemption payments and other items of taxation, under a system known as *krugovaya poruka*. This system held the peasants still in a kind of bondage (to be sure, to the land, no longer to the landowner, but the restrictions on free movement were as great) and prevented them from enjoying the full civil status which the reforms of Alexander II had, in theory at least, granted to all other sections of the population. Village communes were of two types, both of which had origins long preceding the Emancipation. In the type predominant in most of European Russia, the *obshchina*, land was periodically redistributed between households as peasant families grew larger or smaller; this was to ensure, as far as possible, that each family could feed itself from its own holding. In the type of commune predominant in the Ukraine and the west of Russia, on the other hand, land was passed down the family hereditarily, and was not subject to redistribution. In both types of commune, timber, meadows, pastures and water-courses were held in common.

Russian agriculture was inhibited by a technical backwardness which was only partly the result of communal tenure. Partly, too, it was a function of low urbanisation. Where, as in most of Western Europe and much of North America, there was a dense network of towns and good communications between them, then a receptive market existed for a wide variety of agricultural produce. In Russia this was only the case round St Petersburg and in the Moscow area: over the expanses of the main agricultural regions of Russia, peasants scratched the soil with wooden ploughs, grew rye and oats, lived on a diet of ' cabbage soup and gruel ' (as a popular saying had it) and sold very little to the outside world. They farmed their land in strips, narrow (they were sometimes measured in terms of the width of a ' bast shoe ') as a result of redistributions, with wasted border land running alongside each of them; often these strips were miles from their owners' homes, so that a good part of the day's work was lost in getting to and from them. Crop rotation was primitive, amounting either to exhaustion of the soil or to the three-field system current in England before the enclosures.

Russian governmental policy in the late nineteenth century did nothing to help the peasant overcome this backwardness. Rather the reverse, in fact. By fixing the peasant to the commune and its land, it prevented him from leaving the land and going off to the town to join the industrial working class (though many did so for part of each year to complement their meagre agricultural earnings). The communal land tenure insisted on by the government also provided him with a disincentive for land improvement: he never knew when it might be taken away from him and given to someone else. Taxation and redemption payments weighed heavily on him; and even when the poll-tax was abolished in 1887, it was in effect replaced by indirect taxes on the matches, candles, salt and vodka – above all, alas, vodka – which were the few articles the peasant bought at all regularly.

To make matters worse, the peasant population grew consider-able in the years after Emancipation. From about 55 million in 163 it grew to 82 million in 1897. No more land was allotted to them, so the peasants had to feed the new mouths by other means. The lucky few would buy extra land, perhaps getting a loan from the Peasant Land Bank, with its high interest rates. Some, less lucky, would leave the village in the late autumn and winter and seek factory work or other odd jobs in the towns. Others would rent land from local landowners, or work their estates in return for a share of the crops (a form of land-use which demanded maximum immediate returns, and thus discouraged land improvement and even proper use of fallow, and led to rapid deterioration of the soil).

In a sense, it might seem that peasant land shortage was the root of the problem, and this was argued by all the socialists and many Kadets. Yet the total of peasant landholdings in European Russia exceeded that of the landowners by nearly three to one, so that simple expropriation of the latter would not contribute all that much to a permanent solution. Extensive lands were held by the state and the crown, but they were mostly forest, marsh and tundra, quite unsuitable for peasant agriculture without huge investment. Some of Siberia was more cultivable than the region's popular renown might suggest, but resettlement of peasants there was slow and had only just started seriously.

In fact, there was no simple solution to Russia's agrarian problems, as the later experience of developing countries confirms. Only a patient combination of improvements in land tenure and agricultural methods with the gradual development of the political and industrial life of the country could have brought greater prosperity to the village. But the myth that there *was* a simple solution, and that the peasants had a natural right to all the land, was the single most explosive factor in Russian politics between 1905 and 1917.[1]

Bureaucratic reappraisal of the peasant problem was very slow. The famine of 1891-92 merely led the government to tighten the commune's grip on the peasant, in the hope of ensuring minimal social welfare for everybody and avoiding pauperisation and vagabondage. It was only the rural disorders of 1902 in the provinces of Poltava and Kharkov which began to spread inside the government a sense of the need for fairly radical change. In 1903 the system of *krugovaya poruka* was abolished.

[1] The best general work on the problems of Russian agriculture at the turn of the century is G. P. Pavlovsky, *Agricultural Russia on the Eve of the Revolution*, New York, republished 1968, especially pp 66-114. See also H. Willetts, ' The Agrarian Problem ', in G. Katkov, E. Oberländer, N. Poppe and G. von Rauch (eds), *Russia enters the Twentieth Century*, London 1971, pp 111-37; L. Volin, *A Century of Russian Agriculture: from Alexander II to Khrushchev*, Cambridge, Mass., 1970, pp 40-93; A. Gershenkron, 'Agrarian Policies and Industrialisation: Russia, 1861-1917 ', in *The Cambridge Economic History of Europe*, vol 6, pt 2, Cambridge 1965, pp 706-800.

But the critical swing in bureaucratic opinion did not come until the late months of 1905. At that time there were, broadly speaking, three points of view:

(i) the conservative view, represented above all by Stishinsky and Goremykin, that the taxation burden should be eased, but that land-relationships, and in particular the commune, should be preserved for the basic mass of the peasant population;

(ii) the view principally represented by Krivoshein (Assistant Minister of Agriculture) and Gurko (head of the Zemsky Otdel, in the Ministry of the Interior, which dealt with questions of local economy) that peasant land-relationships must be substantially changed: that the open-field system should give way to one based on enclosed holdings, and that the peasant must be given the chance, and even be encouraged, to leave the commune and take out personal title deeds on his plot of land;

(iii) the ' revolutionary ' view expounded by Kutler during his short tenure of the Ministry of Agriculture, and almost certainly supported for a time by Witte, that an essential part of any agrarian reform must be the expropriation of privately owned land to relieve peasant land-shortage.[2]

The period of decision between these three policies came in January and February 1906. In order to understand the decisions which were taken then, it is important to realise that the third view, expounded in the Kutler project, even if it had little chance of being accepted, *was* a violent provocation to serious and radical thinking, by the challenge it posed to private property, especially that of the nobles (we have already seen the role it played in inducing the nobility to rally their forces for action). In the reaction against it, most officials came to take the Krivoshein–Gurko line, but in doing so they altered the latter's emphasis. From being a pragmatic, gradual policy covering the whole field of agrarian relationships, it took on in the eyes of some (including Stolypin) the form of a salvation for private property in land. And this defence of private property became an essential element in the alliance Stolypin reached with the Octobrists.

An early move in the Krivoshein–Gurko direction was the Manifesto of 3 November 1905, halving redemption payments from 1 January 1906 and abolishing them altogether from 1 January

[2] Simonova, 'Agrarnaya Politika Samoderzhaviya v 1905g ', pp 199-215.

1907.[3] With redemption payments abolished a major fiscal reason, and legal justification, for the commune's existence was removed.

But the significance of this act was lost in the wave of peasant outbreaks which swept Russia in the autumn and winter. This was the time when D. F. Trepov remarked to Witte: ' I am myself a *pomeshchik,* and shall be only too pleased to give away half of my land for nothing, as I feel certain that is the only way of saving the other half for myself.'[4] Kutler's agrarian reform project was a product of these disturbed times, and Witte himself almost certainly asked Kutler to draw it up, though he denies this in his memoirs.[5] It was also strongly influenced by the agrarian programme of the Kadet party, with which the government thought it might well have to work in the autumn of 1905. Indeed, one of the leading Kadet agrarian experts, Professor A. A. Kaufman, took a leading part in the drafting of it.[6]

The element in Kutler's project which caused so much controversy was the article stipulating that private land, where required to relieve peasant land-hunger, might be ' compulsorily expropriated '. Such a harsh measure was only to be taken where the Peasant Land Bank could not reach a voluntary agreement with the owner over the compulsory purchase of the necessary land. Furthermore, the terms of the expropriation would lay a considerable burden on the peasant taking over the land: he would have to pay compensation of 5 per cent of the current rent (or average real income over the last three years) for a period of fifty-five years. These terms were more favourable than buying land at current inflated market prices; but for the land-hungry peasants who would benefit from such an operation they would still be extremely onerous over a long period. Nor did Kutler intend otherwise. He was no partisan of a *cherny peredel* (mass transfer of land) or of the creation of a national land fund. In general, he wanted to see the same kinds of improvements in land tenure and in technical methods which Gurko and Krivo-

---

[3] *PSZ*, 3rd Series, no 26871.   [4] Vitte, *Vospominaniya,* vol 3, p 196.

[5] For evidence that the Kutler project was drawn up on Witte's initiative, see Gurko, *Features and Figures of the* Past, p 235; also Kokovtsev, *Iz Moego Proshlogo,* vol 1, p 130; and the letter of Kutler to Witte quoted below, p 62. Witte's denial is in his *Vospominaniya,* vol 3, pp 195-205.

[6] S. M. Dubrovskii, *Stolypinskaya Zemal'naya Reforma,* M 1963, p 91; L. A. Owen, *The Russian Peasant Movement, 1906-1917,* London 1937, p 26. Kutler himself, when his ministerial career was over, joined the Kadets.

shein were recommending. But it was his belief that many peasant households held so little land that they could not even begin to contemplate technical improvements. Therefore some kind of requisitioning of land for them must be undertaken, from whatever source.[7] When the project came before the Council of Ministers, in January 1906, the government was feeling somewhat more sure of itself, having successfully arrested the St Petersburg Soviet and suppressed the Moscow uprising. Those Ministers most opposed to flirtation with revolutionaries felt able to assert themselves. On 10 January 1906, Witte reported to the Emperor: ' The project, at the preliminary general exchange of views, aroused a complete and radical disagreement in the Council of Ministers . . . The objections arose not from the details of the project, but were based on the principle that property is sacred and that dangers threaten the state if that chief foundation of social life is undermined.'[8]

Now that worse threats to the state appeared to have been overcome, most ministers felt able to regard the whole scheme of compulsory expropriation as the most serious threat remaining. The Council of Ministers took no definite decision for the moment, deciding merely that the whole matter would have to come before the newly formed legislative institutions (not a principle to which they invariably adhered thereafter when important legislation had to be passed). The Emperor, however, was quite clear what he thought. He marked against the summary of Kutler's project: ' I do not approve ', and further commented: ' Private property must remain inviolate.'[9]

No less important to the fate of the Kutler project was the meeting of provincial Marshals of the Nobility in Moscow in January 1906 (as mentioned in the previous chapter). It reasserted the inviolability of private property and called for a solution of the land problem based on ' the transition from communal tenure to hereditary ownership of an enclosed plot of land, with the right to free sale of that land '.[10] The Emperor wrote on his copy of the resolution: ' To be examined in the Council of Ministers '.[11]

[7] The text of Kutler's project is in *Agrarnyi Vopros v Sovete Ministrov v 1906g*, ed B. B. Veselovskii, V. I. Pichet and V. M. Friche, Moscow–Leningrad 1924, pp 27-48.   [8] ibid, pp 76-7.   [9] ibid, pp 76-9.
[10] *TsGIAL*, f 434 (United Nobility), op 1, d 1/303, p 22; see above, p 31.
[11] *TsGIAL*, f 1276, op 2, d 2, p 1. The marginal note is dated 27 January 1906.

This clear lead given by the nobles, and the Emperor's unequivocal support of it, was probably decisive in bringing about the victory of those inside the Council of Ministers (always a majority) who were resolutely opposed to the Kutler project. Even Kutler himself began to climb down from his exposed position before he was dismissed in late January 1906. He wrote to Witte, telling him that, after consultation with some of his advisers, he had decided to rewrite his draft Manifesto on the land question ' without predetermining the fate of private property '. He said that he was doubtful about his project for three reasons:

(i) [It] will have no effect on the extreme parties and may alienate the government's friends;

(ii) The pacification of the peasants is not likely to be achieved . . . The peasants will continue to make impracticable demands and to insist on their immediate fulfilment . . .

(iii) By publicising the solution to the problem before the Duma meets, the Manifesto will in effect provide a final answer: there will be no going back.

He added: ' In case Your Excellency should wish to stand by the previous project, I have suggested suitable amendments. But I cannot take it on my conscience to advise that that project be proceeded with.'[12]

Thus the flirtation with ' revolutionary ' and ' Kadettish ' schemes was brought to an end. From February 1906, the government took its stand on the Krivoshein–Gurko line, for which the nobles had indicated their support. This line was worked out, with somewhat different emphases, in two committees. One, under Krivoshein, was concerned with the means by which land-settlement might be improved, and arose out of Krivoshein's concerns in the Ministry of Agriculture. The other, under Gurko, was set up to consider the problems of bringing peasant legislation into line with the Manifesto of 3 November 1905, which freed the peasants from the redemption debt. Since, under the Emancipation settlement, the completion of redemption payment implied that the peasant held the land he had redeemed as private property, the main question here was that of

---

[12] *TsGIAL*, f 1276, op 1, d 172, p 1. The letter is undated, but must be from the period shortly before his resignation. The last part of the letter is interesting in showing beyond reasonable doubt what Witte denies in his memoirs: that much of the initiative in this scheme came from him.

the peasant's ownership rights. In brief, the Krivoshein committee was mainly concerned with agrarian problems, the Gurko committee with legal ones. They both met at the end of January and beginning of February 1906.

The main recommendation of the Krivoshein committee was that land-settlement commissions should be set up in each province and in each district. Their major concern would be to help the peasants in their area enclose their strips in single plots of land, sorting out all the problems that would arise over boundary demarcation, access to meadows or water, the replacing of bad land by good land, or vice versa, residual rights to timber and pasture, and so on. The land-settlement commissions would be formed of representatives of the government, the nobles and the peasants themselves. To make their work possible, legislation should be brought before the Duma ' to facilitate the transfer to hereditary ownership of an enclosed plot of land ', and also to make it possible for individual house-holders ' to take out property deeds on the allotment land accredited to them '. The Emperor wrote on the margin of the committee's report: ' The measures outlined in the note merit complete approval: in view of its urgency, to be discussed immediately in the Council of Ministers.'[13]

The direct result of this report was the Ukaz of 4 March 1906, establishing provincial and district land-settlement commissions.[14] These were the commissions which were to be responsible for the prac-tical application of the Stolypin agrarian reforms in the localities.

The main problem of the Gurko committee was to determine the quantity of allotment land to which any householder should have the right if he decided to take advantage of the ending of redemp-tion payment and leave the commune. In principle, the best solution would have been for each to be entitled to a proportion of the commune's allotment equal to the proportion of the commune's redemption debt which he or his family had met. But, partly because of the complexity of the 1861 legislation, partly because correct and full records had not everywhere been kept, it was usually impossible to determine this proportion accurately. The majority of the com-mittee therefore proposed that each withdrawer should have the right to keep the land he actually held and used; but if the land he

[13] *Agrarnyi Vopros*, ed Veselovskii, Pichet and Friche, pp 102-5.
[14] *PSZ*, 3rd Series, no 27478.

actually held was more than he was entitled to according to the commune's distribution practices (for example, if his family had got smaller since the last redistribution), then he would only be permitted to retain the surplus if he paid for it at the price laid down in the redemption settlement. Since these prices were at the level of 1861, this would constitute something of an incentive for those in this fortunate situation to leave the commune straight away.

The problem about this kind of recommendation was that, in their haste to give the peasant genuine private property at last, the committee did not sufficiently consider what kind of property it would be. For there was not much point in a peasant's taking out title deeds on his strips; indeed, his doing so would constitute a positive obstacle to the later and more important process of converting his strips into enclosed plots of land. Two members of the committee, Rittikh and Smirnov (significantly the only members of the Ministry of Agriculture represented on it), made precisely this point, and urged that instead each withdrawer receive the nominal right to a defined quantity of private land, to be allotted to him as a single plot only when it was convenient for the commune to do so. The rest of the committee rejoined that the whole object of the reform was to give the peasant full right of disposal of his land, including the selling and mortgaging of it, as well as the certainty that he would reap the full yield from careful cultivation or improvement of it. For these purposes, a notional quantity would be inadequate.[15]

In this way the Gurko committee, unlike that of Krivoshein, finished up by separating the question of private ownership from that of land-settlement, and laying stress on the former. And after the government's head-on clash with the First Duma, this tendency was deepened. The whole issue became dramatised as one of Compulsory Expropriation versus Inalienability of Property. The government's agrarian reform came to be seen, both by its attackers and its defendants, as a defence of private property, indeed as a regeneration of the peasantry through private property. Stolypin's rhetoric helped to push matters in this direction, and the defence of private property through agrarian reform became the principal point in his tacit alliance with the Octobrists.

[15] *TsGIAL*, f 1276, op 2, d 366, pp 22-3.

Having formed his new government in July 1906, Stolypin considered the agrarian problem urgent enough (and was sufficiently authoritarian in temperament) to proceed straight to the promulgation of legislation, using Article 87 of the Fundamental Laws, without waiting for the Second, let alone the Third Duma to debate the matter. The Ukazes he issued were directly based on the recommendations of the Krivoshein and Gurko committees. By Ukaz of 27 August 1906, certain state, appanage and monastery lands were transferred to the Peasant Bank to be put on the market for peasants to buy; at the same time conditions of mortgage in the Peasant Bank were eased.[16] A subsidiary Ukaz of 15 November 1906 legalised the mortgaging of allotment land with the Peasant Bank.[17] By Ukaz of 5 October 1906 certain *soslovny* restrictions on peasants were abolished, primarily the right of peasant officials to control the issuing of passports (without which it was impossible to leave the home village for more than a day or two).[18]

The legislative act that was seen at the time as the most important, and which became the centre of debate in the Duma, was the Ukaz of 9 November 1906, which defined the conditions under which a peasant might leave the commune and claim his allotment land as private property. It accepted for the first time in Russian legislation the principle that 'Any householder who holds allotment land by communal right may at any time demand that the parts of this land accredited to him be deeded to him as personal property.'[19]

The other provisions of the bill reinforced this main point in that they gave legal advantages to the withdrawer, following the recommendations of the Gurko committee. He was to have the right to retain all the land which his household held at the time of the demand; if it exceeded the amount which they would receive at a general redistribution (and such a general redistribution *had* taken place in the last twenty-four years), then they had the right to buy the excess at redemption (i.e. 1861) prices (Article 3). Demands for title deeds had to be met by the commune within a month, during which brief time it had to settle the complicated question of which lands, under Article 3, were due to the withdrawer; if it had not decided within this time, all the decisions were to be taken by the land commandant (*zemsky nachalnik*) (Articles 6 and 7). If the

---

[16] *PSZ*, 3rd Series, no 28392.   [17] ibid, no 28547.   [18] ibid, no 28392.
[19] ibid, no 28528, Section 1, Article 1.

withdrawer further wished at any time to have his private land enclosed in one plot, the commune must either satisfy his request (individually or as part of a general redistribution) or compensate him monetarily with a sum to be settled by the cantonal court (Articles 12-14). The withdrawer was still to have the right to certain communal facilities: pasture, meadow, timber, water, etc. (Article 16).

While all these provisions plainly gave the advantage to the withdrawer, and therefore presumably were intended to hasten the dissolution of communes, it cannot be fairly claimed, as some opponents of the bill were to do, that it represents the forcible destruction of the commune. Much depended on the way in which the local land commissions and the land commandants carried out their duties. And in fact, Section 4 of the Ukaz indicated another way in which the commune might be dissolved, without exclusive advantage to any particular individual: 'The transition of the whole commune, with hereditary as with communal land-usage, to ownership in consolidated plots of land may be carried out by a resolution of a two-thirds majority of the peasants having the right to vote at the communal assembly.'

The American investigator of the Stolypin agrarian reforms, G. L. Yaney, maintains that, in the field, the government's officials and the land commissions were pragmatic rather than doctrinaire, and gradually came to favour this kind of collective dissolution of the commune, rather than individual withdrawals which disrupted both agrarian and personal relationships.[20] The Duma's work on the agrarian bill, of course, was being carried on whilst the bill was already being treated as effective outside; this casts Stolypin's respect for the legislative powers of the Duma in bad light, but it did enable the Duma to profit from practical experience in the operation of the bill, and to reformulate it. One such modification was that it permitted, in the final law of 14 June 1910, such collective dissolutions on a simple majority vote (not two-thirds) of the communal assembly. Another, the product of the work of the Duma Land Committee, was the suggestion that communes in which no general repartition had taken place in the last twenty-four years should automatically be considered as having gone over to private owner-

[20] G. L. Yaney, 'The Concept of the Stolypin Land Reform', SR, vol 23 (1964), pp 275-93, especially pp 292-3.

ship.[21] These amendments brought in by the Duma were in the direction of speeding up the transition to private land ownership.

The important point about the debates in the Third Duma on Stolypin's agrarian reform is that the Octobrists and Rights were able to rally together under the umbrella of rhetoric about the defence of private property and the inculcation of healthy patriotic instincts in the peasant. Shidlovsky, reporting for the Duma Land Committee, set the tone:

At the basis of every state founded on the rule of law lies the free, energetic and independent individual. That individual you will not get without granting him the common human right of owning property; and I think that anyone who really wants our state to be founded on the rule of law cannot pronounce against personal ownership of land.[22]

If communal tenure were continued indefinitely, he argued, the result would be that at every setback the peasant would expect the government to allot him a little bit more land. But shortage of land was only one aspect of the agrarian problem. In fact, it was merely a symptom of technical backwardness, of insufficiently intensive cultivation. Russia had reached a stage in her historical development when the commune was already outdated, and she must therefore move on. Peasants should no longer be artificially bound to the land: the surplus population should, as was part of normal historical development, leave and go to live in the towns. The promotion of industry was thus an essential part of the solution to the agrarian problem. So also was the provision of education for the rural population. In fact, the agrarian problem could in the long run only be solved by the all-round development of the country. The introduction of peasant private landed property, Shidlovsky concluded, would do much to release the creative forces which would drive this development forward.[23]

[21] The Octobrist agrarian expert S. I. Shidlovsky claims in his memoirs that this article was added as something that might be sacrificed later to appease the defenders of the commune in the State Council. In the event, there were no defenders. However, Stolypin spoke against it, and the State Council replaced it with an article confining the automatic transfer to private ownership to those communes which had never carried out a general repartition (and then only if those communes had been established before 1 January 1887). (Shidlovskii, *Vospominaniya*, vol 1, pp 179-81; I. V. Chernyshev, *Agrarno-Krest'yanskaya Politika Rossii za 150 let*, Petrograd 1918, p 343.) [22] *GDSO*, III, 2, pt 1, col 171.

[23] ibid, cols 145-98.

This was mostly sensible and perceptive. What was striking was the way in which the conservative side of the house, with very few exceptions, failed to mention the obstacles to change which they were unfailingly to discern when it came to other reforms. Bishop Mitrofan for the Right fraction, for example, welcomed the Ukaz of 9 November with only a cursory backward glance at the established tradition of the commune.[24] It was left to the Kadets to criticise the government's policy – and, even more significantly, to the peasant deputies of all parties.

The Kadets were politically in an awkward position. They had become identified with a policy of compulsory expropriation of private land, even if limited and for just compensation. They were now faced, as in the Second Duma, with the fait accompli of the Ukaz of 9 November, and also with the government bill brought before the house. They were not wholly opposed to the Ukaz of 9 November, and indeed accepted its long-term aims of setting up individual peasant property as the basis of a legally ruled state. But they did not consider it incompatible with a preliminary measure of expropriation in favour of land-hungry peasants. So they had to run the political tightrope between two polar views of the agrarian problem, taking something from both sides.

Shingarev, the Kadets' main spokesman on agrarian matters in the Third Duma, concentrated his attack on the crudity and hastiness of the government's measures for loosening the commune, and on the artificiality of the incentives given to those withdrawing from it. He pointed out that it was meaningless, if not actually harmful, to encourage peasants to take out title deeds on strips: this was not the kind of peasant smallholder who would bring stability to the state. What was more important, he argued, than the theoretical introduction of private property, was the establishment of the rule of law in the countryside. How could the peasant work as a free property-owner when he was still under the administrative caprice of the land commandant, and when any sign of intellectual or cultural life in the village was greeted with suspicion? Reforms of local administration and education were at least as urgent as this artificially hasty measure, and more unequivocally beneficial. In the meantime urgent cases of rural hardship should be dealt with as the Kadets had always proposed, by compulsory expropriation of private land for

24 ibid, cols 198-204.

redistribution where this should prove necessary: it was recognised in all law-abiding states that the inalienability of private property was not something absolute and must be overridden if state or social emergencies required it.[25]

The Kadets tabled an alternative bill on withdrawal from the commune, which embodied their criticisms of the government's programme. The Kadet bill did not separate *ukreplenie* (the mere taking out of title deeds on existing holdings, often in strips) from *vydel* (the separation and enclosure of holdings as one private plot). In effect, any peasant wishing to withdraw from the commune would have at the same time to consolidate and enclose his holdings in one place. The commune would have the right not to carry out such an enclosure till the first general repartition after the withdrawal demand had been made. If the enclosure *was* carried out before such general repartition, then the withdrawer would receive as much land as he was entitled to according to the number of distribution units in his family; except that the commune would not be obliged to give him more land than he had received at the last repartition. Such separate enclosures must be agreed to by a two-thirds majority of the communal assembly. The Kadet bill proposed a time limit of three years between the demand and its fulfilment, either through a separate enclosure, general repartition, or monetary compensation, failing which the intending withdrawer should have access to the courts; nowhere in the Kadet bill did the land commandant figure as a last instance. As a restriction on rural capitalism, the bill forbade any peasant to accumulate, by purchase or enclosure, more than six times the maximum allotment laid down for the area by the Emancipation legislation of 1861.[26]

Compulsory expropriation in favour of land-hungry peasants did not feature in this bill, since it was intended purely as a replacement to the Ukaz of 9 November. But Shingarev made it clear in his speech that it would be an essential complement to their bill.

The Kadet bill succeeded in drawing the votes of a few peasant deputies, even in the Labour group. But the peasant vote was

[25] ibid, cols 223-53, 261-74.
[26] *TsGIAL,* f 1278, op 2, d 59, p 28. The government introduced a similar restriction on peasant landholding (not present in the Ukaz of 9 November) into the bill before the first reading in the Third Duma. It was passed, and became part of the law of 14 June 1910. (*TsGIAL,* f 1278, op 2, d 59, p 5.)

divided by another initiative, the Project of the 47, which was submitted by peasant and priest deputies of all parties. This was quite a serious threat to the government's bill, since it threatened to draw peasant votes from the right wing and the Octobrist fraction, and thus to disrupt the majority on which the government was relying (indeed Avrekh asserts, though without citing any evidence, that it was right-wing peasants who actually took the initiative in drawing up the bill, and that it was only later supported by the left-wingers).[27] The project was forwarded to the government on 14 March 1908, long before the debates in the Duma, and thus was evidently prepared well in advance. It started from the assertion that land shortage was at the root of the peasant's problems, and that legislation should begin by eliminating this. The method it proposed was the estimation of land-norms for each area, the formation of a state land fund from state, appanage, monastery and (where necessary) expropriated private land, and the award of land to peasants on favourable terms to bring their holdings up to this norm. Previous owners would be compensated ' at a just estimate ', and the whole operation financed by the introduction of a progressive land tax. Redistribution would be organised by local land committees elected by the whole local population. In areas where there was not enough land to go round, land-hungry peasants were to be given state aid to emigrate to Siberia or to other areas where land was available.[28]

Whether or not right-wing peasants drew up the bill, they certainly supported attempts to discuss it. M. S. Andreichuk, for example (Moderate Right – Volynia province), after welcoming the Ukaz of 9 November, went on:

Our respected reporter emphasised in his report that, if we pass this law of 9 November, then the agrarian problem will be solved. In my view this is not at all the case. Many other sides of the agrarian problem still need to be settled . . . What is important and urgent is the peasants' landlessness and land shortage . . . In these circumstances I consider partial expropriation necessary.[29]

Ya. G. Danilyuk, a member of the Right fraction from the same province, declared:

We shall not satisfy the peasants with this law. Look at those who have little or no land. Living here in St Petersburg in a clean room

[27] A. Ya. Avrekh, 'Agrarnyi Vopros v 3-ei Dume ', *Ist. Zap.*, vol. 62, p 65.
[28] *TsGIAL*, f 1276, op 4, d 449, p 2.   [29] *GDSO*, III, 2, pt 1. cols 999–1000.

and receiving a tidy salary, you imagine that the whole world has it just as good; but you go and take a look at any village and see what cold and hungry poverty they have there.[30]

G. F. Fedorov, Octobrist deputy from Smolensk, said much the same:

On the one hand we cannot but accept the law of 9 November. On the other hand, we cannot vote for that law because in it nothing is said about the landless and land-hungry who, if the Ukaz of 9 November is accepted, will be left completely without land and will be thrown to the mercy of fate.[31]

Other peasant members of these three right-wing and centre fractions repeated the point. It is clear, in fact, that most of the peasant members of the Duma wanted to supplement the law of 9 November with some kind of additional allotment of land to needy peasants. The Project of the 47 went before the Duma Land Committee, but was never fully discussed in a general session. In effect, it was ' buried '.

Even in the State Council, there were no voices raised in favour of the traditional state protection of the commune. Stishinsky, Stolypin's old antagonist, spoke in support of the Ukaz of 9 November. Most of its opponents objected to the haste of the bill, to the artificial separation between claiming title deeds and carrying out enclosure, to the automatic dissolution of communes which had not carried out repartition in the last twenty-four years. In this, such right-wing figures as Ya. A. Ushakov and D. A. Olsufyev concurred with Witte and the Kadet professors Kovalevsky and Manuilov. They proposed a number of amendments, which aroused lively discussion and some close voting. The most controversial amendment was that put forward by Prince A. D. Obolensky. It would have stipulated that land taken out of the commune should pass into family rather than personal property; in this way an important element of traditional peasant land tenure would be preserved. Stolypin had to appear in person to object to this proposal. But significantly, this and all other amendments unacceptable to the government were rejected by the house. Probably the fact is that, when it was known that the government was determined to pass a bill, and also that the Emperor concurred with this intent, then the State Council would go along with the current. Only when a wedge could be driven between the Emperor

[30] ibid, col 1250.   [31] ibid, cols 1265-6.

and the government did the State Council play an independent, and vital, role.[32]

The agrarian reform, in fact, offers a unique example of virtual unanimity between Stolypin's government, the Octobrists, the right wing in the Duma, the State Council and the United Nobility. This is because it was the keystone of the 3rd June alliance: the defence of private landed property and its extension to the peasant was the central point of the alliance between these various groups which had grown up in the turbulent months following the Moscow December uprising. They all agreed, in effect, that this was the first essential in order to stave off revolution, whether or not they also agreed on the need for further reform.

But this political significance of the bill vitiated somewhat its substantive purposes. The emphasis on dissolving the bonds of the commune and on giving private property to individual peasants was one-sided, and distorted the early stages of the reform's application. From available evidence on its actual operation, it would seem that, indeed, the transfer of the peasant from communal to individual ownership was by itself really of no great significance in changing his way of life. Applications to transfer in this way declined sharply after the early years of the reform, and government policy concentrated more on enclosures and other tasks of land-settlement, especially where these could be undertaken by whole villages at a time. In this it achieved a respectable measure of success, enclosing something over 10 per cent of all households in European Russia by 1915.[33]

One of the leading Western investigators of the Stolypin reform, G. P. Pavlovsky, has concluded that this overemphasis on individual withdrawals from the commune added a dangerous element of friction in a countryside still alive with the memories of revolution. This conclusion is corroborated by the statistics of the Soviet scholar S. M. Dubrovsky, who shows that the peak of peasant disturbances against the Stolypin smallholders came in 1910-11, closely following the peak year of individual withdrawals, but then dropped sharply in

[32] GSSO, Sessiya 5 (1909-10), cols 1179-86, 1189-1207, 1525-33, 1601-7, 1661.
[33] See Dubrovskii, Stolypinskaya Zemel'naya Reforma, pp 241-4; G. T. Robinson, Rural Russia under the Old Regime, New York 1932, p 225; Yaney, 'Concept of the Stolypin Land Reform', pp 285-6; W. E. Mosse, 'Stolypin's Villages', SEER, vol 43 (1964-5), pp 257-74; Pavlovsky, Agricultural Russia on the Eve of the Revolution, pp 134-41.

1912-13. The pioneers of individual withdrawal and enclosure were also among the first victims of the renewed upheavals of 1917.[34] The agrarian reform also suffered from the disadvantage that it did not satisfy most of the peasants, as can be seen from their speeches in the debates on the Ukaz of 9 November. This was something that no responsible government could have done anything about, but the peasants' continued unsatisfied land-hunger, whetted in 1905, left the threat of a mass uprising hanging over the heads of all politicians. This fundamental threat could have been parried if Russia's élites had co-operated better. But in fact, as we shall see, the easy passage of Stolypin's agrarian reform through Duma and State Council was not to be repeated in the case of his government's other reform projects. In fact, the 3rd June system was a really firm alliance for one issue only.

[34] ibid, pp 144-5.

4

The Naval Staffs crisis

Military and naval questions in the Duma

From the beginning of the Third Duma, the Octobrists set out to make the military and naval field one in which they could both exercise independent influence and yet also work with the government, and in general leave their mark upon Russia's future. At first sight it might appear odd that they should choose this field, for Article 14 of the Fundamental Laws appeared not to leave the Duma (or the State Council) many powers at all in the ordering of naval and military matters, in which new dispositions, unless they entailed fresh expenditure, were to be decided directly by the Emperor.

Yet in fact this was an excellent field politically for the Octobrists to take up. For one thing, the constitutional position was not as clear as it is portrayed above: Article 96 of the Fundamental Laws actually seemed to contradict Article 14 by confining the Emperor's direct authority to the combat, technical and supply areas of military life. At any rate, the confusion of general with specific provisions gave the Octobrists the opportunity to profit by ambiguity in a way which was to be a characteristic part of their parliamentary tactics. Furthermore, the backward and depleted state of both army and navy after the Japanese War ensured that huge new expenditures would in fact be required, and that the Duma would be able to exercise influence through budget debates.

Most important of all, the disasters of the Japanese war had exposed glaring deficiencies in the equipment, organisation and leadership of both army and navy. The Octobrists were therefore in an excellent position to make outspoken demands for reform in the armed forces: by boldly criticising the government's record, and then working with them to improve it, the Octobrists could project themselves as a party both patriotic (perhaps more patriotic than the government, or at any rate the court) and also fearlessly independent, not at all a party of lackeys with an electoral system tailor-made for them, as they were usually represented in the opposition press.

Public involvement in the improvement and expansion of the armed forces was a tradition in the major polities of Europe at this time. In Germany this was the era of the Navy League and the Army League, with which the old parties of the Right allied themselves. In France the anti-Dreyfusards banded to defend the honour of the French army. In Britain there was also a Navy League: while schoolchildren went about in sailor suits, the Harmsworth press called for a navy strong enough to protect the Empire against all comers, and Lord Roberts's National Service League pressed for the introduction of universal military service. There were ample precedents to suggest that this kind of agitation could win a great deal of public attention and even votes.

The Octobrists' enthusiastic espousal of military causes also owed much to the personality of their leader. Guchkov was a man of ebullient and vigorous character, and imbued with a strong love of his country. He was deeply interested in military affairs, and had gained considerable experience of them in Bulgaria, in Armenia, in fighting for the Boers against the British, and in the Japanese War. There was indeed much in him that resembled his British contemporary (against whom he may have fought in South Africa), Winston Churchill: the same fascination with war, the same devotion to parliamentary institutions, mixed with the emotional need to play an unorthodox, sharp-shooting role in them (Guchkov could only compromise with the government so long as such a role made him an odd man out among Russian liberals), and the same capacity to arouse either strong loyalty or intense hostility in those who had to deal with him.[1] The other Octobrists, however, did not always appreciate Guchkov's love of ' playing soldiers ', and felt he would do well to spend less time with officers of the General Staff and give more attention to the unwieldy fraction he had set up for himself in the Duma.[2]

The keystone of the Duma's involvement in military politics was its Committee of Imperial Defence. This was established at the opening of the Third Duma to study military and naval questions, and Guchkov was elected its chairman. Members of the opposition, from the Kadets leftwards, were excluded from it,[3] and the

[1] The similarity was noted by Sir Bernard Pares: see his article 'Alexander Guchkov', *SEER*, vol 15 (1936), pp 121-2.
[2] See, especially, Shidlovskii, *Vospominaniya*, vol 1, p 204.
[3] Against Guchkov's wishes, and at the insistence of the Rights, according

committee became a closely knit and homogeneous group of centre and right-wing deputies, well placed to establish contact with some of the younger officials of the War and Naval Ministries. As soon as the committee was formed, a delegation of twelve from it visited the Minister of War, Rediger, and discussed the Ministry's programme with him. Rediger, for his part, was also pleased with the consultation: he hoped that the Duma's co-operative disposition might be used to gain more credits in his perpetual rivalry with the Naval Ministry.[4] Contacts were continued on a more informal level: a group of young staff officers of the War Ministry, impatient at the slow rate of reform in the army, began to meet with members of the Duma Committee at the private flat of General I. V. Gurko (who knew Guchkov well from the Boer War), to discuss necessary reforms and to mobilise public opinion in favour of them. Rediger, and at first his successor, Sukhomlinov, allowed these meetings to take place and even to make use of confidential material. The meetings were also encouraged and sometimes attended by the Assistant Ministry of War, A. A. Polivanov, who got to know Guchkov well, and was always ready to help with information and advice, not always to the approval of his superior. In the end, apparently about 1910, Sukhomlinov became alarmed by the group's sharp criticisms of ministerial policy and stopped its meetings, but not before it had done much to make the Duma, and through it the newspaper-reading public, more aware of the kinds of military reform that were needed.[5]

to A. Ya. Avrekh, 'Stolypinskii Bonapartizm i Voprosy Voennoi Politiki v III Dume', *Vop. Ist.*, 1956, no 11, p 23; see also A. I. Zvegintsev, 'The Duma and Imperial Defence', *Russian Review*, vol 1 (1912), p 50.

[4] A. A. Polivanov, *Iz Dnevnikov i Vospominanii po Dolzhnosti Voennogo Ministra i ego Pomoshchnika* (1907-16), M 1924, pp 34-5.

[5] 'Iz Vospominanii A. I. Guchkova', *Poslednie Novosti*, 19 August 1936; *Padenie Tsarskogo Rezhima*, vol 6, Moscow–Leningrad 1926, pp 251-2, 291-2; Polivanov, *Iz Dnevnikov i Vospominanii*, pp 40-3, 57; *Dnevnik Velikogo Knyazya Andreya Vladimirovicha*, L 1925, pp 57-8; W. A. Suchomlinow, *Erinnerungen*, Berlin 1924, pp 199, 279; A. S. Lukomskii, *Vospominaniya*, Berlin 1922, vol 1, pp 28-9; A. I. Denikin, *Put' Russkogo Ofitsera*, New York 1953, pp 250-2. Very little published information seems to exist on these consultations, beyond the scattered references noted here. The records of the Duma Imperial Defence Committee (in the Central State Historical Archive, Leningrad) were not made available to me.

In its relations with the Naval Ministry, however, the Imperial Defence Committee took the path not of co-operation, but of direct attack. They used the opportunity offered by the huge credits the Ministry required to rebuild the fleets lost in the Japanese War. Early in 1908 the government came before the Duma requesting an annual credit of 30 million rubles for four years in order to construct four Dreadnought-type battleships in the Baltic. The Octobrists and Moderate Rights decided to refuse these credits and thus bring pressure on the government for the reform of the Naval Ministry, and indeed of the whole command of the armed forces. The house, with the support of even the Right fraction, voted to withhold over $8\frac{1}{2}$ million rubles from the credits requested for naval construction, and on a motion of the Budget Committee called for

(i) the integration of the measures of the naval Ministry into a future plan of the nation's defences;
(ii) a radical reorganisation of the naval administration;
(iii) the preliminary tabling before the State Duma of a financial programme of naval construction covering a sufficiently extensive period.[6]

In effect, the Duma was saying that it had no confidence in the ability of the Naval Ministry to use the credits effectively, nor did it feel certain that the Supreme Command had co-ordinated the plans of the Naval Ministry with other strategic planning. The Emperor was very annoyed at this refusal of a most important credit. On 25 May 1908, he wrote to Stolypin complaining of the Duma's ' blind and totally unjustified refusal of credits for the reconstruction of the fleet . . . just before the arrival of the English king ' (who was coming on an official visit to Reval). Stolypin, too, was worried by the Duma's failure to reach an agreement with the Naval Ministry: before the debate on the credits, he had arranged a private conference of the two sides to try to sort out their differences unobtrusively. He had also appeared in person before the Duma Imperial Defence Committee to support the credits. Now, in a speech to the State Council on 13 June 1908, he fired a warning shot over the Duma's bows: the Duma, he said, had acted in a high-handed and irresponsible manner, which threatened to disrupt the delicate equilibrium of Imperial prerogative and legislative institutions.[7]

[6] *GDSO*, III, 1, pt 3, cols 1412-16, 1472-3.
[7] *KA*, vol 5, p 118 (Correspondence of Nicholas II and Stolypin); A. L. Sidorov, ' Iz Istorii Podgotovki Tsarizma k Pervoi Mirovoi Voine ',

The State Council then passed the credits which the Duma had rejected, and in accordance with the budget regulations the previous year's credits came into force, and actually provided enough for the naval construction programme to be started.

Before this, however, Guchkov had widened his attack, moving on from the Naval Ministry to the Supreme Command itself. The criticisms he made of it grew out of his constitutional concept of the new Russia. The key word was ' irresponsibility '– both in its everyday and its constitutional sense. The War and Navy Ministries had remained unaffected by the constitutional changes of 1905-6: they were not responsible to the unified Council of Ministers (as were all other Ministries save that of Foreign Affairs), but rather, in an imprecisely defined hierarchy, to the War and Admiralty Councils, the Council of Imperial Defence, headed by the Grand Duke Nikolai Nikolayevich, and thence to the Emperor. These bodies were supposed to co-ordinate the armed forces of the Empire. Indeed, the last-named had been set up only in 1905 in view of the patent lack of co-ordination between army and navy in the Japanese War. But in fact, as Guchkov saw it,[8] these bodies only caused confusion and duplication of functions, and created sinecures for members of the royal family. They should be replaced by bodies answerable to the Naval and War Ministries, and indirectly to the Council of Ministers. This was an important part of the struggle for the fulfilment of the new constitution. In an article for an English journal, Guchkov's close associate of these years, A. I. Zvegintsev, showed how the changes they envisaged were connected with the ending of autocracy and the establishment of responsible unified government:

In the old autocratic system of government, there was no cabinet, and co-operation between Ministers was impossible. Each branch of the administration pursued its own objects, and the jealousy which ordin-

---

Istoricheskii Arkhiv, no 2, 1962, p 121; *GSSO*, Sessiya 3 (1907-8), cols 1706-9; K. F. Shatsillo, *Russkii Imperializm i Razvitie Flota*, M 1968, pp 170-1, 185-6.

[8] And here, if nowhere else, his testimony agrees with that of his later military bête noire, Sukhomlinov: see the latter's *Erinnerungen*, pp 198-9. Also Yu. N. Danilov, *Velikii Knyaz' Nikolai Nikolaevich*, Paris 1930, p 70. A pity in many ways, for the idea seems basically a good one: the Council of Imperial Defence had much in common with the Imperial General Staff being set up in Britain at that time.

arily exists in all countries between army and navy had resulted in a complete ignorance among the staff of each as to what the other was doing; in fact, the Admiralty had no General Staff at all. The same absence of a common responsibility in army organisation had gone very far to create a whole number of Departments, not responsible to the Minister of War; several were directed by persons whose birth put them above the law; some had no real organisation, so that practically they could not carry out the ideas outlined in their central offices.[9]

In a notorious speech in the Duma on 27 May, Guchkov made the same points in more sensational form by naming certain Grand Dukes, 'irresponsible by their very position, at the head of responsible and important branches of military life'. As he reeled off the names, the left wing of the Duma, and much of the centre and right wing breathlessly applauded him.[10] In his autobiography, Guchkov reports that after his speech, Milyukov came up to him and asked him excitedly: 'Alexander Ivanovich, what have you done? After that they will dissolve the Duma!' 'No', answered Guchkov, 'for that they will not dissolve the Duma. I am convinced that in this matter the army and the people are with us. For that reason they will not dare to dissolve.'[11] One may doubt whether this altercation ever in fact took place, but Guchkov's telling of it well represents his intentions at the time: he wanted a *succès de scandale*, and at the same time the feeling that he represented the majority of military and civilian opinion and therefore could afford to throw down a challenge to the government and the court.

Yet in some ways, it is doubtful if this speech was advisable or well-timed. The government was already well aware of the Duma's attitude, and, as Stolypin remarked to him, Guchkov could more properly have made his criticisms of the Grand Dukes to the Emperor privately, instead of seeking the maximum publicity and not warning anyone in advance. It is certain that the speech alienated the Emperor and royal family; and their distrust, even hatred, of Guchkov was an important political factor in the following years. Furthermore, the speech contributed to a poisoning of the level of political discussion in the country, which was more and more tending to become scurrilously personal rather than revolutionary (a tendency which reached its apogee, of course, in the campaign over Rasputin).

[9] Zvegintsev, 'The Duma and Imperial Defence', pp 52-3.
[10] *GDSO*, III, 1, pt 3, cols 1578-1600.   [11] *Poslednie Novosti*, 19 August 1936.

On the other hand, the speech undoubtedly impressed the parliamentary correspondents both at home and abroad. And it also had practical effect: it was not long before the Grand Duke Nikolai Nikolayevich resigned, the other Grand Dukes were given honorary positions, and the Council of Imperial Defence was abolished.[12]

The Naval General Staff bill

In some respects, Guchkov was hammering at an already open door. One of the most important reforms of the type he was demanding in the naval command had already been set under way: this was the creation, in June 1906 (under Article 87), of a Naval General Staff, to undertake naval strategic planning and to ensure the fleet's overall readiness for mobilisation. The initiative had come from a group of young officers in the Naval Ministry, who had studied the lessons of the recent naval disasters – a group not unlike that of Gurko and his colleagues in the War Ministry, recently trained ' young Turks ', anxious to adopt the latest weapons and to introduce more systematic strategic planning. They formed the nucleus of the new Naval General Staff.[13]

The new Staff was clearly subordinated to the Naval Ministry. In fact, it accorded in every way with the spirit of the reforms the Octobrists and the Duma Imperial Defence Committee were demanding. They decided, however, to try to make additional political capital out of it. When the government requested annual credits of around 95,000 rubles necessary to establish the Staff on a permanent basis, the Duma passed them and also, on the recommendation of its Imperial Defence Committee, confirmed the establishment lists, together with the salaries, of the Staff. It did so on the grounds that, being part of the Naval Ministry, the Staff formed part of the governmental structure of the Empire and its establishment was therefore

---

[12] Polivanov, *Iz Dnevnikov i Vospominanii*, pp 48-9; Danilov, *Velikii Knyaz' Nikolai Nikolaevich*, pp 70-1.

[13] One of these young officers was Captain Kolchak, of later fame. See his testimony to a Bolshevik Investigatory Commission: *Dopros Kolchaka*, Moscow–Leningrad 1925, pp 13-18; also Eroshkin, *Ocherki Istorii*, p 287; Amburger, *Geschichte der Behördenorganisation Russlands*, p 356; Shatsillo, *Russkii Imperializm i Razvitie Flota*, pp 173-4.

subject to the confirmation of the legislature in substance and not only from the budgetary point of view.[14]

This step was fully in accord with the Imperial Defence Committee's policy of asserting the Duma's influence in military affairs wherever possible, and also with the Octobrists' policy of exploiting ambiguities such as were represented by Articles 14 and 96 of the Fundamental Laws. It laid them open to attack, however, from those who wished to cut down the Duma's influence by interpreting Article 96 unequivocally in the opposite sense. Such defenders of autocratic prerogative were in the ascendancy in the upper house, the State Council. We have already seen that this body, at its reform in 1906, was intended as a guarantee of the continuity of the state system in an era of change. In effect, it became a kind of institutional embodiment of the Emperor's ambivalence towards his own constitution. The mechanism by which he influenced it was the annual appointment system; on 1 January each year he had the right to transfer his previous appointees, if they did not satisfy him, to other, non-legislative departments of the State Council, and to replace them in the chamber with more reliable candidates. In principle, these appointments were to be made in consultation with the President of the Council of Ministers, but this practice was apparently dropped very early, and neither Stolypin nor his successor, Kokovtsev, were able to influence the appointments except when they were in particular favour. The result was that the appointed half of the State Council constituted a solid conservative bloc; and together with some of the elected representatives of the nobility and zemstvos, it formed a permanent majority which was a formidable barrier to legislative change, especially where the interests of the nobility or the prerogatives of the autocracy were in question. The nucleus of the bloc was a ' group ' (the Duma word ' fraction ' was shunned) of Rights under the former Minister of the Interior, P. N. Durnovo. One of its staunchest members, M. G. Akimov, was appointed President of the State Council in 1907, and from then on exercised a considerable influence on the annual appointments. In fact, only where the government was determined on a particular reform measure, and the Emperor agreed with it (as in the case of the agrarian reform), could it transverse this barrier. If there was the

[14] *GDSO*, III, 1, pt 3, cols 1420-3; *Proekty Zakonov, prinyatye Gosudarstvennoi Dumoi*, 3 Sozyv, 1 Sessiya, 1907-8gg, SPB 1909, pp 198-9.

slightest hint of displeasure or doubt from Tsarskoe Selo, then a majority could no longer be ensured, and ministers themselves often began to have second thoughts about measures which they had piloted through the Duma with all apparent conviction.[15]

The Naval Staff bill was the first to face this kind of conservative opposition. P. Kh. Shvanebakh, former State Controller, asserted in the Finance Committee of the upper house that, while the Duma had every right to confirm or reject the *credits* for the new Staff, it had no right to confirm the establishment list itself, since according to Articles 14 and 96 of the Fundamental Laws, this right belonged to the Emperor alone. Akimov, President of the State Council, and Durnovo, leader of the Rights, supported this view. Kharitonov, State Controller, speaking for the government, replied that before 1905 all the establishment lists of the War and Naval Ministries had been subject to the general legislative procedure, and that the government had simply continued this system under the new post-1905 legislative procedure. The establishment lists of the Naval Ministry were part of the general administrative network of the Empire, not part of the combat and organisational structure of the navy, which was withheld from the legislative chambers. When Rediger was asked for his view, he replied that, as a member of a united cabinet, he shared the State Controller's view, though he appears to have said this with implied reservations.[16] Polivanov noted in his diary: ' In everything that was said one felt a desire to undermine Stolypin for having supposedly sanctioned in the Council of Ministers a restriction of the supreme power.'[17] The State Council Finance Committee with one dissenting vote recommended the rejection of the bill for the following reason:

The legislative institutions may take decisions only on the general magnitude of sums requested for the salaries of officials. The supreme leader of the army and navy is the Emperor, and it would be inconsistent with the very concept of a supreme leader to restrict him by

[15] Chasles, *Le Parlement Russe*, pp 112-17; Kokovtsev, *Iz Moego Proshlogo*, vol 2, p 6; M. M. Kovalevskii, 'Vospominaniya', *Ist. SSSR*, 1969, no 5, pp 84-94; A. D. Stepanskii, 'Politicheskie Gruppirovki v Gosudarstvennom Sovete, 1906-7gg ', *Ist. SSSR*, 1965, no 4, pp 49-64.

[16] *Rech*[1], 25 June 1908; Polivanov, *Iz Dnevnikov i Vospominanii*, p 47, reports that ' Rediger replied diplomatically that there was no doubt about his own view, but that he associated himself with the government's opinion '.   [17] Polivanov, *Iz Dnevnikov i Vospominanii*, p 47.

THE NAVAL STAFFS CRISIS

directions as to the number of persons or offices which should exist in the combat bodies of the army and navy, and as to their conditions of service.[18]

The State Council duly rejected the bill in full session on 3 July. Shvanebakh and Kharitonov took up the same opposing positions as before. All the Ministers (who were ex officio members of the State Council) voted for the bill, and therefore in support of the Duma's position.[19]

The elements of a crisis were already fully in the making here, and it was a matter of considerable importance when estimating the place of the new state institutions, the Duma and the Council of Ministers, in Russian politics. It was precisely such precedents which would determine the practical operation of the ambiguous 1906 constitution. The extremities of interpretation which could be wrung out of the Duma's stance were shown in the State Council by Kasatkin-Rostovsky, when he asked: 'We are defending a very serious question of principle: who . . . will stand at the head of the armed forces, the Council of Ministers or the Emperor?'[20] It was presumably because of these far-reaching implications that both sides held firmly to their views against opposition, in spite of the obvious political costs of doing so: for the Council of Ministers and the Duma in terms of promoting a crisis in which they would embarrass the Emperor and quite possibly suffer a humiliating defeat, for the State Council in terms of rejecting and therefore at the least seriously delaying the proper financing of an important reform in the Empire's naval administration. The intentions of the Council of Ministers are in many ways particularly difficult to assess: in his memoirs, Kokovtsev claims that the Naval Ministry had given the establishment lists to the Duma for information only, and that they had been confirmed along with the credits by oversight. The Council of Ministers, according to him, had then supported the further passage of the bill in view of its importance.[21] This is not a satisfactory account. As we have seen, the Duma's attitude was clearly expressed and was certainly not the result of an oversight. In any case, the Council of Ministers could have asked the State Council to pass the bill immediately with an appendix noting the procedural

[18] *Rech'*, 25 June 1908.
[19] *GM*, 4 July 1908; *Rech'*, 4 July 1908; *GSSO*, Sessiya 3 (1907-8), col 2230. [20] ibid, col 2228.
[21] Kokovtsev, *Iz Moego Proshlogo*, vol 1, pp 338-42.

irregularity and annulling it as a precedent. This it did not do; indeed, Kharitonov argued that the Duma's procedure had been correct. On the available evidence, we must conclude that Stolypin's cabinet regarded the matter as one of principle, and supported the Duma.

However, since the State Council rejected the bill in July 1908, it did not at this stage come before the Emperor, and for the time being crisis was averted. Because of the matter's importance, the Naval Ministry submitted the same bill to the legislative institutions in the next session, and it went on the same path as before through the Duma, though this time the Naval Ministry tried, according to Kokovstev, to persuade the Duma Imperial Defence Committee to confine itself to the simple confirmation of credits. This it refused to do, for the reasons already stated the previous year.

In the State Council, the bill went before a joint session of the Finance and Legislative Committees, which this time voted to pass it. Manukhin, the joint reporter for the two committees, stated why in full session on 19 March 1909. They had decided, he reported, in spite of the State Council's previous vote, that the State Controller had been right in his speech of 3 July 1908 to maintain that the new Staff did not form part of the combat, technical or supply organisations of the navy, but was part of the central governmental administration, and therefore came under the jurisdiction of the legislative bodies as defined in Article 96 of the Fundamental Laws. He also pointed out that further delay was most undesirable, and urged the State Council to pass the bill immediately without amendments.[22]

This sharp change of opinion by the State Council's committees must have represented their reaction to the government's evident determination to pass the bill in its present form, and may indeed represent a reaction to direct government pressure on them. The Rights in the State Council, however, were not to be moved in this way: indeed, they must have felt that it was an appropriate point at which to resist what they by now saw as a joint conspiracy of the Octobrists and Stolypin's government to whittle the Emperor's prerogatives away. Durnovo put their view:

We, the members of the State Council occupying the places on the right wing of that chamber, cannot approve extensive interpretations of the Fundamental Laws, in the direction of widening the jurisdiction

[22] *GSSO*, Sessiya 4 (1908-9), cols 1335-43.

and powers of the legislative institutions. In the case before us, we are convinced that the law indicates precisely the procedure we should follow. Any deviation from that procedure we consider a conscious or unconscious attempt to use an apparent unclarity in the law with the aim of involving the legislative institutions in the field of military administration, which does not belong to us. Through such impatient intrusions, military administration will gradually pass into the hands of the State Council and State Duma, which is contrary to the Fundamental Laws, to our rooted beliefs, and to our vision of the exalted mission of that Power which created Russia and embodies her strength and might.[23]

Stolypin was ill and unable to attend the debate, though he considered it so important that he declared himself ready, if need be, to rise from his sickbed. However, Kokovtsev agreed to make the government speech, and in doing so relied almost entirely on a draft which Stolypin gave him.[24] This time he avoided the direct question of whether or not the Duma had acted correctly, perhaps in order not to offend the Right, but noted that the State Council had passed analogous bills before, and asserted that this bill would not affect the constitutional position of the army and navy any more than the previous ones had done. On the contrary, he said, it was Durnovo who was trying to make political capital out of a military matter, while the cabinet was working untiringly to strengthen the armed forces and to uphold the authority of the supreme power.[25] This time victory went to the government, but only just. The bill was passed by a majority of 87 to 75, in which seven Ministers voted.[26]

Dissension in the Octobrist fraction – the Gololobov affair

This, however, was far from being the end of the matter, for by now the Naval General Staff bill had become a focal point for wider issues. What was beginning to be at stake by now was in fact the composition both of the government and of the Duma majority.

As far as the Duma majority is concerned, the Octobrists had up till now managed to maintain the very strong position they had occupied in the centre of the house since the opening of the Third Duma. Yet they were vulnerable because of the unwieldy and uncertain nature of the fraction's organisation and its lack of any definite programme.

[23] ibid, cols 1345-50.   [24] Kokovtsev, *Iz Moego Proshlogo*, vol 1, pp 341-2.
[25] *GSSO*, Sessiya 4 (1908-9), cols 1410-18.   [26] ibid, col 1442.

In general, during the first and much of the second session of the Third Duma the Octobrists succeeded in maintaining a substantial measure of unity, while their tactics aimed first of all at keeping the Duma in existence, as a permanent feature of the state system, and secondly at making the broadest possible use of the Duma's rights, supporting the united Council of Ministers against the old, uncoordinated, ' irresponsible ' bureaucracy. Strains and disagreements had occasionally been in evidence, but on the whole the fascination of the new parliamentary politics, the absence of controversial bills in fulfilment of the October Manifesto (not for nothing were the Octobrists sometimes known as the ' Party of the Missing Document ') and common work on the agrarian reform had proved enough to hold the fraction together. By the spring of 1909, however, the impatience of reactionaries at the consolidation of the Duma and of Stolypin's government, the ripening of trouble over the Naval General Staff bill, and the imminent appearance on the agenda of the first reform in the spirit of the October Manifesto (the bill on religious freedom) threatened the fraction's internal unity more seriously.

Those who wished to undermine the political influence of both Stolypin and the Octobrists were aiming at a reshuffle of the parties, so that a minority of Octobrists on the left wing of the fraction would break away and join the Kadets and Progressists in opposition, while the majority of the fraction would form a new majority bloc along with the Moderate Rights and Nationalists: such an alliance would certainly number at least 200 in a house of 430, and would receive the support of the 48 Rights on many issues. This is the setting in which we must now see the Naval General Staff bill.

A week after the bill's passage through the State Council, as rumours began to circulate that the Emperor was perhaps not going to confirm it, the influential right wing journalist of the immensely respectable *Novoe Vremya*, Menshikov, wrote :

It has long been perfectly obvious to everyone that the party of 17 October really represents two or perhaps even three parties welded into one for no clear reason. It is obvious to everyone that the left Octobrists are camp followers of the Kadets, and that their natural place is under the wing of a bird like Mr Milyukov. Let this detached part of the flock find its home at last. The right Octobrists, on the other hand, are undoubtedly moving towards the Moderate Rights – or vice versa. Why delay these natural alliances in favour of unnatural ones? . . .

Without the extreme Rights, a powerful centre is possible, composed of the parties of liberal-nationalist turn of mind. These parties are disunited not so much by principles as by the petty ambitions of their leaders.[27]

This bloc, it could be hoped, would act on good nationalist principles, take the sting out of necessary reforms, not assert the Duma's rights as stridently as the existing Octobrists, and perhaps some even hoped that it might eventually allow the Duma to drift into being a purely consultative body.

The elements which favoured this kind of rearrangement, led by the Rights in the State Council, now used the Emperor's indecisiveness to make the Naval General Staff bill a wedge which could be driven between Stolypin's government and the Octobrists, and which could split the Octobrists internally.

They had their first opportunity to achieve this aim from February 1909, when an 'incident' blew up inside the Octobrist fraction around the conduct of Ya. G. Gololobov, a wealthy land and property owner from Ekaterinoslav province, who was one of the fraction's more distant 'adherents'. He had been a consistent opponent of any attempts by the fraction to enter into closer relations with the Progressists or Kadets, and had made his view known in the earliest fraction meetings.[28] The general position of the fraction, in so far as it had one, was that it was perfectly justifiable to ally with the Progressists and Kadets to speed social reforms where the right-wing parties and the government might be inclined to drag their feet, or for the purpose of forthrightly revealing the shortcomings and abuses of the bureaucracy. The Gololobov affair blew up as a result of one of the Octobrists' attempts to use the Duma's rights to a controversial extent to create constitutional precedents,

---

[27] *NV*, 26 March 1909.
[28] A. S. Vyazigin, *Gololobovskii Intsident: Stranichka is Istorii Nashikh Politicheskikh Partii*, Khar'kov 1909, pp 6-7. Vyazigin, professor at Khar'kov University, had been a member of the early right-wing group 'Russkoe Sobranie', and edited the journal issued by its Khar'kov branch. His pamphlet on the Gololobov affair was itself a piece of ammunition in the political fight. The author represents Gololobov as a true Octobrist, in the spirit of the majority of the fraction, and as a man concerned to save his party from the petty ambitions, unworthy intrigues and Kadet leanings of Guchkov. He ends by drawing a glowing picture of a Duma dominated by just such a coalition as Men'shikov recommends above, embodying a genuine union between Emperor and people.

4

reinforce the position of the legislature and awaken public attention to grievances. The occasion was a Social Democrat interpellation which asserted that the Rules on Associations of 4 March 1906
hindered the formation of trade unions and prevented workers
from effectively protecting their interests. The interpellation cited
instances of oppressive administrative action taken on the basis of
these Rules. The Duma Committee on Interpellations (whose reporter was Gololobov) recommended that it be declined, without
discussion, since there was no question of illegal activities having
been carried out by officials.[29] However, Guchkov, anxious that the
opportunity should be used to probe the government's policy on an
important issue, and also to demonstrate support for the workers'
grievances, hurriedly called a fraction meeting on 18 February, and
proposed that the Octobrists should support the discussion of the
interpellation in spite of the committee's known recommendation.
Those present at the meeting supported his proposal, though Gololobov warned that, as the committee's reporter, he would have to take
the latter's position. It was typical of the haphazard way in which
the Octobrists were organised that very few members of the fraction
were present at this meeting, and that it was held only just before
the debate on the subject was due to start. Other members of the
fraction present at the debate were then hastily informed of the
decision.[30]

Gololobov opened the debate by giving the Interpellation Committee's report and supporting it. Lyuts then immediately replied
by announcing the opposition of the Octobrist fraction to this report,
and requested that the debate on the problem of whether to accept
the interpellation for discussion should be closed forthwith, as the
decision of the Octobrist fraction to vote for it decided the fate of
this question.[31] This unusual attempt to rush the house's vote was
doubtless motivated by the fear of acrimonius discussion in which
the Octobrists might take opposite sides. It sparked off a lively
debate, which had to be continued on 25 February. On that day
Gololobov, confident perhaps that the current political situation

[29] *GDSO*, III, 2, pt 2, cols 1929-38.

[30] Vyazigin, *Gololobovskii Intsident*, pp 21-3. That this meeting was hastily
    conducted is confirmed by the fact that there appears to be no record
    of it in the Octobrist archives in Moscow – not that the Octobrists were
    ever very methodical in recording their doings.

[31] *GDSO*, III, 2, pt 2, cols 1929-41.

favoured an attack on his fraction from the right, and annoyed by what he considered Guchkov's underhand tactics, made a speech going beyond a discreet defence of his committee's position, and attacked the Octobrists rather bitterly.[32] In the vote which followed the debate several Octobrists supported Gololobov and voted for the immediate rejection of the interpellation.[33]

The Octobrist fraction bureau met and discussed Gololobov's speech. They decided, as it was later reported in the press, ' to express censure to deputy Gololobov for his speech on the interpellation concerning trade unions, in which the bureau considered certain judgments to contradict the views of the Union of 17 October.'[34] This for the Octobrists most unusual decision was communicated privately by Kamensky to Gololobov, who replied by writing a letter to the bureau complaining that they should at least have asked for an explanation from him before taking this unilateral step, and asserting that many members of the fraction agreed with him on the issue of the interpellation. In a letter to Kamensky he further expressed the view that the bureau was a purely executive organ and had no right to pass censure of its own initiative on members of the fraction.[35]

At the same time, it began to be publicly mentioned that Gololobov might be trying to split the fraction and form a group of his own in order to leave the Octobrists and joint the Moderate Rights. Gololobov himself vigorously denied any such intention, but admitted that the fraction was indeed divided within itself and that relations between the dissident groups and fraction discipline as a whole would have to be improved.[36] The natural corollary of a rightward move by one wing of the fraction would have been a leftward move by the opposite towards closer alliance with the Progressists and Kadets. Both these parties, however, seemed to be clear about the dangers such a development would present to the constructive work of the Duma, and neither of them encouraged it, despite the increase in numbers it might have brought them. The Progressist leader Efremov publicly denied that the Progressists were looking for such an alliance, and *Rech,* the unofficial organ of the Kadet leadership, reporting the possibility of split and re-alliance among the Octobrists, took care not to suggest

[32] ibid, col 2466.   [33] *Rech*[1], 26 February 1909.   [34] ibid, 3 March 1909.
[35] ibid, 3 March 1909; Vyazigin, *Gololobovskii Intsident*, pp 42-9.
[36] *Rech*[1], 3, 6 March 1909.

that the left Octobrists and Kadets should work together more closely.[37] On the other hand, the first sign that the government was yielding to pressure on the possibility of a realignment came in a leading article at this time in the semi-official newspaper *Rossiya,* which commented that the Duma as at present constituted was perfectly capable of working constructively if there was closer consultation between the Octobrists, Moderate Rights and Nationalists, who together could form a solid majority bloc.[38]

Sensing the political danger, Guchkov tried at two fraction meetings on 11 and 15 March to tighten the Octobrist fraction's discipline. Raising the question of Gololobov's speech and his letter to the bureau, he called upon the fraction both to regularise its discipline and to consider whether it could afford to retain elements that were unsympathetic to Octobrist principles and censured the party's activities. Zvegintsev and Opochinin supported this proposal, calling the present state of fraction discipline ' anarchical ': inside it, they said, supporters of the constitution were rubbing shoulders with proponents of return to unlimited autocracy. On the right of the party, Gololobov, who was absent, found a number of defenders. Their views reflected the revulsion of the whole right wing of the Duma against party politics, against the ' cliques ' which they considered parliamentary fractions to be. Polovtsev maintained that the fraction had no right to pass censure on one of its own members, still less to exclude him. Baron Cherkasov supported this view, claiming that the electorate, not the fraction, had given Gololobov his place in the Duma as an Octobrist, and the fraction had no mandate from anyone to reverse this election; he accused Guchkov of putting artificial pressure on members of the fraction. Shidlovsky went deeper into the causes of the fraction's ill-discipline when he said that it stemmed from the absence of any programme beyond a generally agreed opposition to the methods of the now long defunct Union of Liberation; this was insufficient – the party was probably now going to have to stand up against ' drunken reaction ' and had to have a positive programme, such as would sort out the convinced supporters from the waverers and time-servers. Volkonsky, from the left wing, warned the fraction that it was harbouring Black

[37] ibid, 7, 10 March 1909.
[38] J. F. Hutchinson, ' The Union of 17 October in Russian Politics, 1905-17 ', unpublished Ph.D. thesis, London 1966, p 120.

Hundred elements, and likened it to a robin's nest in which cuckoo's eggs were being hatched.

Daunted perhaps by this revelation of the bitter feeling long bottled up inside the fraction, Guchkov withdrew his implied proposal to exclude Gololobov from it, but stated that, as a long-recognised member of the conservative wing of the fraction, he had overstepped the line separating the Octobrists from the Rights, and the fraction should therefore pass censure on him by accepting the bureau's formula, based on their letter to him. This proposal was eventually passed unanimously.[39]

Guchkov was not, however, entirely satisfied with this result. He had not succeeded in tightening fraction discipline to the point where he could be sure, with the help of either the right or the left wing of the Duma, of passing measures which accorded with the Octobrists' general principles. On 15 March, the newspaper *Golos Moskvy,* which generally acted as Guchkov's mouthpiece, commented (in its first admission of trouble inside the Octobrist fraction):

The Gololobov incident, which has created such a stir, poses the question of party discipline, to which, unfortunately, the Octobrist fraction in the past has been insufficiently attentive. The fraction has been too tolerant to certain individual members and has thus prepared the ground for incidents like that of Gololobov. This tolerance, though it springs from a worthy principle – respect for others' opinions – must in the end be restricted by the bounds of party discipline, without which work becomes very difficult.

and, after mentioning speeches contradicting the fraction's decisions, by Gololobov and others, the leading article went on:

This state of affairs is utterly abnormal, and we are convinced that we must put an end to it in the interests of our broad general aims. It is possible, of course, that the strengthening of fraction discipline will cause the defection from the fraction of a few individual members, but

---

[39] *TsGAOR*, f 115 (Union of 17 October), op 1, d 19, p 100; *Rech¹*, 12, 13, 17 March 1909; *GM*, 17 March 1909. According to Vyazigin (*Gololobovskii Intsident*, pp 59–60), 'only' seventy members, mostly from the left wing, came to the second meeting. At the end of it, he claims, Guchkov invited those who did not consider Gololobov's speech of 25 February 'ill-timed and inadmissible' to stand. When no one did, he declared the bureau's resolution to have been passed 'unanimously'. If indeed seventy members attended, then this was a better record of attendance than Octobrist fraction meetings usually enjoyed. On the other hand, there is no record of the meeting in the Octobrist archive.

we can say in advance that their number will be very small and will not have any effect on the balance of forces in the Duma.

The ministerial crisis

This was the state of the Octobrist fraction when rumours began to circulate in the press that the Emperor was about to decline the Naval General staff bill. The first victim of his displeasure had been the Minister of War, Rediger, who was dismissed at the beginning of March as insufficiently staunch in his defence of the army's reputation against the Duma's attacks. On 18 March the Emperor wrote to his mother: 'I had to dismiss the War Minister, Rediger, because twice in the Duma he not only failed to rebut Guchkov's speeches but even agreed with him and thus did not defend the honour of the army.'[40]

His successor, Sukhomlinov, was warned by the Emperor on his appointment: 'I created the Duma, not to be directed by it, but to be advised.' Sukhomlinov acted on this warning by summoning Guchkov and P. N. Krupensky (the latter a prominent member of the Moderate Right fraction) and telling them to raise military matters less in the house, on the grounds that enemies might through these debates receive valuable information.[41]

The considerations which had moved the Emperor to dismiss Rediger applied just as much to the whole government, and over a broader range of issues. It is not surprising, therefore, that the Rights in the State Council felt that the narrow majority for the Naval General Staff bill in the State Council gave them the opportunity to influence the Emperor to reject it and thus weaken if not dislodge Stolypin's government. Two days after the vote in the State Council, Akimov had an audience with the Emperor, expressed his sorrow to him that the Council had agreed to a limitation of the Emperor's powers and offered his resignation as president of it. The Emperor declined his resignation, but told him that he had not yet decided whether to confirm the bill or not. Akimov came away in hope.[42] Rumours began to circulate that a cabinet change was

---

[40] ' Iz Perepiski Nikolaya i Marii Romanovykh, 1907-1910gg ', *KA*, vols 50-1, p 188; see also Polivanov, *Iz Dnevnikov i Vospominanii*, p 63; Suchomlinow, *Erinnerungen*, pp 277-8.

[41] *Polivanov, Iz Dnevnikov i Vospominanii*, pp 62-3, 68-9.

[42] ibid, p 65; Kokovtsev, *Iz Moego Proshlogo*, vol 1, p 342; *GM*, 21, 23 March 1909.

iminent. On 25 March Guchkov wrote to Zvegintsev: ' The general situation is bad: the resignation of Stolypin and part of the cabinet is possible.'[43] Replacements were expected to include Goremykin, Durnovo, Akimov, Shcheglovitov, V. F. Trepov, Pikhno and Stishinsky.[44] Stolypin was away in the Crimea convalescing after his illness, and so was unable effectively to take part in events, though in any case his nature inclined him against stooping to intrigue.

Those who were pressing for a right-wing reorientation of the Duma majority and a general loosening of fractional discipline found an unexpected ally: this was E. J. Dillon, Russian correspondent of the *Daily Telegraph,* who was an associate of Witte. Early in April 1909 he wrote a number of articles in the British press on the ministerial crisis, and they caused a furore inside Russia because they reflected so closely the views of the Rights in the State Council:

At this very moment headstrong political currents are being formed by the clash of the Radical parties, who seek to whittle away imperceptibly the Tsar's prerogatives, as safeguarded by the Constitution, with the Conservatives, who vainly endeavour to preserve them. The essential surprise in the situation lies in the significant fact that arrayed on the side of the whittlers of the Imperial prerogative are the Prime Minister and the Cabinet. They have scored a victory in the State Council by a majority less than a dozen, obtained, it is alleged, by means which should have been sedulously eschewed, and now if the Emperor should endorse the self-denying ordinance, the friends and enemies of Russian monarchism will draw the obvious practical conclusions from the voluntary renunciation by the autocrat of his rights, belonging not merely to an autocrat, but to every Constitutional monarch, nay, to the Presidents of Republics.

Commenting on the possible successors to the present cabinet, Dillon remarked that Stolypin had shown himself a less than convinced monarchist by drawing into the cabinet ' the three Ministers of War, Marine and Foreign Affairs, whom the Constitution expressly emancipates from Cabinet control '. He concluded:

A grave crisis, not of the Cabinet only, but of the Government system, has declared itself, and it is the opinion of the most devoted loyalists in the Empire that unless it is settled in a monarchical sense the chances of saving Russia from a catastrophe may disappear . . . In case the

[43] *TsGAOR*, f 932 (A. I. Zvegintsev), op 1, d 132, p 1.
[44] *GM*, 24, 27 March 1909.

Premier's forces resign, Mr Durnovo now appears the most likely successor. He is certainly the strongest man of all parties.[45]

This attempt to play on the fears of a military ally about the command of Russia's armed forces and the strength of her political system in general must have reached the Emperor's ears, and we may imagine that they weighed with him.

News that the Sultan of Turkey had been deposed by the Young Turks, which reached St Petersburg on 14 April, provided more fuel for the press campaign against the Octobrists inside Russia. For in 1908 Guchkov had paid a visit to Turkey, and had been impressed by the constitutional efforts of the Young Turk party; on returning to Russia he had written articles about his impressions, describing the Young Turks as 'Turkey's Octobrist Party'. This phrase now rebounded on him: the irrepressible Menshikov used the news of the Sultan's overthrow to make insinuations about the aims of Russia's own 'Young Turks':

Today a minor divergence from the precise meaning of Article 96 of the Fundamental Laws – tomorrow a slightly bigger one – the day after still bigger – and before you know where you are, instead of the written law an unwritten one contradicting it is in force, and has become a habit.

Mr Guchkov, imitating the leader of the Kadet party, went to Turkey to acquaint himself with the political movement there. As a result there appeared the famous declaration: 'The Young Turks are their Octobrists'. If the Young Turks are Octobrists, then the reverse must also be true, mustn't it? If one is to believe Mr Guchkov that Octobrists are our Young Turks, then a lot of simple Russian folk will vaguely be wondering what is the 'fullness of power' for which the Octobrists are struggling.[46]

To strengthen the organisation of those groups on the right who might hope to profit from a split in the Octobrists, the Moderate Rights were preparing to broaden themselves from a loosely organised Duma fraction into a nation-wide political party. In St Petersburg on 19th April a foundation congress took place. P. N. Balashov, member of a large landowning family, and deputy from Podolya, was elected chairman of the party committee. In his speech to the delegates, he spoke of the aims for which the party was being set up:

[45] Daily Telegraph, 7, 9 April 1909.   [46] NV, 15 April 1909.

Greetings to a young growing force! In the depths of Podolya province was born the idea of organising an indisputably progressive and fearless national party. The seed of this idea was brought by deputies to St Petersburg, and has here sent forth its shoot. We hope to join all streams of national thought into a mighty torrent which will water the plains of our state, dried up by the sharply changing winds of political moods.[47]

It was of course no accident that the origins of this party lay in Podolya province, in that western region of Russia, only won in the eighteenth century from the Poles, where the Rights, Moderate Rights and Nationalists had their strength. This was similar to the north-western region with which Stolypin was familiar, and the nationalism of the new party had much in common with his own. As the imagery of Balashov's speech shows, it also had much in common with the monarchist parties, and this represented the first attempt to organise a right-wing party both in the Duma and in the country as a whole. Later, in October 1909, it was amalgamated with the Nationalist fraction to form the Russian National Union, which had a regular parliamentary voting strength of about 120.[48]

Meanwhile, the Central Committee of the Union of 17 October sought to rebut the charges which the right was bringing against the Duma fraction. It issued an official statement denying that the Octobrists were attempting to encroach on the imperial prerogative, and reaffirming the conviction that careful but progressive activity on the part of the Duma would continue to promote the renewal of the country. It expressed ' deep indignation ' at the insinuations of the Rights.[49]

On 21 April, Stolypin having returned from the Crimea, the Council of Ministers held a meeting at which they discussed the political situation, and all the ministers (with the possible exception of Krivoshein) affirmed their solidarity with Stolypin and their intention of resigning if he were dismissed. On the following morning, Stolypin went to the Emperor, reported on this meeting, and consulted with him. He found that the Emperor was still undecided whether to confirm the Naval General Staff bill in the form in which it had reached him. Stolypin tried to smooth his fears about the establishment of a legislative precedent in the military sphere, and about the alleged attempt to limit his prerogatives. He came away

[47] *Rech¹*, 20 April 1909; *GM*, 21 April 1909.   [48] *GM*, 27 October 1909.
[49] *GM*, 18 April 1909.

with the impression that the Emperor would let the bill go through.[50]
But on 25 April he received the following letter from the Emperor:

Peter Arkadyevich!

After my last conversation with you I have been constantly thinking about the question of the Naval General Staff lists.

Today, having weighed every consideration, I have finally decided not to confirm the bill submitted to me.

The necessary expenditure is to be charged to the 10 million credit.[51]

There can be no question of confidence or no confidence.

Such is my will.

Remember that we live in Russia, and not abroad or in Finland [Senate], and therefore *I do not permit any thought of any one resigning.* Of course there will be talk about this in Petersburg and Moscow, but the hysterical cries will soon die down.

I charge you to draw up in the next month, with the War and Naval Ministers, the necessary rules to end the present unclarity in the examination of military and naval bills.

I warn you that I categorically reject in advance your or anyone else's request to be relieved of his office.

Respectfully your Nicholas[52]

Stolypin commented to Kokovtsev: 'After a letter like that has been sent to me, I ought, of course, to tender my resignation. But I shall not do so; I don't want to upset the Emperor simply because of the passing irritation aroused in him by some outside person.'[53]

It was a double blow to the Octobrists that the bill had been rejected and that Stolypin had been instructed to draw up rules on the legislative procedure in military matters (which, in the circumstances, could scarcely fail to restrict the Duma's part in them). It undermined their working alliance with the government, and hampered their freedom of action in a field where they had hoped to make their mark and establish the Duma's reputation for professional competence, patriotism and independence. Stolypin's dismissal, furthermore, would have allowed them to go unequivocally into opposition, with the loss, doubtless, of some of their right wing. But his survival posed them the task of continuing to try to work

[50] *GM*, 23 April 1909; Polivanov, *Iz Dnevnikov i Vospominanii*, pp 68-9; Kokovtsev, *Iz Moego Proshlogo*, vol 1, p 343.
[51] The government had an emergency fund of 10 million rubles per annum, for unspecified expenses, free of Duma control. See Chasles, *Le Parlement Russe*, p 184.   [52] *KA*, vol 5, p 120.
[53] Kokovtsev, *Iz Moego Proshlogo*, vol 1, pp 344-5.

with a government which would now be more sensitive to Right and Nationalist pressures, whilst endeavouring neither to lose all their credit with their electors, nor to surrender completely over the reforms they considered necessary. On 6 May, Guchkov's *Golos Moskvy* gloomily surveyed the political situation:

The incident is far from exhausted, and the postponement of the ministerial crisis seems to us far from comforting. The task laid on P. A. Stolypin touches the most sensitive side of our national life, and Russia's future depends to a significant degree on what direction is taken in carrying it out. The Third Duma, remembering the terrible and cruel lessons of the past, pays particular attention to questions of national defence. Although in this sphere the powers of the people's representative body are extremely limited, the Duma has nevertheless succeeded in taking up an independent and influential position, which is recognised not only in this country, but also abroad, where the Duma's work and its defence policy is watched with keen interest. Its criticisms of the negative side of the management of our military problems was, of course, resented by a large number of gentlemen, and it is precisely in this field, the restriction of the Duma's rights in military and naval affairs, that the treacherous blow has been struck, disguised by the mask of devotion to the law.

The aftermath – the beginning of the Octobrists' decline

The immediate reaction of the Octobrist leadership in this difficult situation was to throw down the gauntlet on a question of principle over which it was known there would be differences in the fraction. If their working alliance with the government was to fail them, then they could only hope to maintain their authority in the Duma by reaffirming the principles which they were in danger of compromising in the interests of that alliance. If, as Shidlovsky had both forecasted and recommended, such an affirmation should mean the loss of certain elements within the fraction, then their unity and moral strength would only gain from the process.

The question on which the Octobrists made their reassertion of principle was that of religious freedom, the first of the basic individual liberties promised in the October Manifesto to come before the Duma in the form of a legislative bill. If successfully handled, the issue would also have the effect of restoring Guchkov's authority in the fraction, which had been shaken by the setbacks of March and April: being a member of a prominent Old Believer family, he was anxious to join the Kadets in fighting for the freedom of Old Believers to form communities, worship and preach their faith.[54] It was on this issue that he now chose to force the pace. On 1 May, the Octobrists issued in the Duma a declaration that the Old Believers' bill should be debated not later than 11 May, since it had already passed through the Duma Old Believer Committee, and the other committee responsible for its preliminary examination, the Orthodox Church Committee, could complete its study of the question by then. The house voted to accept this declaration.[55]

On 6 May an Octobrist fraction meeting discussed the recommendations of the two Duma committees and decided to support the amendments to the government bill proposed by the Old Believer Committee but opposed by the Orthodox Church Committee. The three main amendments concerned were:

(i) that Old Believers should have the right not only to ' profess ' ther faith, but also to ' preach ' it, i.e. to have the right to public demonstrations of their faith;

(ii) that they should not have to request preliminary administrative permission every time they wanted to open a new commune, but could do so *yavochnym poryadkom* (without specific permission), provided that it met the stated requirements of the law;

(iii) that Old Believer priests should be allowed to bear their clerical titles just like priests in the Orthodox church.

The decision was not unanimous, for V. N. Lvov and Sheideman, among others, supported the findings of the Orthodox Church Committee.[56]

In the debate on 12 May, the amendments of the Old Believer Committee were expounded by its reporter, the Kadet Karaulov. Then V. N. Lvov reported for the Orthodox Church Committee against the views of his own fraction. He maintained that to allow the Old Believers freedom to ' preach ' amounted to allowing them freedom of ' propaganda ', which was intolerable, as not even the Orthodox church had such freedom. He further argued that preliminary permission for the establishment of each commune was

---

[54] Though Guchkov himself was apparently baptised in the Orthodox faith. See L. Menashe, ' "A Liberal with Spurs ": Alexander Guchkov, a Russian Bourgeois in Politics ', *Russian Review*, vol 26 (1967), p 44.

[55] *GDSO*, III, 2, pt 4, cols 504-5, 688.

[56] *Rech¹*, 28 April 1909; *TsGAOR*, f 115, op 1, d 19, p 107.

essential because the definition in law of what constituted an Old Believer commune was so loose, and that to allow Old Believer clergy to assume titles only appropriate to the hierarchy of the true faith would be in effect an attempt on the supremacy of the Orthodox Church within the Empire. Like Lvov, Sheideman approached the question not as one of freedom of conscience, in the spirit of the October Manifesto, but as one of the unity and strength of the Russian state and church: 'Gentlemen! the land of Russia was gathered together by Holy Orthodox Rus'. (Voices from right: True!) 'Do not loosen the cement which binds together the great unshakable strength of Russia . . . (Voices from right: Bravo!)', and he drew a picture of Old Believers, moving from village to village, visiting peasants in their homes and seducing them from the true faith.[57]

Kamensky hastened to reaffirm the Octobrists' support for the amendments of the Old Believer Committee, and took his stand on the principle of freedom of conscience, of which the right to preach one's faith was an integral part. Count Uvarov joined him in protesting against the identification of ' preaching ' with ' propaganda ', and praised the loyalty and industry of the Old Believers, who were among the finest of Russia's citizens.[58]

However, on Guchkov the effect of the speeches of Lvov and Sheideman was decisive; and characteristically he acted with an immediate headstrong gesture, making no attempt at diplomacy or compromise. On the morning of 15 May he gave M. V. Rodzyanko, his deputy, a letter in which he announced his resignation as chairman of the fraction, and publicly made it quite clear that he was doing so because he was dissatisfied with the fraction's discipline, and that a condition of his return was that it should agree to be bound by a compulsory vote on matters of principle. He also wanted to make his own speech on the Old Believer question free of any fractional responsibilities. Rodzyanko immediately called a fraction meeting: the first issue before it was who should now speak that evening in the name of the fraction in the Old Believer debate. A known opponent of freedoms for Old Believers, Father Spassky, was rejected by the relatively narrow margin of 51 votes to 21, after which Guchkov was given authority to speak for the fraction. The relatively high vote against him on an issue on which he was an

[57] GDSO, III, 2, pt 4, cols 1006-23, 1286-9.   [58] ibid, cols 1041-2, 1061-5.

acknowledged authority shows the extent to which his actions had by now alienated many Octobrists.[59]

When Guchkov spoke in the Duma on the afternoon of 15 May, therefore, he was defending not only the beliefs with which his family was identified, but also his position within the Octobrist party, and his conception of the nature and the tasks of the party, and indeed of the Duma as a whole. He rejected the notion of the Old Believers as subversive of Russia's unity or strength. This was a field in which, he said, freedom of conscience could and should be applied. The Emperor had taken the first step towards this in the Ukaz of 17 April 1905, proclaiming religious toleration and freedom. Would the Duma really refuse to complete this work in the first major legislative test of the principles of the October Manifesto? 'Gentlemen, we are discussing not only the bill on the Old Believers' communes, we are passing judgment not only on the Old Belief. It is ourselves on whom we are passing judgment. And the verdict which you bring on yourselves when you vote on this bill will be signed for you by history.'[60]

When voting followed on the vital amendments, they were passed, but among the minority which voted against them were up to fifteen Octobrists, including (according to *Rech*, in a report which does not seem to have been denied) Rodzyanko.[61] What was worse, there were indications that this dissident group had organised itself, perhaps with a view to rapprochement with the moderate Rights, and that the government had approved and encouraged its action. On the day before the vote, Sheideman and Cherkasov had visited Stolypin to sound the government's views and intentions, and according to some reports, denied by Cherkasov himself, had given Stolypin a list of those members of the Octobrist fraction who could be relied on to vote for the government's version against the Old Believer Committee's amendments.[62] In two articles in *Novoe Vremya*, A. A. Stolypin (the Premier's brother and a member of the Octobrist party, who sometimes rather mysteriously acted as a spokesman for the left wing of the party) asserted that these and other back-stage manoeuvres were being carried out with the deliberate purpose of winning the Octobrists away from Guchkov's leadership and into a permanent bloc with the Moderate Rights formed for

[59] *GM*, 16 May 1909; *Rech*¹, 17 May 1909; *TsGAOR*, f 115, op 1, d 19, p 109.   [60] *GDSO*, III, 2, pt 4, cols 1379-86.
[61] *Rech*¹, 16 May 1909.   [62] ibid, 20 May 1909.

docile co-operation with a government which, in its turn, could then afford to yield smoothly to reactionary pressures. He hinted that offers of important party posts had been made, and that one member of the Octobrist fraction had been offered the chairmanship of the new bloc. This reference could more or less only be to Rodzyanko, deputy chairman of the fraction, and the most authoritative figure on its right wing.[63] Because of these allegations, Rodzyanko followed Guchkov and resigned his deputy chairmanship of the fraction.

On 16 May, the fraction bureau met to discuss the situation created by the resignations of Guchkov and Rodzyanko. It passed a resolution noting that Guchkov had resigned because of the 'insufficient unity' of the fraction, and stated that for the same reason the bureau as a whole no longer felt it could speak for the fraction. It proposed that, in order to resolve the crisis, all members of the fraction should be made to submit to a secret ballot among the other members to determine whether they should remain in the fraction. A fraction meeting of 18 May accepted that, on the demand of thirty members, any member of the fraction should be submitted to ballot in this way. At the same time the fraction appointed a deputation of five to visit Guchkov and ask him to take back his resignation.[64]

Gololobov and V. N. Lvov announced their resignation from the fraction without waiting for the ballot; they declared that they could not remain members of a body which insisted on submitting its members to this kind of procedure. Polovtsev announced his resignation at the next fraction meeting, before the vote began, and was accepted into the Moderate Right fraction a few days later. On 28 May Cherkasov was submitted to ballot and expelled. At the same time Rodzyanko asked the fraction to submit him also to the ballot, in view of the serious accusations he considered had been directed against him in A. A. Stolypin's articles. Guchkov, however, rose to his defence, reminding the meeting that Rodzyanko had been among the founder members of the Union of 17 October and always faithfully followed its banner. He proposed that the fraction should unanimously reinstall him as deputy chairman. This proposal was accepted amidst applause. Guchkov then announced that, on the

[63] *NV*, 17, 22 May 1909.
[64] *TsGAOR*, f 115, op 1, d 19, p 109; *GM*, 17 May 1909.

fraction's request, he would withdraw his own resignation and resume its leadership.[65]

Guchkov had achieved part of his aims: he had held the Octobrist fraction together, whilst disembarrassing himself of the most obvious dissidents. But, on the other hand, he had not persuaded the fraction to adopt stricter discipline in future votes. And since the practice of resigning from the fraction proved later on to be contagious, we must mark the decline of the Octobrists in the Duma from this point. By the beginning of the next Duma session, indeed, fourteen members had left, eleven of them to form their own little fraction, which called itself the Right Octobrists.[66]

The tide of political events continued to move against the Octobrists. On 24 August, Stolypin published the new rules defining the Duma's rights in the examination of military questions: all organisational matters were now unequivocally defined as lying in the Emperor's prerogative, and the Duma's jurisdiction was strictly confined to the consideration of budget credits.[67] In September, in a by-election in the Moscow first curia, caused by the death of the distinguished Octobrist lawyer F. N. Plevako, the Octobrist candidate was defeated by a Kadet. This was a major shock, as Moscow, especially the first curia, had always been considered the Octobrists' most reliable stronghold; indeed, the other seat there was held by Guchkov himself.[68]

In October a nation-wide congress of the Union of 17 October was held, the first since the opening of the Third Duma. It was called by the party leadership in order to rally Octobrists in the country at large behind the Duma fraction. Right-wing members of the party had protested that the Duma fraction existed in a little world of its own, having no regular contact with local branches and exercising a virtual dictatorship over a party which was supposed to have numerous provincial organisations as well as two Central Committees.[69]

Guchkov made the principal speech at the congress, summing up the work of the Union of 17 October in the first two sessions. Its

---

[65] *Rech¹*, 23, 27 May 1909; *GM*, 29 May 1909; *TsGAOR*, f 115, op 1, d 19, p 112-13.   [66] *GM*, 6 October 1909.

[67] The text of the rules is in Kalinychev, *Gosudarstvennaya Duma v Rossii,* pp 404-5.   [68] *GM*, 29 September 1909.

[69] See, for example, the letter from the Dvinsk branch of the Union of 17 October, in *Rech¹*, 19 April 1909.

greatest achievement, he said, was that the constitutional monarchic form of government had firmly implanted itself in Russia. The Octobrists had played a major role in bringing this about by giving support to a government which declared its resolve to suppress revolution and carry through reforms. He denied, however, that the Octobrists crawled to the government, as some ill-wishers insinuated. On the contrary, the Octobrists had never failed to illuminate the darker side of the government's activity. But they had never allowed criticism to degenerate into ' making a political career out of oppositional attitudes '. For the most part, the Octobrists in the Duma had maintained a working alliance with the Moderate Rights, but this majority bloc had not always proved stable, and this instability had weakened relations between the Duma and the government. The Octobrists had co-operated with the Progressists and Kadets for limited purposes, but could not form a regular bloc with them: the Progressists were insufficient in number and unclear in aims, while the Kadets' past and their still essentially agitational aims disqualified them as regular allies. Another line which divided the Octobrists from the opposition parties was the national question: the Octobrists believed that in the Russian Empire the interests of the Russian nationality should have pride of place, as the natural unifiers of the state, though not at the expense of enslaving other nationalities, as the Extreme Rights seemed to wish to do.[70]

The congress as a whole passed a resolution calling for the passage of further bills fulfilling the promises of the October Manifesto. It also took organisational decisions, which, however, failed to define clearly the vital relationship between the party's Central Committees and the Duma fraction. In future, all-Russian congresses of the Union were to be held, if possible annually, and never with an interval of more than two years – a pious hope which was not to be realised.[71]

Golos Moskvy concluded that the Octobrists had moved leftwards, though there was no very obvious reason for this conclusion, except perhaps that the paper wanted to emphasise that no movement in the opposite direction had taken place, in spite of the recent successes of the reactionaries.[72] In fact, however, that part of the congress which was to come to mind most often in the next

[70] *GM*, 6 October 1909; *Rech*[1], 5, October 1909.
[71] *GM*, 6, 8, 9 October 1909.   [72] ibid, 9 October 1909.

two years was Guchkov's proclamation of the paramount place of the Russian nationality within the Empire, as the Octobrists gave support, despite internal splits, to Stolypin's nationalist bills on the Finnish and Western Zemstvo questions.

The belated termination of the Naval Staffs affair came with an interpellation, brought by the Social Democrats, on the publication of the rules of 24 August. The interpellation claimed that the rules constituted a violation of the Fundamental Laws, in that they introduced a new category of 'military legislation' not therein provided for. Guchkov felt the matter was most important and that the interpellation, in spite of its questionable origin, should be accepted for discussion, and referred first of all to a committee for reformulation.[73] The Octobrist fraction, however, decided to avoid discussions embarrassing to the government by declining the interpellation, arguing that the rules of 24 August constituted merely an administrative instruction, binding on government officials but not on the Duma. This interpretation had already been accepted by the party congress of October 1909.[74]

Stolypin accepted this compromise. In his speech for the government he combined the themes of Russian national greatness and of the necessity for government and representative institutions to continue to work together:

Russia is discontented with herself. That discontent will pass when from its present uncertain outlines the Russian state consciousness becomes clear and firm, when Russia once again feels herself Russia. And that can be achieved under one principal condition: correct common work of the Government and the representative institutions, work which can be so easily disrupted by distortion of the Government's aims and tasks.

On the other hand, he insisted again on the Emperor's authority in military matters:

The history of revolutions, the history of the fall of states teaches us that an army falls into decay when it ceases to be united, united in obedience to one sacred will against which there is no appeal. If you inject the poison of doubt into that principle, if you give our army the slightest notion that its organisation depends on a collective will, then

[73] *GDSO*, III, 3, pt 1, cols 162-6, 169-71.
[74] *Rech¹*, 9 October 1909. See also Shubinskoi's speech in the Duma, 26 March 1910, *GDSO*, III, 3, pt 3, cols 1965-73.

its might will cease to rest on the sole inflexible force uniting it – on the Supreme Power.[75]

The interpellation was rejected, though some Octobrists abstained from voting.[76]

Conclusions

The Naval Staffs affair as a whole represented a serious blow both to the Octobrists and to Stolypin's government. It undermined the Octobrists' influence in a field where they had hoped to achieve creative if watchful co-operation with the government in the interests of the reform and strengthening of Russia's armed forces. The process continued thereafter, so that in 1910 Guchkov resigned as chairman of the Duma Imperial Defence Committee, and in 1911 the Octobrists gave way to the Naval Ministry on the issue of credits for battleship construction. In 1912 a majority of the Octobrists accepted an even larger construction programme, against the vehement advice of Guchkov, who thus became isolated from most of the party on this cardinal issue.[77]

The affair began the diminution and factionalisation of the Octobrist fraction, which was to go on for the next four years, and strengthened the Moderate Right and Nationalist groups; it thus ensured that the ground on which government and Duma majority could best co-operate in the coming years was less one of social and political reform than of nationalism. Furthermore, the Rights, especially in the State Council, had found that they could attack Stolypin and the Octobrists with success. In fact, in every respect, the ground had been laid for the Western Zemstvo crisis, which occurred two years later.

[75] *GDSO*, III, 3, pt 1, cols 2521-30.

[76] *GDSO*, III, 3, pt 4, col 709; *Rech¹*, 2 April 1910.

[77] Avrekh, ' Stolypinskii Bonapartizm ', p 33; Shatsillo, *Russkii Imperializm i Razvitie Flota,* pp 186-7; see below, p 183.

5

The Western Zemstvo crisis

In the changed political situation after the Naval Staffs crisis, Stolypin's co-operation with the Octobrists had perforce to be limited to fields in which they were not likely to embarrass him. At the same time he sought closer relations with the new Nationalist fraction to the right of the Octobrists. The result was a kind of 'constitutional nationalism', attempting constitutional initiatives only in areas where they could be combined with a centralising Great Russian nationalism. The mixture was similar to that which Joseph Chamberlain had been preaching in Britain a few years earlier: an Empire for the common man. In an era of rapid and confusing political change, when the first attempts were being made to establish centres of authority other than the autocracy, the notion of the 'people' was important, particularly when interpreted as the 'Russian people'. Nationhood was being sought as a new basis for political cohesion.

I will explore some of the implications of this search in the last chapter. For the moment, I want to examine two 'constitutional nationalist' ventures on which the Octobrists embarked in 1909-11, working with Stolypin in the attempt to patch up the threatened relations between them. These were the Finnish and the Western Zemstvo bills, the second of which eventually led to a crisis that discredited Stolypin as a statesman and drove the Octobrists into opposition.

Finland

The root of the Finnish question was that Finland had long been a constitutional state whose titular head was an autocratic Monarch. The Russians had conquered it from the Swedes in 1808-9, and it had pleased the then Russian autocrat, Alexander I, to confirm the Fundamental Laws, rights and freedoms Finland had enjoyed under the Swedes. In theory, Finland was joined to the Russian Empire only by a personal union, through the sharing of a common Monarch. But after the reforms of 1905-6, when the Monarch ceased by himself to embody the state, the whole problem of Finland's place within the Empire had to be raised anew. By claiming a share in the sovereignty over Finland, the Duma was paralleling its constitutional initiatives in other fields.

During the nineteenth century the Finnish executive had been headed by a Minister State Secretary for Finland in St Petersburg, and a Governor-General in Helsingfors, both appointed by the crown and responsible to it alone. Finland's internal legislative affairs were handled by a Diet, elected by the four estates of the nation (clergy, nobility, burghers and peasantry), and possessing from 1886 the right of legislative initiative in all matters except the Fundamental Laws, the armed forces and the press.

In the late nineteenth century the rise of a Russifying policy in St Petersburg and of a strong anti-Russian nationalism in Finland made these arrangements difficult to work. The Finnish Diet began to make separatist demands, and passed, for example, a law reducing Russian citizens in Finland to the status of foreigners. Nicholas II reacted by appointing Russians wherever possible to the Finnish civil service and making Russian the official language in certain branches of government. This policy reached its climax in 1898 with the appointment of the unimaginative General Bobrikov as Governor-General, and the issue of an Ukaz integrating the Finnish armed forces with those of the Empire. The Diet refused to accept this measure, whereupon by Ukaz of 3 February 1899 it was passed into law without the Diet's consent. This Ukaz asserted that it was the Emperor's prerogative to determine which legislation was of ' imperial concern ', and therefore not subject to the Diet's veto but to be passed by the normal imperial legislative channels. The Finns responded to this with a campaign of passive resistance, which quickly took on more active forms and culminated in the murder of General Bobrikov.[1]

The October Manifesto, since it changed the legislative system of the Empire, by implication changed the system governing Finnish legislation of ' imperial concern '; but no subsidiary act was promulgated making this clear. However, another manifesto, issued on

---

[1] A. G. Mazour, *Finland between East and West*, New York 1956, pp 10-26.

24 October/6 November 1905, granted full civil freedoms to the Finns and repealed the Finnish legislation of 'imperial concern' which had been passed since 1899. In particular, the Finns were provisionally relieved of the obligation to do military service and were required to pay a compensatory tax instead. The Diet met again and re-formed itself as a single-chamber legislature elected by universal, free, equal and secret ballot, the vote being extended to women as well as men. In the subsequent elections the Social Democrats became the strongest single party and initiated a broad programme of social reform, which met strong opposition from the other more conservative parties.[2]

The decline of the revolutionary movement inside Russia, however, left the imperial government time to think about resuming practical exercise of its sovereignty over a nation so close to its capital and so hospitable to subversive elements. In this aim it was supported by the majority in the Third Duma. Viewing the Empire as one and indivisible, and also as a constitutional monarchy, the Octobrists could not tolerate the existence of a semi-autonomous unit joined to the Empire only by personal union. They wanted Finland brought under the Empire's new state institutions, the Council of Ministers and the State Duma (together with the reformed State Council), instead of being subject to the crown through institutions (the State-Secretary for Finland and the Finnish Diet) which bypassed both. Their aim here was the same as that which they pursued in military and foreign affairs: to consolidate the influence of the Council of Ministers and the new legislative institutions against the old 'irresponsible' bureaucracy, acting and taking decisions through private reports to the Emperor.

The question of Finland was first raised in the Duma through three interpellations, one by the Octobrists, and two by the Rights, submitted in the first session. The two Rightist interpellations pointed out that revolutionary groups in Finland had been active in organising crimes committed in Russia, and claimed that the secret society 'Voima' was preparing an armed uprising to separate Finland from the Empire. They urged that the Minister of the Interior, through the Finnish Governor-General, should promote greater vigilance and more active counter-measures.[3] The Octobrists' inter-

[2] J. H. Hodgson, 'Finland's Position in the Russian Empire, 1905-10', *Journal of Central European Affairs*, vol 20 (1960), pp 158-73.

[3] *GDSO, Prilozheniya*, III, 1, pt 1, pp 509-13, 591-4.

pellation was focussed on Finland's position in the state structure. It pointed out that the Ukaz of 19 October 1905 required all Ministers and heads of departments to communicate the contents of their personal reports for the Emperor to the Council of Ministers, in order that the latter could carry out its task of co-ordinating the administration. The State-Secretary for Finland was certainly under this obligation as much as any other Minister, since Finland in the Fundamental Laws was described as a constituent part of the Empire. The interpellation maintained that, nevertheless, the State Secretary for Finland had ignored the Council of Ministers, and by doing so had inaugurated measures harmful to the state and enabled the Finnish Diet to infringe on the domain of imperial legislation.[4]

The interpellations were welcomed in the Duma by Stolypin himself. He spoke at some length of the danger which revolutionary societies in Finland represented for the Russian state. He also confirmed that the situation regarding Finnish legislation of imperial concern was unsatisfactory: at present the State-Secretary for Finland, acting on the basis of a law of 1891, decided for himself which matters to communicate to the Council of Ministers, and which to decide on his own initiative. In this way a law had been promulgated in April 1906 reducing the use of the Russian language in Finnish institutions, without any reference to the Council of Ministers. Similarly, a press law had been drafted of which he, Minister of the Interior for the whole Empire, had learnt only by chance. At one stage, too, Russian revolutionaries had been completely safe on Finnish soil, as the authorities there did not treat them as revolutionaries at all. The root of the evils exposed by all three interpellations lay, Stolypin asserted, deep in the history of Russia's constitutional relations with Finland. The Finns had constantly taken their fundamental laws to be proof of their nation's existence as a separate state, whereas their legal position was that of a constituent part of the Russian Empire. Their fundamental laws guaranteed them internal autonomy, but in matters of imperial concern they must be subject to the normal imperial legislative institutions, newly established in 1905-6. Until a procedure was defined by which these matters could be dealt with in the new state system, persistent confusions would arise:

[4] ibid, pp 503-8.

This, gentlemen, is abnormal and, I repeat, it is not in the inactivity of the authorities, nor in their illegal activities, that the roots of the abuse lie: they lie in the fact that a whole area of our legislation, the huge area of our mutual relations with Finland, is completely unregulated. Gentlemen, this deficiency is intolerable, and it must be overcome . . . And I would remind you that you now have one unequivocal means of settling all legislative issues, laid down by Article 86 of the Fundamental Laws. That is to pass them through the State Duma and the State Council.

He called on the Duma to reject the interpellations, and instead to bring forward a bill defining the legislative relations of Russia and Finland. In this way, he specifically encouraged the Octobrist rather than the Rightist approach to the problem. He denied that such a bill would be reactionary, as the Finns would probably suggest; on the contrary, it would demonstrate the new patriotism, of which Russia's representative bodies were the bearers. For Stolypin, the significance of the Duma was that it was the voice of the Russian people, ready to work with the Monarch in the consolidation of Russia's greatness.

Previously only the government had the concern and the duty of defending the sovereign historical rights and acquisitions of Russia. Now it is different. Now the Emperor is endeavouring to put together once more the crumbling temple of the Russian national feeling. It is you who are the bearers of that feeling, gentlemen, and you cannot spurn the responsibility for the preservation of these sovereign rights of Russia.[5]

For the Octobrists, Count Bennigsen immediately announced that the fraction was entirely satisfied by Stolypin's declaration, and that they would therefore withdraw their interpellation, which they had brought in order to ensure that this very important question was aired. They would now work with the government in preparing legislation.[6] The Rights declined to withdraw their interpellations, but the Duma rejected them for the reasons which Stolypin had suggested.[7]

One immediate result of the interpellations was the imperial Ukaz of 20 May 1908, by which the Finnish administration was subordinated to the Council of Ministers.[8]

[5] *GDSO*, iii, 1, pt 2, cols 2919-41. [6] ibid, cols 2941-2.
[7] *GDSO*, iii, 1, pt 3, cols 721, 723. [8] *PSZ*, 3rd Series, no 30379.

The preliminary drafting of a bill to regulate Russo-Finnish legislative relations was entrusted in March 1909 to a special committee under the State Controller, Kharitonov. Its two main tasks were to decide

(i) which legislative issues might be deemed to lie in the category of ' imperial concern ';
(ii) the procedure by which such legislation should be passed.

The committee consisted of five Russians and five Finns, under the chairmanship of Kharitonov, whose casting vote was to be decisive. For the committee, as is scarcely surprising, found a ' fundamental divergence of views ' between its Russian and its Finnish members. The committee's report detailed these divergences, but the draft bill which it laid before the Council of Ministers was that of its majority of one.[9]

It proposed a very broad definition of matters of ' imperial concern ', including such items as ' the use of the state language ', ' the basic principles of judicial organisation and procedure ', ' the basic principles of education in Finland and the organisation of their supervision ', ' the organisation, rights and conditions of activity in Finland of companies, societies and unions, as also of public meetings ', ' post, telephone, air flight and other means of communication '.[10] Deprived of jurisdiction in these fields, the Finnish Diet would, practically speaking, be reduced to the status of a provincial zemstvo assembly.

The committee's proposals concerning legislative procedure were no less centralising, as the government and the Octobrists wished. The Finnish members had suggested that legislation of imperial concern should be handled by delegations (on the Austro-Hungarian model) appointed by the parliaments of Russia and Finland. The idea was that they would meet separately in St Petersburg and communicate with each other in writing. If they failed to reach agreement in this way, then each delegation would elect members to a conciliatory commission (*soglasitelnaya kommissiya*); and if agreement was not reached here either, then the proposed legislation would be dropped.[11] The Russian members rejected this on the grounds that it placed the Russian and Finnish legislatures on a basis of equality, which was unacceptable, and held out the prospect of

[9] *TsGIAL*, f 1278, op 2, d 1159; A. Ya. Avrekh, *Stolypin i Tret'ya Duma*, M 1968, pp 63-4.   [10] *TsGIAL*, f 1278, op 2, d 1159, p 203.
[11] ibid, p 163.

bills being indefinitely delayed because of Finnish stonewalling. Their proposal (and the one that accordingly came before the Duma) was that legislation of imperial concern should be handled through the regular imperial legislative channels. The Finnish Diet would be invited to send a fixed number of deputies to the Duma and State Council and would be asked in a consultative capacity to give an opinion on any bills.[12]

The bill submitted by the Kharitonov committee had an abnormally swift passage through the Duma. Its 'urgency' was voted at an early stage,[13] and all three readings were completed in a week (21-28 May 1910). The unusual haste was a result of the political circumstances surrounding the bill's passage. Only a week or so earlier the confused progress of the Western Zemstvo bill through the Duma had shown the Octobrists barely able to muster a majority for a version remotely acceptable to the government. So it was important both to the government and to the Octobrists to pass this Finnish bill with a minimum of fuss. In the process, the debates took on an indiscriminately chauvinist character, which not only awoke the resentment of the Finns and the indignation of international opinion, but also caused dissension in the Octobrist fraction. As soon as the bill came before the house, indeed, Baron A. F. Meyendorf, a left-wing Octobrist from the Baltic provinces and a member of the fraction bureau, was reported to have written to Guchkov, asking to be released from the fraction because he could not accept its view of the Finnish issue. A lawyer by training and profession, Meyendorf frequently impressed the house by the independence of his standpoint and the thorough legal grounding he always gave his case. On this occasion, he was persuaded to retract his letter and even take his stand with the fraction, but when, three years later, he did finally resign from the Octobrists, the Finnish question was generally cited as being the main reason for his decision.[14]

The fraction's point of view was put by Anrep. It was one of uncompromising Russian state centralisation, unconcerned with the niceties of Finland's constitutional history:

It is my view that inside the Russian Empire there has never been, is not, and never will be a 'Finnish state'. (Applause from centre and

[12] ibid, p 203.   [13] *GDSO*, III, 3, pt 4, col 1958.
[14] *Rech¹*, 19 March 1910; *GM*, 4 May 1913.

right) . . . We must emphasise and hasten to fulfil our state duty. In this way we shall be replying to those unsolicited interferences from West European scholars and those who wish to make a lawsuit out of an imperial duty. Between Finland and Russia there is no plaintiff and no defendant, and the Duma is not a law-court: it is an establishment charged with the interests and needs of the state, and it will carry out its duty.[15]

He asserted that Russia must do what any great power, be it Britain, France or Germany, would do with regard to territories under its sovereignty, and establish unified governmental control:

Only those states and those nations can be strong which uphold as something sacred their own interests and their own mission . . . There must be definite and immutable means of deciding issues which concern the nature of the Empire itself, and there must be no concessions. Which, then, is the best means? Plainly that which has been chosen on the present occasion, that is, the passing of legislation through the imperial representative institutions, since here the representatives of the whole of Russia are gathered together, expressing the real interests of the people.[16]

Milyukov was certainly right when he called this speech ' worthy of Markov 2 '.[17] It was also, surely, an imitation, conscious or unconscious, of the Bismarckian mode, and of the rhetoric of the National Liberals in the Reichstag. Germany was the model to which the centre and right in Russian politics tended to look as an example of the successful integration of an authoritarian monarchy, an imperial patriotism and parliamentary institutions. And Anrep, as we shall see, was not the most chauvinist of the Octobrist fraction in his approach to Finland.

The Kadets did not feel it was either right or possible to absorb Finland into the Empire as though it were a mere province. Their view of the Russian Empire had always envisaged wide cultural and political autonomy for the constituent nationalities. Indeed, it was over this issue that the future Kadets had first broken with the future Octobrists in 1905. All the same, the Kadets were not united among themselves on the Finnish problem. Their differences came

[15] GDSO, III, 3, pt 4, cols 1957-8.
[16] ibid, cols 2004-6.
[17] ibid, col 2024; ' Markov 2 ' was N. E. Markov, the extravagant Rightist from Kursk, a prominent figure in the United Nobility as well as on the right wing of the Duma.

out in a Central Committee meeting of 21 October 1909, while the Finnish bill was still before the Kharitonov committee. Milyukov considered the bill a gross infringement of Finland's liberties: what he recommended was parallel legislation by Duma and Diet for matters of imperial concern, perhaps along the lines suggested by the Finnish members of the committee. Another group, however, led by I. I. Petrunkevich and P. B. Struve, believed that the imperial legislative bodies had the overriding right to deal with matters of 'imperial concern', provided only that this concept could be moderately defined, in such a way as to leave a satisfactorily broad field within Finland's 'internal autonomy'. They hoped to be able to persuade the Finns to make concessions if a sufficiently broad sphere of jurisdiction was left to them in this way.[18] The uncompromising conclusions of the Kharitonov committee excluded this possibility, however, so that the Milyukov view prevailed within the Kadet fraction.

Interestingly, in his speech on the subject in the house, Milyukov framed his own vision of a 'constitutional nationalism'. This was one in which all the peoples of the Empire, bound in their relations with one another by the rule of law, would contribute in their own way towards the greatness of the Russian state. The 'zoological nationalists' of the right and centre would only plunge the Empire into civil war by the crudity of their Russian chauvinism. 'The Third Duma', he said, 'is not the Russian people. The Finns realise that perfectly well . . . They know that it is not the Russian people who are their tormentors.' And, turning to the Rights, he warned them: 'It is we and not you who will bear the Russian imperial idea through this chaotic world of brutish arbitrariness into which you have strayed. And it is we who will save Russia's state unity from the civil war, from the national feuds and the devastation into which you are about to plunge it.'[19]

For the Progressists, I. N. Efremov warned that the Duma's rights might in their turn come to be belittled if they first trampled on those of the Finnish Diet.[20]

The Rights, naturally, greeted the bill as a direct expression of their national ideals. Their two main speakers, V. M. Purishkevich and G. G. Zamyslovsky, both emphasised that it was intolerable to

---

[18] *TsGAOR*, f 523, op 1, d 30, pp 29-30.
[19] *GDSO*, III, 3, pt 4, cols 2072-89.   [20] ibid, col 2125.

have only a few miles from the capital of the Empire a rebellious nation preparing armed uprising with impunity. Purishkevich, with characteristic bravura, declared that it was the Duma's mission to arrest the disintegration of the borderlands which had started in 1905, and to restore to Russia the strength and unity which would be required for the mighty national and racial struggles of the twentieth century.[21]

The decisive moment in the second reading of the bill was the decision, supported by the Rights, Nationalists and most of the Octobrists, to discuss Article 2 (the proposed list of legislative fields of 'imperial concern') as a whole, not point by point.[22] The aim here was to speed up the debate, and avoid messy disagreements on each point. But the Kadets and some of the Octobrists had been intending to use the second reading to alleviate the harshness of the bill by contesting some of the more objectional items in Article 2. Taking the whole article together made it virtually impossible for them to initiate a serious discussion of individual items. Accordingly, Milyukov announced that the Kadets would walk out, as their further participation was pointless. They were joined by the Progressists and the rest of the opposition.[23] For this they were reproached by *Golos Moskvy,* which argued that they should have stayed, in order to help the Octobrists pass mitigating amendments.[24] The voting pattern of the rest of the sitting, however, suggests that too many Octobrists supported the whole of Article 2 for the opposition's absence to have made any difference.

At any rate, it was left to a few dissident Octobrists to propose amendments which had no chance of being passed. G. G. Lerkhe and M. Ya. Kapustin protested against the steamroller treatment of Article 2, and proposed that three fields, education, the press and the right of meeting and association, should be removed from the list and left to the Finns as purely internal matters. Anrep also signed these amendments,[25] in spite of his earlier speech. Most of the Rights, Nationalists and Octobrists felt, however, that the educational system was vital, as it inculcated Finnish hostility to Russia, and the freedom of press, meeting and association were what had made Finland such an ideal refuge for Russian revolutionaries in 1905.[26] The amendments were defeated. However, when the entire

---

[21] ibid, cols 1982, 2233-45.   [22] ibid, col 2469.   [23] ibid, cols 2472-3.
[24] *GM,* 27 May 1910.   [25] *GDSO,* III, 3, pt 4, cols 2477-80, 2499, 2581-2.
[26] ibid, cols 1952-3, 2025, 2032, 2041.

bill, after its third reading, came up for the final vote, Yu. N. Glebov read a statement on behalf of nineteen members of the Octobrist fraction:

We recognise the necessity of an imperial legislative procedure for matters of imperial concern, but only on the firm condition that Finland shall be fully autonomous in her internal affairs. After the rejection of the amendments to Article 2, Section 1, proposed by deputies Lerkhe, Anrep and Kapustin, the bill in the form in which it is being passed by the State Duma at the third reading, is unquestionably at odds with this principle. For that reason we are voting against the bill.[27]

The bill was then passed by 164 votes to 23, to the accompaniment of an exultant shout of ' Finis Finlandiae! ' from Purishkevich.[28] It passed the State Council without difficulty, and became law on 17 June 1910.

In the end, then, what the Octobrist leaders intended to be a demonstration of the Duma's patriotism, and of its inherent right to a voice in all imperial legislative affairs, turned into an exhibition of ' zoological' nationalism and into a resurrection of the repressive Russification associated with Bobrikov. Sensing that the focus of influence in the house had shifted towards the Nationalists and Rights, many Octobrists expressed views in no way different from theirs, cast votes with them, and aided the feverish passage of the bill. The Octobrist leadership was here defeated by the rank and file of its own fraction, its position was correspondingly weakened, and the later complete split of the party was foreshadowed.

The origins of the Western Zemstvo bill

The political significance of the Western Zemstvo bill was very similar to that of the Finnish one: it aimed to extend elective local government institutions to western areas of Russia, where they had not existed previously, and also to strengthen the position of Russian inhabitants there at the expense of the Poles and Jews.

[27] ibid, col 2581; the 19 were Kamensky, Glebov 2, Iskritsky, Golitsyn, Bergman, Lerkhe, Godnev, Klyuzhev, Zvegintsev, Khomyakov, Boratynsky, Vasich, Guz, Belyaev, Favorsky, Zuev, Rotermel, Mufty-Zade, Zakharov 1. This included many leading members of the fraction: Glebov, Kamensky, Lerkhe and Golitsyn were members of its bureau.
[28] ibid, col 2582.

For Stolypin personally, and for his conception of the new ' great Russia ' which he wanted to begin building, the Western Zemstvo measure was even more important than the Finnish one. The Western region of Russia was the one in which Stolypin had his roots, and was the area of Russia which he knew best. The nine provinces of Vilna, Kovno, Grodno, Minsk, Vitebsk, Mogilev, Kiev, Podolya and Volynia, i.e. Lithuania, Belorussia and the Right-Bank Ukraine, had lain almost entirely under Polish rule until the partitions of the eighteenth century. The Polish landowners remained strong, and after the rising of 1863, Alexander II did not set up zemstvos in these provinces, fearing that the Polish landlords would dominate them to the detriment of stable and loyal local government. The rest of the population was pretty miscellaneous: there were many Jews in the towns, in the countryside there were many Lithuanians in the three north-western provinces, and elsewhere Belorussian and Ukrainian peasants, some of whom were Catholic or Uniate, and economically often dependent on Poles or Jews. The Great Russian inhabitants of the region tended to be military personnel, government officials, or recently established landowners (often absentee). These were the people who formed the backbone of the Nationalist fraction in the Duma.

On the face of it, it might seem an unpromising area for Russian nationalist experiments. But Stolypin always saw the Belorussians and Ukrainians, provided they were Orthodox believers (and most were), as bearers of the Russian national idea. And the western region had another great advantage for his concept of Russia's political development: faster than anywhere in European Russia, the peasant commune was breaking up and being replaced by private peasant smallholdings. If local government institutions could be set up there which gave strong representation to these smallholding Russian peasants, then a working model could be established for the transformation of Russia à la Stolypin.

The introduction of zemstvos in Lithuania, Belorussia and the Right-Bank Ukraine was first mooted by Stolypin in his energetic period of legislation following the dissolution of the First Duma. But his motives then were somewhat different. He believed at that stage, as he reported to the Council of Ministers on 22 November 1906, that the former hostile attitude of the Poles in the region towards the Russian state had been replaced by peaceful and co-operative work for the benefit of the area. Furthermore, as he said, Russian landownership had been encouraged to the point where in some of the western provinces it actually exceeded Polish landownership. He saw no reason for the government to persist in the mistrust of 1863, and recommended that zemstvos be introduced in the western provinces under Article 87 in order to

give the population of the western region the same institutions for the conduct of their local affairs as have long been active, to the benefit of the nation, in the internal provinces of the Empire – and to provide the population with a further demonstration of the government's inflexible resolve to put into effect the principles proclaimed in the Imperial Manifesto of 17 October 1905.[29]

In his recommendations regarding the details of the legislation, Stolypin recognised that national differences might still pose problems, but did not give them the central position they occupied in the bill he put before the Duma four years later. He proposed to allow electors to split into separate national groups at the electoral meetings, if they wished to do so, each group returning a number of deputies proportional to its own numbers. Similarly, provincial governors were to have the right to divide electoral meetings in this way on their own initiative if they felt it necessary. In six of the nine provinces, he said, it might be necessary to add a further safeguard for Russian interests by laying down in advance a minimum number of Russian deputies to sit in each district zemstvo assembly, and of Russian officials to serve on each district zemstvo executive board.[30]

This scheme was never put into effect, however, as the government was also planning a general zemstvo reform, and decided to wait until it had been determined what form zemstvos should take in the rest of the Empire before trying to introduce them in the western region.[31]

In a more nationalist form, the western zemstvo scheme was revived as a result of a right wing pressure at the time of the Naval Staffs crisis. On 8 May 1909, Pikhno, a Rightist in the State Council, made a speech criticising the way in which deputies to the State Council were elected from the Western provinces. Since there were

[29] *TsGIAL*, f 1276, op 2, d 60, pp 2-10.   [30] ibid, pp 13-15.
[31] Kryzhanovskii reported this to the Duma early in 1908: *GDSO*, III, 1, pt 2, col 2800.

no zemstvos there,[32] deputies were returned to the State Council by the local assemblies of the nobility, whose active members were mainly Polish and therefore naturally returned Polish deputies. As a result, there was at that time in the State Council not a single Russian deputy from the nine western provinces. This, Pikhno said, was an intolerable state of affairs in a region the great majority of whose population was Russian.[33] Thirty-three members of the right wing of the State Council tabled a legislative motion proposing a new system for electing deputies from the western provinces: the whole population would be represented, not just the nobility, and would be divided for the elections into national curiae, with the number of deputies to be fixed at six Russian and three Polish for the whole region.[34]

This was a moment when it was very difficult for Stolypin to resist right-wing pressure. Besides, the proposal was one with which he must have had a lot of sympathy. The problem was to make it more acceptable to the Octobrists, especially their left wing, since he still relied on the fraction as a whole for his continued Duma majority. His solution was to revive his own idea of introducing zemstvos in the western provinces. The new zemstvos would appeal to the strong ' zemstvo ' sentiment in the Octobrist party, and would at the same time serve as the institutions through which specifically Russian deputies could be returned to the State Council. Both the Rights in the State Council and the Octobrists in the Duma would support him.

But the problem was to ensure that the new zemstvos *would* be Russian, and yet also serve properly as zemstvos should, representing local opinion, but with a particular bias towards landed property. This is why, in his 1910 version of the bill, Stolypin decided to erect a compulsory system of national curiae, with an elaborately worked out distribution of Russian and Polish deputies between them.

[32] Deputies were elected to the State Council by the provincial zemstvo assembly in all provinces where zemstvos existed, but by the provincial assembly of the nobility where they did not.

[33] *GSSO*, Sessiya 4 (1908-9), cols 1933-41; A. S. Izgoev, the contemporary Kadet commentator, says that Pikhno actually made this proposal with Stolypin's knowledge and agreement (*P. A. Stolypin*, pp 87, 90).

[34] *GSSO*, Sessiya 4 (1908-9), col 1950; *TsGIAL*, f 1278, op 2, d 885, pp 3-4 (note from the Minister of the Interior to the President of the Duma, 9 May 1909).

5

Feeling, perhaps, a little unsure of his reception in the Duma, Stolypin first of all flew his western zemstvo idea as a kite. When, on 9 May 1909, he wrote to the President of the Duma, forwarding the proposal of the thirty-three members of the State Council, he mentioned the possibility that the introduction of zemstvos in the western provinces might solve the problem of the State Council elections there. But he went on to say that probably this move should wait for the general zemstvo reform, and that the best plan for the moment was to postpone the State Council elections in the western provinces for a year while a new electoral system was worked out on the lines suggested by the thirty-three.[35]

However, the Duma committee responsible for the preliminary examination of legislative proposals responded as he had probably hoped they would, by seizing on the western zemstvo idea.[36] More important, the Octobrists reacted favourably to Stolypin's implied proposal. At a fraction meeting on 28 May they recommended that the deputies returned to the State Council at the forthcoming elections in the western provinces should have their terms of office limited to one year, so that in the meantime a bill could be worked out for introducing zemstvos in the region.[37]

In the Duma on 30 May Stolypin personally welcomed this response:

The Government, as I have indicated, did not take upon itself the initiative of such a proposal, simply because it considered it impossible to pass in such a short time a bill extending the activity of the zemstvo institutions. But recently the Duma has taken a new point of view: it has itself expressed the wish that in certain internal provinces the current Zemstvo Statute should be introduced. I must say that this considerably eases the Government's position, and, agreeing with it, the Government can and does undertake to table in the autumn session a bill extending the current Zemstvo Statute to the nine western provinces, with a few alterations, naturally, in the system of electing deputies, to conform with local conditions and peculiarities.[38]

For the Octobrists, Antonov on the same day expressed dismay that the government could not pass the general zemstvo reform reasonably quickly, but welcomed the promised bill as one that

---

[35] ibid, pp 5-6.   [36] ibid, p 8.   [37] TsGAOR, f 115, op 1, d 19, p 113.
[38] GDSO, III, 2, pt 4, col 2756.

conformed with a basic demand in the Octobrists' platform, the extension of elective local government.[39]

The Western Zemstvo bill in the Duma

Having thus felt his way and assured himself on the general support of the majority of the Duma, Stolypin drafted his bill. Since there were so many conditions to be fulfilled, and so many diverse interests to be satisfied, the result was a very complicated piece of legislation. The main difficulty, from which all others sprang, was to ensure Russian predominance in a zemstvo which should nevertheless contain sufficient active and educated local people to be able to function at all. This was why Stolypin decided to leave nothing to chance, to abandon the idea of allowing groups to form freely at electoral meetings, and instead to erect a system of closely defined national curiae. Even then, there remained the question of how seats should be distributed among the various nationalities (and here the main problem, as far as Stolypin was concerned, was the division between Russians and Poles). If seats were distributed by the criterion of population, then indeed a Russian majority would be assured, but, Stolypin felt, a primarily uneducated majority who would not conduct local government well and would certainly not be to the taste of such influential groups as the United Nobility and the Rights in the State Council. On the other hand, if seats were distributed according to a property qualification, there was a considerable danger that the Poles, profiting by the probable absence of many Russian landowners, would emerge triumphant and dominate the new zemstvos in a manner unacceptable to the Nationalists and most of the Octobrists in the Duma, as well as to Stolypin himself. Eventually he decided to distribute the seats between the two principal nationalities not exclusively on the basis of either population or property, but on a mixture of both. The proportion of deputies, in his proposed bill, to be elected by each national group in any given district was to be the arithmetical mean of (i) the percentage of the population represented by that nationality in the district, and (ii) the percentage of the total value of the property in the district owned by that nationality.[40] This was not all: since in

[39] ibid, cols 2757-61.
[40] *TsGIAL*, f 1276, op 5, d 73, pp 9-10 (explanatory note to the Ministry's bill).

some districts this would have meant a majority elected by the communal peasantry, he further stipulated that in no district was the representation of the communal peasantry to exceed one-third of the total. Other medium and small landholders (many of whom would be the ' Stolypin ' peasants) were, however, to be encouraged. Whereas by the Zemstvo Statute of 1890 large landowners, holding a full electoral qualification (*tsenz*) or more, had separate representation from the medium and small landowners, in the new western zemstvo all landholders owning down to one-tenth of the electoral qualification (equivalent to a rateable value of 1,500 rubles) were to vote in one curia. This would weaken the Polish landowners and strengthen the non-communal Russian peasantry, and was a move towards the kind of classlessness which Stolypin still claimed to want to introduce in a general zemstvo reform.[41]

There were one or two other important departures from the Zemstvo Statute of 1890. Russian Orthodox clergy were to receive increased representation, four deputies in the district zemstvo and three in the provincial one, instead of just one in each. A further buttress to Russian influence was the stipulation that the chairman of the executive board (*uprava*) and his deputy and also the chairman of each of the zemstvo's committees, together with their deputies, should be Russian; certain offices in the administration, to be decided by each provincial governor, would be open only to Russians; and one-half of the employees of the executive board should be Russian. Jews were to be excluded altogether from the zemstvos (even though the great majority of Russia's Jews lived in these western provinces).[42]

Finally, since not even this concatenation of complications would ensure the realisation of Stolypin's purposes in the three north-western provinces of Vilna, Grodno and Kovno, he decided, on the advice of his Council for the Affairs of the Local Economy, to drop them from the bill.[43]

From the start, the bill's complicated provisions ran into trouble. At nine heated meetings lasting most of March 1910, the Duma

[41] ibid, pp 4, 15-16.
[42] *TsGIAL*, f 1278, op 2, d 1171, pp 45-46 (the text of the bill as submitted to the Duma). Jews were to be banned altogether from the zemstvo elections, as in the law of 1890.
[43] *TsGIAL*, f 1276, op 5, d 73, pp 10-12. For an explanation of the Council for the Affairs of the Local Economy, see below, p 160.

Local Self-Government Committee examined the bill and altered or even rejected many of the provisions to which Stolypin ascribed particular importance. They lowered the property qualification by half (i.e. to a rateable value of 750 rubles), but at the same time altered the electoral system so that property-owners holding one-fifth or more of the qualification would vote in one curia, while those holding between one-tenth and one-fifth would vote in another. The effect of these amendments would be to increase the number of smallholders involved in the election, without allowing the medium landowners to be swamped by them. Antsiferov, representing the Ministry of the Interior in the committee, did not raise any objection to these two amendments.[44]

As far as the national curiae were concerned, the majority of the committee was prepared to accept them only with reservations, as a necessary but temporary evil. It therefore proposed that in any district the two national curiae might vote together, provided that two-thirds of the members of each wanted to do so. Antsiferov immediately expressed the government's unqualified opposition to this proposal: 'Any such proposal radically undermines all the principles of the Russian zemstvo which have formed the basis for the committee's decisions.' The proposal was carried in the committee by the votes of the Octobrists and the opposition against the Nationalists and Rights.[45]

Another amendment disruptive of the government's intentions was that the distribution of seats between the national curiae in the district zemstvo should be calculated solely on the basis of property. This would ensure the Poles a somewhat higher proportion of seats, though to ensure that they would not be dominant in any single district, the committee recommended that the proportions of property should be calculated at the level of the province, not of the district, since there were one or two districts where Poles actually held half or more of the landed property.[46]

The committee also rejected the limitations placed by the government on national composition of the executive board and its various committees, considering these limitations ' incorrect and superfluous '. Antsiferov spoke out again to declare that

---

[44] *TsGIAL*, f 1278, op 2, d 1171, pp 205-8 (meetings of the Duma Local Self-Government Committee).   [45] ibid, pp 198-201.
[46] ibid, pp 215-20.

The Government insists on the preservation of Articles 21-23 in the present bill, and considers this question to be one of principle. As has already been agreed, from the point of view of the state the zemstvo in the western provinces must be a Russian one; it is to this aim that the provisions of the Government bill are directed, including the articles being discussed. More specifically, since the direction taken by the zemstvo's activity depends on the executive board and its chairman, the Government . . . decided that it was absolutely essential that control over the activity of the zemstvo and its various branches should be in Russian hands.

Nevertheless, the committee voted to reject these articles, the only palliative being that they proposed to reserve the administration of education to a Russian official.[47]

The cumulative result of these various amendments was to produce a hybrid bill satisfactory to almost no one. For their different reasons, the Right-Nationalist bloc and the opposition were so dissatisfied with it in its present form that when the committee came to vote on the bill as a whole the majority of them turned out to be against it. The committee was thus in the absurd position of having to recommend the Duma to reject the bill which it had just worked out.[48]

The debates on the floor of the house were even more protracted and difficult, in spite of the fact that the government was trying to hurry the bill through. Objections to the bill, in principle and in detail, were made from every side. The Octobrists were placed in a very difficult position. They were not, as it transpired, in agreement among themselves on the issues, yet they had to try to sense the mood of the whole assembly and gather a consensus for a composite bill which would be acceptable to the government. Antsiferov's firm stand in the committee suggested that the government would not be easy to please, and might even withdraw the bill. Nor could the Octobrists afford a repetition of the fiasco of the committee.

In the first reading, Stolypin made the main speech for the government. Formally, since the Duma's committee had rejected its own bill, only the government's version was before the house. But the amendments suggested by the committee were very much in everyone's mind, and it was against them that Stolypin directed the burden of his speech. He gave particular attention to the national curiae. It

[47] ibid, pp 233-8.   [48] ibid, p 255.

was a mistake, he declared, to suppose that they were a temporary evil, designed to yield eventually to co-operation between all nationalities in the area. On the contrary, the Russian zemstvo was a projection of the Russian state into the western provinces, and the system of national curiae which ensured its Russian character was intended to be permanent. His justifications were largely historical. The vast majority of the population there, he maintained, had always been Russian in nationality and religion, even when the region lay within the Polish state, and when Polish landowners had undisputed economic and cultural supremacy. The peasant population and clergy had successfully resisted these influences, so that when Russia resumed her rights over the region in the eighteenth century, they found a suppressed population still faithful to Orthodoxy and the Russian state. Was the government now to abandon this population to an alien people? 1830, 1863 and 1905 had shown that, whenever Russian state influence was weakened, the Poles tried to resume their sway over the Russian peasantry. And in the Duma the Poles and Lithuanians had insisted on maintaining separatist national political parties, refusing alliance with any of the Russian parties. It was for these reasons that the government had altered its original intention to make the national curiae facultative. If the two curiae voted together, the elections would become political, nationalist passions would be inflamed, and only the Poles could benefit from such a situation. The Russian state must make absolutely clear its intention of preventing any such possibility.

Most of the other amendments were equally unacceptable to Stolypin, for the same basic reason. Although in theory, he admitted, zemstvo representation should be determined by taxable property alone, the peculiar features of the region must be taken into account, and these demanded a system which gave a less prominent place to the Poles: the distribution of seats proposed by the committee would, he claimed, give 70 per cent more representation to the Poles than the government bill. Nor was it safe to assume that a Russian majority in the zemstvo assembly guaranteed a Russian dominance in the executive board and its subordinate organs: very often it was easier to employ trained Poles from the immediate neighbourhood rather than invite Russians from far away. The Poles' good reputation and their personal connections made it extremely difficult to refuse them employment unless some precise law restricted their admission.

The object of the government's bill, he submitted, was not to oppress the Poles, but to defend the Russians in the western region:

The bill gives legitimate representation to all classes of the local population, and to all interests: it simply puts an end to centuries-old tribal political strife. It does this by shielding with a powerful and decisive pronouncement the Russian state principles. The ratification of these principles here in this chamber by you, gentlemen, will perhaps destroy not a few illusions and hopes, but will also prevent not a few misfortunes and misunderstandings by proclaiming openly and without hypocrisy that the western region is and will remain a Russian region for ever.[49]

The Nationalists entirely supported Stolypin. S. M. Bogdanov (Kiev province) announced that the only amendment they were prepared to accept was that lowering the property qualification by half. If the committee's other amendments were passed by the house, they would vote against the bill as a whole, preferring no western zemstvo to a bad one.[50] The Rights also gave their support. N. E. Markov said that he personally doubted whether there were enough Russian landowners in the western region for the scheme to be wholly advisable, but he would vote for the government bill as the best way of achieving it.[51] V. V. Shulgin, the author of a pamphlet advocating the establishment of zemstvos in the western provinces, gave whole-hearted support to the government's bill, calling it an improvement on his own scheme. It would put an end to the perpetual national strife in the area and encourage a stable Russian middle class to settle there.[52]

The peasant group in the Rights, however criticised the government's bill for giving the peasants – and here they meant the communal peasants – insufficient representation. In this criticism M. S. Andreichuk (Right) found common ground with his Nationalist colleague A. F. Kuchinsky, and even with A. A. Bulat, a Lithuanian from the Labour fraction.[53] Here the peasants of all fractions, as in the agrarian debates, were expressing their opposition to the new 'Stolypin' smallholders. The Social Democrat N. S. Chkheidze went so far as to see the main significance of the bill in the way in which it benefited the Russian landowners at the expense, not only

[49] GDSO, III, 3, pt 4, cols 774-91.   [50] ibid, cols 791-7.   [51] ibid, cols 910-26.
[52] ibid, cols 947-60; V. V. Shul'gin, Vybornoe Zemstvo v Zapadnom Krae, Kiev 1909.   [53] GDSO, III, 3, pt 4, cols 825-30, 849-58, 1018-21.

of the Poles, but also of the Russian peasants. In 45 out of 67 districts, he pointed out, the Russian landowners would have an absolute majority over Poles and peasants combined, and in 10 more would have half of the votes. Nationalism, he concluded, was a screen behind which the government was continuing its narrow class-based policy of restoring and extending the political and economic power of the landowners.[54]

The Octobrists were in great confusion. Yu. N. Glebov put forward the position which was to emerge as the fraction's officially approved line in the second reading. It was about half way between the government's and the committee's versions. He agreed with the committee's view that national curiae were a temporary necessity. But, unlike the committee, he also believed that the statutory minimum of 50 per cent Russian representation on the executive board and its subordinate organs was necessary, since the composition of these bodies depended in practice on many other factors besides the composition of the zemstvo assembly, which in any case met only infrequently. On the other hand, he attacked the government's dilution of the property criterion for distributing seats in the zemstvo assembly. The Minister himself, he said, had recognised that in principle property should be the sole criterion: in this case it was time that such principles were put into effect, especially since in many districts no very significant increase in Polish representation would result. Nor could he accept the need for defining certain posts which non-Russians might not hold: this was only symptomatic of the government's distrust of local government organs. ' I am ready ', he concluded, ' to support what is dictated by national pride, but not what is dictated by hatred for everything non-Russian.'[55]

Virtually no other Octobrist speaker took exactly the same position. Baron Felkersam, for example, maintained that if the division into national curiae was not sufficient to protect Russian interests without further safeguards, then they had no business introducing zemstvos into the western region anyway.[56] One or two other Octobrists supported the government's bill in its entirety.[57] Worst of all, I. S. Klimenko, an Octobrist from Chernigov, openly attacked the whole position his fraction seemed to be taking up. Their party's original programme, he pointed out, called for ' a broad

[54] ibid, cols 751-61.   [55] ibid, cols 858-69.   [56] ibid, cols 1131-5.
[57] ibid, cols 1021-7, 1135-40.

development of local government throughout the Empire, on the firmly established basis of civil freedom and with the equal participation of all Russian citizens, without distinction of nationality or faith, in the exercise of administrative authority '. He continued:

The bill presented for our examination is constructed on different principles – on the principle of separate national curiae – and therefore, since it contradicts the principles of the party to which I belong, I shall vote against it on the first reading. (Prolonged applause on the left.) Furthermore, I invite my colleagues of the centre to do the same. The attention of the whole country is focussed on the centre of the Duma, since the votes of the centre are of decisive importance. And the country sees with bitterness that the centre does not hold firm, is not guided by firm principles. The Third Duma has existed for three years, and for three years we orthodox Octobrists have had to be patient, to give way, and to forego our principles. I consider that we have reached the limit, and in future I intend to act according to the programme of our Union. (Stormy applause left.)[58]

For the Kadets, Shingarev made a detailed criticism of the government's bill from the radical constitutional viewpoint. He singled out five basic faults:
  (i) the division into national curiae, which was contrary to the express intentions of the October Manifesto, and would inflame national hostility;
 (ii) lack of trust in the ability of the local zemstvo men to select the right people for their administrative organs;
(iii) the electoral qualifications laid down by the government discriminated unjustly against medium and small property-holders;
 (iv) the distribution of seats within the zemstvo discriminated unjustly against the peasants;
  (v) the Jews were to be permitted no part in the zemstvos.[59]

This position was broadly reiterated by the Polish and Lithuanian deputies, who, however, laid special emphasis on the injustices done to their own peoples.[60]

In the event, the first reading was carried by 196 votes to 140, the Rights, Nationalists and most of the Octobrists constituting the majority. Fifteen Octobrists, however, voted against the first reading, including Klimenko. Five other Octobrists abstained.[61]

58 ibid, cols 1229-30.   59 ibid, cols 975-94.   60 ibid, cols 810-24.
61 ibid, cols 1233, 1275-6; the Octobrists who voted against the bill were
   Klimenko 1, Belyaev 2, Princes Volkonskii 1 and 2, von Kruze, Leonov,

This significant thinning of the Octobrist ranks gave ground for trepidation over the treatment some of the bill's detailed provisions might get in the second reading. On 14 May 1910, *Novoe Vremya* expressed extreme disapprobation at the disarray of the Octobrists and reminded them their standing on this question would be taken as a test of their reliability as a party: ' In such an important question as the zemstvo, the chief Duma party, if it wants to retain any right to respect, must look for authoritative directives in itself, and certainly not from some other source.'

The Octobrist fraction was, indeed, in a seriously fragmented condition. Only a couple of months before, in March, Khomyakov, the President of the Duma, had resigned over a particularly unpleasant incident involving the Rights. In a surprise move, Guchkov had put forward his own candidacy and gained the support of the Octobrist fraction after a stormy meeting.[62] This was typical of the impatience of the man: disillusioned with the Octobrist fraction and with the Duma Imperial Defence Committee as vehicles for his personal influence, he sought another path. As President of the Duma, he would have the right of personal report to the Emperor. Interestingly, he had the support of Stolypin, who wrote to him as soon as Khomyakov's resignation was announced; perhaps he hoped thereby to renew his slackening ties with the Octobrists and improve their relations with the Emperor. If so, then of course he had chosen the wrong man.[63]

Guchkov was duly elected as President of the Duma, and had to resign his post as chairman of the Octobrist fraction, not for the first or last time. The fraction immediately split over the choice of a successor. The majority wanted to elect Anrep, but a significant minority insistently supported Rodzyanko. Rumours circulated that Rodzyanko, being certain that he would not be elected, intended to leave the fraction, taking twenty or so members with him, and form

Meyendorf, Rozen, Rotermel', Favorsky, Fal'ts-Fein, Khomyakov, Shilling, Ergardt. Those who abstained were Alexeenko, Zhdanov, Leus, Tizengauzen and Timirev.

[62] *Rech'*, 7 March 1910.

[63] On 3 March 1910, after Khomyakov resigned, Stolypin wrote to Guchkov: ' For the good of the cause, the new President of the Duma must be Alexander Ivanovich Guchkov. If you will call on me tomorrow, I will explain my reasons in detail.' (*TsGAOR*, f 555 (A. I. Guchkov), op 1, d 1112, p 3.)

a new Right Octobrist group, alongside that which Gololobov had already formed. In the event, to avoid any such open split, the fraction decided to postpone any election of a chairman till the autumn.[64]

The Octobrists were thus leaderless during the debates on the Western Zemstvo bill, and they behaved like it. At two fraction meetings, on 11 and 14 May, they discussed what to do, and how much of the government's bill they could accept. Rodzyanko spoke in favour of the government's bill, and Anrep, in the chair for the occasion, went so far as to warn the fraction that very serious political consequences might follow their rejection of it. I. V. Godnev protested that Anrep was using unworthy methods to force the fraction's compliance, and proposed that for the sake of their reputation in the country they should vote for the committee's version. He was supported by Prince A. D. Golitsyn, Yu. N. Glebov, A. E. Favorsky, M. A. Iskritsky, D. A. Leonov and Baron Meyendorf, who all affirmed that they could not vote for the government's bill. In the end, a compromise was reached: the fraction accepted an amendment distributing seats between the national groups on a criterion of property alone, and rejected the government's wish that the chairman of the executive board and certain of its officials were to be Russian. But they supported the government in refusing to permit any possibility of a combined vote of the two curiae, and in retaining the provision that at least half of the executive board was to consist of Russians.[65] This was exactly the stand which Glebov had taken on first reading.

In the second reading, the Octobrists were too divided and uncertain for their version to be accepted. But, in fact, a compromise not unlike it emerged. The amendment distributing seats according to the sole criterion of property was rejected by 171 votes to 168 (on recount 182 to 165). There was no official list of the Ayes and Noes, but a large number of Octobrists must have voted against the fraction's resolution, and *Rech* reported that they were split into two almost equal halves by this vote.[66] A further victory for the government was the rejection of the amendment allowing the two national curiae to amalgamate if they wished to.[67]

[64] *GM*, 7 March, 4, 15 April 1910; *Rech*[1], 12, 20, 27 March 1910.
[65] *Rech*[1], 12, 15 May 1910.   [66] ibid, 18 May 1910.
[67] *GDSO*, III, 3, pt 4, col 1507.

In other respects, the government's bill suffered heavily in second reading. The electoral qualification was lowered by half[68] (though this the government was by now prepared to accept). On the question of the national composition of the executive board, Article 23, which stipulated that half its personnel should be Russian, was accepted, with the additional clause that the official responsible for education should be Russian. But Articles 21 and 22, reserving for Russians the chairmanship of the executive board, as well as certain other posts to be defined at the discretion of the provincial governor, were rejected.[69] This was the compromise on which the Octobrists had agreed.

Finally, the government's wish to see the Orthodox clergy strongly represented in the new zemstvos was thwarted. The Duma reduced the representation of the clergy to the level envisaged in the 1890 Zemstvo Statute: one in the provincial and one in the district assembly.[70]

No major changes were made in the third reading, and the bill thus came up for the final vote in a compromise form which satisfied no one completely. Summing up for the Octobrists, Anrep admitted that the bill was not all that could be wished: ' I and my political associates vote for the acceptance of the bill in full consciousness of its imperfections . . . But it has one merit: it brings new life into the region.'[71]

For some of the Rights, of course, the bill was even less satisfactory. Purishkevich declared that only splinters and fragments of the government's intentions were left, and that the government should have withdrawn the bill when it saw the Duma was doing everything it could to belittle the importance of the Russian nationality in the western provinces.[72] Shulgin admitted that much had been lost, but was glad that certain essentials had been retained: the establishment of national curiae, the fixing of the number of deputies of each nationality, and the Russian majority on the executive board. He announced his intention to vote for the bill, in the expectation that further improvements could and would be made later.[73]

In the final vote, the whole bill was passed by 165 votes to 139, with 8 abstentions.[74]

[68] ibid, cols 1498-1500.   [69] ibid, cols 1647-9.   [70] ibid, cols 1736-7.
[71] ibid, col 2835.   [72] ibid, cols 2929-31.   [73] ibid, cols 2831-2.
[74] ibid, cols 2838-9.

The Western Zemstvo bill in the State Council

The compromise bill as it emerged from the Duma contained so many diverse features that it was very vulnerable to attack. And indeed the discussion of it in committee in the State Council was very protracted (the debate in the chamber did not begin till January 1911). Yet at first there were few signs that the bill would suffer shipwreck in the upper house. In fact, the outcome of the committee's deliberations was very favourable to the government: most of the incisions the Duma had made into the government's version were restored.[75]

In the first reading, criticism focussed on the national curiae. The interesting point to note is that it did *not* come from the Right, but rather from the centre and left, and of course from the Poles. Prince A. D. Obolensky, for example, called the division into national curiae a ' violation of the principle of a unified imperial nationality '. A. A. Donetsky, spokesman of the landowners of the Don, complained that the bill deliberately infringed the theory of local self-government, by which citizens were represented according to the taxes they paid: this bill would diminish the Poles' just representation. A. E. Meysztowicz, speaking for the Polish landowners of Kovno province, warned that recent experience suggested that the really important divisions in Imperial Russia were not between nationalities, but between those who supported and those who wanted to overthrow the social order: ' but this bill divides Russian and Polish conservatives into national chambers, and so sharpens disunity '. The liberal M. M. Kovalevsky characterised the national curiae as an ' abandonment of the imperial idea in favour of recognition of the demands of the nationalities '.[76]

Apart from N. A. Zinoviev, the only speaker from the Right who spoke against the bill was V. F. Trepov, who emphasised that he was speaking for himself, not for his colleagues. And he did not condemn the national curiae: rather he maintained, somewhat mysteriously, that the ' conservative monarchical principle' of the zemstvo was being drawn into the same card game as the navy, the church and the schools.[77] What he presumably meant by this was that, by lowering the electoral qualification, the government was diluting the predominance of the nobles in the zemstvo by a large admixture of ' Stolypin ' peasants. In this manner he saw the Western

[75] *GSSO*, Sessiya 6 (1910-11), cols 752-81.
[76] ibid, cols 880-9, 901-12, 913-25, 1224.   [77] ibid, col 927.

Zemstvo bill as part of a deliberate campaign by Stolypin to usurp the Emperor's autocratic prerogatives.

Even in the second reading, no Rights except N. P. Balashov and N. A. Zinoviev attacked the national curiae. Yet the vote on this vital clause went against the government.

The reason for the sudden change lay in intrigues taking place in the right wing of the State Council. The Rights' positive vote at the end of the first reading had been the result of instructions from Stolypin. These instructions had been communicated to Durnovo by Akimov in a telephone call. Akimov told Durnovo that 'in the highest spheres there exists the wish that the bill should be passed', a formula for saying that the Emperor wished the bill to be passed. Durnovo had replied that he could not tell how the Rights would react to this message, but that he was prepared to try to incline them to the wishes of the 'highest spheres'. Many Rights were annoyed at this procedure, which they felt was tactless and arrogant on the part of Stolypin: usually the wishes of the 'highest spheres' were made known to them in some more private fashion. What is more doubtful is whether they were opposed in principle to national curiae as a keystone of the new zemstvo. We have seen that, in the form of the Project of the 33, they had actually recommended national curiae as a means of ensuring better Russian representation in the State Council, and there is no obvious reason why they should have objected to the same means of establishing a 'Russian zemstvo' in the western region.

In fact, the main reason for the Rights' opposition to what Stolypin regarded as the keystone of his bill was political opportunism. They saw this as a suitable way of weakening Stolypin and the Duma further. They therefore sent a letter to the Emperor expressing deep gratitude for the trust shown to them in the 'highest spheres', but stating that they had many doubts about the bill before them; they would do their best to resolve these doubts and vote as conscience dictated. V. F. Trepov conveyed this letter to the Emperor and had an audience with him, from which he returned with the message that the Rights were freed from any external obligations and should vote each as his conscience dictated.[78] According to Kokovtsev, both Durnovo and Trepov, in private audiences with the

---

[78] The most detailed account is given in *Rech*[1], 9 March 1911, but is confirmed in outline by other sources: *NV*, 8, 9 March 1911; *GM*, 6

Emperor, objected to the favour shown to the local peasants in the bill, a feature which they felt would alienate educated and conservative elements in the region, and lead to the creation of a revolutionary zemstvo dominated by the intelligentsia. They were presumably referring to the peasants with non-communal, private property. This objection certainly seems more characteristic of the views of the Rights in the State Council, and of the United Nobility whose ideological partners they often were, and probably represents a genuine motive for rejecting the bill.

However, it was against the national curiae that the blow fell – not probably because it was the feature of the bill which the Rights found most repugnant, but because it was the feature to which Stolypin attached the greatest importance. He had no idea of the blow which was being prepared: when he came to the chamber on 4 March for the debate on the national curiae, he probably imagined he would command the same majority as on first reading. Instead, all but two speakers in the debate spoke against national curiae, Pikhno and Stishinsky, two Rights who in the first reading had supported national curiae, were silent now. Stolypin reiterated his own position towards the end: ' I can and ought to confirm one thing: the government considers that the question of national curiae is one of state significance, the central issue of the present bill.'[79]

But this did not prevent the vote going against him by 92 to 68.[80] The majority included 28 Rights who thus, by voting contrary to their group's original decision, played the decisive role. They were joined by the left, the Poles and many of the centre.[81]

This defeat was clearly the result of intrigue. It is also true, however, that the Western Zemstvo bill was a measure whose hybrid and complex nature, its labyrinthine bureaucratic nationalism, laid it open to attack. The Rights' victory, even if artificially engineered, was also the logical result of the growing sterility of Stolypin's projects.

The ministerial crisis

The ministerial crisis which followed was long drawn-out and undignified. But it did reveal very clearly the assumptions underlying

March 1911; Kokovtsev, *Iz Moego Proshlogo*, vol 1, pp 451-3; ' Dnevnik A. A. Bobrinskogo ', *KA*, vol 6, p 144.
[79] *GSSO*, Sessiya 6 (1910-11), cols 1240-1.　　[80] ibid, col 1256.
[81] *NV*, 8 March 1911; *Rech¹*, 9 March 1911.

Stolypin's conception of his political position as head of a united cabinet in an autocratic monarchy working with a popular representative body.

The unexpected defeat in the State Council had an immediate and violent effect on Stolypin. When he heard of it, he stood stock still for a moment in sheer astonishment, and blushed a brilliant red.[82] Having ascertained that it was the result of Trepov's audience with the Emperor, he drove out to Tsarskoe Selo next morning to tender his resignation. The Emperor was evidently torn between two considerations: on the one hand, the view, zealously repeated to him by Trepov, Durnovo and other former high officials in his entourage, that Stolypin was setting himself up as a kind of dictator, and endeavouring, with the help of the Duma, to narrow the Emperor's prerogatives; on the other hand, his impression that Stolypin was the only man capable of leading the government in the still difficult period Russia was living through. Stolypin was still shaken and furious at the reverse he had suffered. He felt insulted both as a man and as the leader of the government by the intrigues which had been directed against him behind his back. Alone with the Emperor, he attacked Durnovo and Trepov, calling them liars and intriguers, and declared that he could not continue his work if he was to be exposed to the obstructions of such people. Nicholas, who had made the decisive contribution to the success of their manoeuvres, could not help being conscious of the reproach to him implied in the Premier's words, but insisted that he could not afford to lose Stolypin. He suggested that Stolypin pass the bill once more through the Duma, and he, the Emperor, would make sure that there was no repetition of the débâcle in the State Council. Stolypin replied that the State Council would never admit its mistake, and that, in any case, he, as Minister of the Interior, could not be dependent on the intrigues of factions and seek his support in the inconstant currents of public opinion. He insisted, in fact, that there was only one condition on which he would withdraw his resignation: this was that his constitutional supremacy over the State Council and its reactionary intriguers should be unambiguously demonstrated by the Emperor's closing both legislative chambers for a token period of three days, and issuing the Western Zemstvo bill under Article 87. At the same time Durnovo and Trepov should be requested by the

[82] *Rech¹*, 9 March 1911.

Emperor to leave St Petersburg for the remainder of the present session, in order that it might be clear that a repetition of their activities would not be tolerated. The Emperor, while anxious to retain Stolypin, would not immediately agree to such stringent conditions, and said he would think about what he should do. He concluded by urging Stolypin again not to resign.[83]

The matter had now reached the stage of a personal and decisive duel between Stolypin and the reactionary forces which had worked against him and influenced the Emperor in his disfavour ever since it seemed that he might be achieving some kind of stable partnership with the Duma and firmly consolidating the new state system. Stolypin would have been the last to admit that his policy tended to weaken the Emperor's independent power – indeed, he considered the source of his own authority to lie in the fact that it had been entrusted to him by the autocratic monarch. Yet, inevitably, that was the effect of his policy, since he realised that in modern conditions the state could only be strengthened against revolution by increasing in it, through parliament, the influence of the landowning, professional and educated classes. And this could only happen at the expense of the Emperor's own independent power. It was this undeniable fact which gave the reactionaries' arguments such force in the mind of the Emperor.

Probably the only way to parry the intrigues effectively would have been to use such influence and trust as he still commanded among these new participants in government. In other words, in this case, he should have returned his Western Zemstvo bill to the Duma for a renewed expression of their support,[84] after which, if the Emperor indicated that he was in favour of the bill, the State Council would either have to accept it or expose themselves as

---

[83] We have two detailed accounts of this interview: Stolypin's own account, given to the Council of Ministers the next day, and expounded in Kokovtsev's memoirs (*Iz Moego Proshlogo*, vol 1, pp 452-7), and a written memorandum in the Central State Historical Archive in Leningrad, on notepaper headed 'President of the Council of Ministers', apparently transcribed from Stolypin's words shortly after the event (*TsGIAL*, f 1662 (P. A. Stolypin), op 1, d 325, pp 1-2).

[84] This support would certainly have been forthcoming. As soon as the news of the government's defeat in the upper house reached the Duma, a document was signed by over two hundred of its members, expressing willingness to pass the bill again as fast as possible. (*GM*, 12 March 1911.)

saboteurs of the legislative process. Such manoeuvres, however, Stolypin considered beneath him, and he declared to the Council of Ministers when such a course was suggested: 'Let him who values status seek compromises: I consider it more worthy and honourable to stand aside altogether if it is necessary to defend one's personal position in the conditions I have experienced.'[85]

Rather than resort to the 'politicking' which he so much despised, but which was going to have to be characteristic of the constitutional system if it was to survive, Stolypin preferred to cut the knot at one blow by a dramatic gesture. For four years he had retreated rather abjectly in the face of reactionary pressure; now he tried to undo all the work of his opponents at one go. His decision was certainly influenced by ill health, exhaustion and irritability, the result of conducting government business with considerable energy during a transitional period under very trying conditions. But it also had its roots in the conception he had often expounded of the new state system. He saw the government's power as derived from the autocratic monarch bound to his people by the Duma. This view gave him every justification for passing the Western Zemstvo bill under Article 87, for it had been passed by the Duma and rejected only by the State Council as the result of the manoeuvres of a minority group. If the Emperor approved it, it ought, in Stolypin's conception, to be passed, whatever 'artificial' obstacles might be put against it. Only in this way could the common will of the Monarch and the people's representatives be put into effect.

For four days the Emperor pondered whether he could allow Stolypin the fulfilment of the harsh conditions he had demanded. Then, on 9 May, he wrote to Stolypin:

Peter Arkadyevich,
For the last four days since our conversation I have weighed and considered my reply from all angles.

I do not wish to allow you to resign. Your devotion to me and to Russia, your five years' experience in the post you hold, and, most of all, your courageous upholding of Russian political principles on the borders of the Empire, move me to retain you at all costs. I tell you this with complete sincerity and conviction, not on impulse. Look at what people are saying and thinking around you. What unanimous regret and even gloom has been aroused by the mere rumour of your resignation. After all this can you really continue to be stubborn?

[85] Kokovtsev, *Iz Moego Proshlogo*, vol 1, p 457.

Of course you will not. I know in advance that you will agree to remain. This is what I demand and what is desired by every true Russian. I request you, Peter Arkadyevich, to come to me tomorrow, Thursday, at 11 a.m. Remember – my trust in you has remained as complete as it was in 1906.[86]

In the audience which followed, Nicholas agreed to all Stolypin's conditions. Stolypin was by now so suspicious of Nicholas's conduct that he insisted he should make a written record of the terms he had accepted, which Nicholas did with a blue crayon on a large note-pad.[87]

On 12 March, the Ukaz was published suspending the legislative chambers for three days. The Duma parties, and particularly the Octobrists, reacted violently. The Octobrists had for the time being buried their differences and, under pressure from Stolypin, elected Rodzyanko as chairman of their fraction.[88] They responded immediately to the dissolution of the chambers, and stated in a fraction revolution that, if the government now passed the Western Zemstvo bill under Article 87, the Octobrists would vote against it when it came before the Duma again, and would bring before the house an interpellation directed against the Premier. With unwonted unanimity, members of the fraction declared that the suspension of the chambers was utterly artificial, that no emergency existed of the kind designated in Article 87, and that if the government were permitted to establish a precedent of this kind, there would be nothing to stop them passing any future legislation whether or not the Duma and State Council approved of it. Guchkov, for once, spoke for the whole fraction when he said : ' The question is clear and straightforward: we cannot agree to any concessions. In this case a collision with the government is inevitable. If we make no protest, what kind of a party shall we be? Our role will be reduced to nil.'[89]

---

[86] *TsGAOR*, f 601 (Nicholas II), op 1, d 1125, pp 3-4.
[87] Shidlovskii, *Vospominaniya*, vol 1, p 194.
[88] Diary of I. S. Klyuzhev, *TsGIAL*, f 669, op 1, d 3, pp 62-5; also d 4, p 7. According to Klyuzhev, Guchkov deliberately deceived the fraction in order to have Rodzyanko elected. At a special meeting in Lerkhe's apartment on 20 November 1910, he told them that Anrep, the left-wing favourite, had withdrawn his candidacy, which was untrue; and he went on to persuade Alexeenko to stand down.
[89] *TsGAOR*, f 115, op 1, d 19, pp 213-14; *TsGIAL*, f 669, op 1, d 7, p 30; *GM*, 13 March 1911.

A deputation from the Octobrists (Rodzyanko, P. V. Kamensky and Glebov) visited Stolypin to convey the fraction's resolution to him. Stolypin expressed genuine surprise that the Octobrists should object to his act: when he had read that two hundred members of the Duma had signed a letter offering to pass the bill through the lower house again, he had imagined that they had done so because they were anxious to see the bill passed, a purpose which would be served by the application of Article 87. Such an act, he protested, would not in any way be directed against the Duma; indeed, he intended to promulgate the bill in the form in which the Duma had passed it, in spite of the government's objection to some of their amendments. He was using the bill as a weapon to break the resistance of the Rights in the State Council, and thus open the way to more fruitful relations between the upper and lower house in the passing of urgent reforms. He commented that already a number of reforms passed by the Duma had got stuck in the upper house. When Rodzyanko reiterated that the act was illegal, Stolypin disagreed, but conceded that it was a strain on the law. When he read the Octobrists' resolution he was visibly dismayed, but reaffirmed that the government had by now taken its decision and would not go back on it.[90]

On the same day, Guchkov tried his personal influence on Stolypin. He wrote a letter warning him:

I consider it my bounden duty to implore you to desist from this step. Its consequences are incalculable: such a blatant infringement of the letter and spirit of the Fundamental Laws, such a bitter blow to the dignity and independence of the legislative institutions, will cause utter havoc in the country. You know what an ardent and convinced supporter of yours I have been . . . how hateful to me are your enemies, how in particular I supported the Western Zemstvo bill. Nevertheless, I must say to you: the step you are taking is a fateful one, not only for you personally . . . but for Russia, for the now reformed Russia which is so dear to you, and for which you have done so much.[91]

This did not help either. On 14 March the Ukaz was published passing the Western Zemstvo bill, in the Duma's version, under

[90] *GM*, 15 March 1911.
[91] E. D. Chermenskii, ' Bor'ba Klassov i Partii v 4-oi Gosudarstvennoi Dume ', unpublished doctoral dissertation, M 1948, pp 31-2.

Article 87. At the same time it was announced that Durnovo and Trepov were being allowed a vacation.[92]

Guchkov immediately resigned his Presidency of the Duma as a demonstration of protest.[93] The Octobrists, along with the Kadets, the Progressists, and the Social Democrats, submitted an interpellation to the President of the Council of Ministers, arguing that neither an emergency nor any real ' break in the activities of the legislative institutions ' had existed such as might have justified the application of Article 87, and reminding the Premier that no law could take effect without the approval of the Duma and State Council.[94]

Stolypin, apparently genuinely taken aback at the reaction to his step, invited Guchkov for a private conversation to try to smooth over the difficulties. Guchkov, however, was adamant in maintaining the stand which the fraction had taken publicly; he told Stolypin that his action had destroyed the mutual trust which had been built up with such pains, and which were necessary to the fruitful co-operation of government and legislature.[95] He then ended any further possibility of personal contact with Stolypin by embarking on a journey to the Pacific coast, and made it publicly known that he was doing so because he could make no contribution to the Duma's work at the present time, as the constitutional principles to which he had devoted himself had been so rudely overridden.[96] *Golos Moskvy*, as his mouthpiece, summed up the whole affair very uncompromisingly:

For four years much labour and energy have gone into creating relations of trust between the government and the people's representatives. The results of this great and difficult work were beginning recently to be apparent, but this has all been destroyed at one blow. What matters here is not the attitudes which have been taken on this or that question, but the basic infringement of mutual trust.[97]

Interpellations by both houses

As a result of his actions, Stolypin faced interpellations from both houses. The State Council's maintained that

(i) no emergency had existed to justify the use of Article 87;

(ii) the act which the government had passed was not an urgent

[92] *NV*, 15 March 1911.   [93] *GM*, 18 March 1911.
[94] *GDSO*, iii, 4, pt 3, cols 719-20.   [95] *GM*, 22 March 1911
[96] ibid, 25 March 1911.   [97] ibid, 22 March 1911.

measure, but a legislative bill of far-reaching implications which the State Council had just rejected.[98]

Answering this, Stolypin asserted that, although Article 87 should not be turned into a regular method of legislation, the present circumstances were such as made its use a natural expression of the government's constitutional position. In a representative system as yet young and inexperienced, methods had to be used which would be inappropriate when Russia's political culture was more developed. It was the Monarch's right, in consultation with the Council of Ministers, to decide whether an emergency existed such as would justify the use of Article 87; and once the existence of an emergency was established, one could not, without falling into parliamentarism, deny the Monarch the right to dissolve the chambers and issue decrees. Russia was not a parliamentary monarchy, and in an issue of such moment for Russia's national policies, it was right that the government should have used the powers granted to it.[99]

It was not until 27 April, after the Easter recess, that Stolypin came before the Duma to answer the interpellations brought against him there. This was a major political event in the life of the capital, and the Tauride Palace, where the Duma met, was packed out. Foreign diplomats and members of the royal family were present in the spectators' gallery.

In his speech at the start of the debate, Stolypin repeated the arguments he had used in the State Council, but coloured them to appeal to his present audience. He recalled the way in which many bills passed by the Duma had got stuck in the upper house, and characterised the State Council as the ' representative of interests, not of the population '. To have passed the Western Zemstvo bill again through the legislative chambers, as many of his critics maintained he should have, would, he said, only have led to the same result, an indefinite burial in the State Council. For that reason, recourse to Article 87 had been unavoidable, but the government had only felt able to take this step in the knowledge that the bill already had the approval of the people's representatives. For that reason, it had been promulgated in the form in which the Duma had sanctioned it. In making this claim, Stolypin was not only seeking the Duma's support by implying that its opinion should carry more weight than that of the State Council: he was describing

[98] *GSSO*, Sessiya 6 (1910-11), cols 1043-6.   [99] ibid, cols 1781-95.

the kind of co-operation between government and Duma which he felt, and had always felt, should form the basis of the new state system:

Only in the reign of Nicholas II has trust in the people manifested itself in the summoning of them to decide national affairs; and it is possible that from this point of view, gentlemen, no more serious bill has yet come before the State Duma than the question of the Western Zemstvo . . . However severely you may judge and even condemn the form of what has been done, I know, I believe, that many of you admit in your hearts that what happened on 14 March did not infringe but strengthen the rights of the young Russian representative body. The Duma's patriotic fervour in creating a Russian zemstvo in the west of Russia was understood, appreciated and warmed by the approval of the Supreme Power. (Right and centre applause and cries of ' Bravo!' On the left hissing.)[100]

Stolypin's only supporters were the Nationalists and one or two Right Octobrists. Count V. A. Bobrinsky virtually repeated Stolypin's own arguments, but denied that the Nationalists were slavishly following the government: ' Gentlemen, we are not following behind the government, we are walking with the government, and we are together following one common banner, shared by them and us – the Russian national banner, and while the government continues to follow this banner, we shall be with the government.'[101]

Gololobov, of the Right Octobrists, bitterly attacked his own former party. Having become the leading party in the Duma as a result of the act of 3 June 1907, he said, they now had the effrontery to wax indignant over the act of 14 March 1911. However much the Octobrists liked to think they ruled the country, there was no parliamentarism in Russia, and their opposition to Stolypin would not harm him since the Emperor, whose authority was paramount, would maintain him in power.[102]

The Rights, who had supported Stolypin in the Duma on the Western Zemstvo issue, turned against him now that their colleagues in the upper house had been so successful. Purishkevich, their flamboyant representative from Bessarabia, held forth on the familiar right-wing theme that the government was appropriating to itself too many powers, was becoming bureaucratic and dictatorial at the

[100] *GDSO*, III, 4, pt 3, cols 2850-63.   [101] ibid, cols 2986-97.
[102] ibid, cols 2931-44.

expense of the rights both of the Monarch and of the people. He claimed that Stolypin had wrung the act of 14 March from the Emperor in a wholly unworthy manner, and he mocked Stolypin's 'zoological nationalism', according to which nationality was defined by local *chinovniki*. Finally, he asserted that the government had reneged on many undertakings by passing the bill in the Duma's version, in which it was so ill-suited to serve the real needs of the Russian population of the western provinces.[103]

P. V. Kamensky, official spokesman for the Octobrists, emphasised that the arbitrary nature of the government's action in dissolving the chambers had its roots in the worst of the autocratic past. The government had merely been 'playing at legality', and this alarmed public opinion because it was seen as a return to the pre-1905 traditions of lack of respect for the law, to conditions which encouraged any minor provincial official to say, 'the power of my superior is above the law'.

The Octobrist fraction considers that the Duma cannot remain a silent spectator of what has happened, for silence, in this case, would justly be considered a sign of acquiescence and approval of a policy which ignores the requirements of good faith as well as the new legislative methods, and which, in fact, delays the normal and natural development of our young constitutional system.[104]

The speeches which threw the major issues into clearest relief were those of the Octobrist Baron Meyendorf, and the Kadet V. A. Maklakov. Meyendorf took his stand on the Fundamental Laws. The existence of these laws meant, he argued, that the basic principle of the state was not the Monarch's will, nor, even worse, the government's, but the rule of law. It was plainly not the sole prerogative of the Monarch or of the government to state that an emergency existed: if that were the case, there would be no point in including the word 'emergency' (*chrezvychainye obstoyatelstva*) in the text of Article 87, or at least it would have no more force than that of a general instruction to government departments. Once the word was included, it was implied that there were some objective criteria by which an 'emergency' might be shown to exist, and by which the government should be bound. In fact, one expected from the government what one expected of any citizen, or of any party to an agreement, that they should interpret the law in good faith.

[103] ibid, cols 2877-2914.   [104] ibid, cols 2864-8.

It was precisely as a result of the feeling that the government was acting not in good faith, but in order to get its own way, that the Octobrists now no longer trusted it. Nor, continued Meyendorf, was it sufficient to argue that the government was struggling for the sake of its ideals and had therefore taken the initiative by the means within its power.

I ask the President of the Council of Ministers: (pointing left) do these illegal parties not also have their ideals? What distinguishes them, then? Is it not that they fight for those ideals by *illegal* means? . . . The achievement of the zemstvo reform in the six provinces a few years later – all this is not a question of life or death for Russia. What *is* a question of life and death for Russia is something else: the population's immediate sense of the state idea. You should be inspiring the broad population, its deepest layers, with the state idea, you should be kindling in them the fire of faith in the law and in the possibility of relative earthly well-being under a normal government.[105]

Maklakov, speaking for the Kadets, had in some ways a much easier task than Kamensky and Meyendorf. The whole course of the crisis showed the correctness of the thesis which the Kadets had maintained since the opening of the Third Duma, that there could be no long-term co-operation between the government and any constitutional party, since their views on the nature of the state, and on the rights and duties of the various political forces composing it, were bound to be fundamentally opposed. He took as an example of this the formal objection which Stolypin had made at the beginning of his speech: that an interpellation could not be made to the Council of Ministers as a whole, only to individual Ministers. Maklakov saw in this argument not merely a legalistic quibble, but an expression of Stolypin's fundamental outlook, and a sign of that which made the Duma's co-operation with him impossible:

To assert that the decisions of the Council of Ministers lie outside the criticism, supervision, and verification of the legislative institutions is to manifest that political arrogance, that *mania grandiosa,* which better than any learned references explains to us the reasons for the conflict we are discussing here. If the decisions of the Council of Ministers are above the supervision of the state institutions, then is it surprising that the law itself can be replaced by a decree of the Council of Ministers? Here we have the subversive and fatal idea which lies at the root of this affair and of the explanations we have heard today.[106]

[105] ibid, cols 3005-6.   [106] ibid, col 2872.

He was prepared to accept that, from the formal viewpoint, the act of 14 March contained no direct infringement of the Fundamental Laws, but insisted, as Meyendorf had done, on the importance of good faith. That this good faith was missing was evident in the mere fact that the government had not hastened to bring the new law as soon as possible before the legislative chambers for confirmation. No, as everyone perfectly well realised, the government would wait the full two months allowed under Article 87, and would dissolve the Duma just before this period was up, in the middle of May, so that the new western zemstvos could be set up during the summer recess. Then the Duma, if it still insisted on rejecting the bill, would be destroying live institutions. In fact, the government was not seriously trying to co-operate with the Duma, in the sense in which the Duma understood that word:

Here – and I am repeating the words of the President of the Council of Ministers – two conceptions of the state have collided, two types of idea, which can no more be reconciled or understand one another than the Hottentot can understand European Christian morality . . . The President of the Council of Ministers has not realised one thing, that for the Duma the question of whether there is to be a zemstvo in the six provinces is a triviality compared with the question of whether Russia is to be a state based on the rule of law or Stolypin's private domain.[107]

And in this failure of understanding, as Maklakov saw it, lay the real difference between Stolypin's conception of the new state system and that of the constitutional parties in the Duma. Stolypin could not see that the method by which he proposed to help the Duma's position to triumph in one question would undermine the Duma's entire constitutional position; he could not understand that the whole of constitutional politics is compromise; he could not wait for the upper house to yield, as in every constitutional nation it always eventually has to yield, before the express wishes of the people. Maklakov predicted that the consequences of this failure of understanding would be Stolypin's ruin.

Gentlemen, there are victories which do not pass without trace, and this is one of them . . . The President of the Council of Ministers may still remain in power: he will be kept there by fear of revolution – revolution which his own agents are fermenting – he will be kept there by the

107 ibid, cols 2875-8.

fear of creating a precedent. But, gentlemen, this is the final agony. You may take what attitude you will towards this, but I shall say, in the words of the President of the Council of Ministers himself: 'there is no such thing in politics as revenge, but there are consequences'. These consequences have overtaken you and you will not avoid them now.[108]

On a Kadet motion, Stolypin's reply to the interpellations was rejected by the house as unsatisfactory. The majority against him was 203 to 82.[109]

The Octobrists went unequivocally over into opposition, abandoning the alliance with the goverment which had been the keystone of their policy in the Third Duma. On 26 April a leader in *Golos Moskvy* made it clear that the Octobrist leaders were disavowing completely their position as ' government party ' and whetting their knives for opposition: ' Conditions have changed completely. After the terrible blow that has been dealt to the cause to which the Octobrists have devoted themselves, organic work in the Duma has become impossible for them. They can no longer take any responsibility for the direction which the Duma's activities may take.'

Guchkov began to draw the consequence, that the fraction must now shed still more of its less convinced members, in order to become a more unified and disciplined group, ready for the new task of struggle against the government.

At the same time, the struggle has become sharper, more serious and has shifted to another plane. This new struggle demands united and well-disciplined forces, firm and uncompromising. There is no room for the hesitant and doubtful in this struggle. If such should prove to be in the fraction's ranks, their withdrawal is quite inevitable in the situation that has arisen, and it should not frighten the fraction.

As a result, on 7 May, the fraction worked out new rules for its internal discipline. It was resolved that the old practice of allowing virtual freedom of vote must now be discarded. In future, any decision taken at a meeting at which sixty or more members of the fraction were present, provided it was approved by a three-quarters majority, automatically became binding on the entire fraction, and those who did not submit themselves to it would be considered as having left the fraction.[110]

[108] ibid, col 2887.   [109] ibid, col 3025.
[110] *GM*, 8 May 1911. Note that these rules were almost exactly the same as those they had adopted at the opening of the Third Duma. They had

The end of the Stolypin era

The 'consequences' of which Maklakov had spoken did not take long to manifest themselves. Stolypin became isolated from the main political forces in the country. On the one side he had earned the permanent distrust of the constitutional parties in the Duma, including the Octobrists, on whom he had relied; on the other, he had infuriated and further alienated the whole State Council, as well as the palace hierarchy, by the manner of his ' victory ' over them.

The Emperor had hitherto, despite waverings, given Stolypin much needed support. Now even he resented the humiliating way in which he had been persuaded to yield to Stolypin's demands. He remained sensitive to the right-wing pressure, and late in April 1911 wrote to Stolypin saying that he proposed to invite Durnovo and Trepov to return to St Petersburg. Stolypin, realising that such a step would undermine a large part of the demonstrative triumph which he had won in March, urged the Emperor to refrain from it.[111] The very fact that this proposal could come so soon after the March crisis shows how much Stolypin's standing had suffered.

All observers agree that during the summer of 1911 Stolypin was a man broken in health and in spirit, and obsessed by the feeling that he had come to the end. As early as the middle of the crisis, in March, he told Kokovtsev: ' The Emperor will not forgive me if he has to fulfil my request. But that is a matter of indifference to me, since I well know in any case that I am being attacked from all sides, and that I shall not be here much longer.'[112] And, after the crisis, Kokovtsev recalls: ' Something had given way inside him, his former self-confidence had departed, and he seemed to feel that everyone around him, secretly or openly, was hostile to him.'[113]

But his end came in another way. At the end of August and beginning of September, festivities were held in Kiev, among whose events was the opening of the new zemstvo there. The Emperor and

---

evidently not been much observed, and the rules adopted now did not fare much better.

[111] The Emperor's letter does not appear to have survived, but its general content is clear from Stolypin's reply to it, in *KA*, vol 30, pp 87-8.

[112] Kokovtsev, *Iz Moego Proshlogo*, vol 1, p 458.

[113] ibid, p 463. A very similar picture is painted by Stolypin's daughter in her memoirs: M. P. Bok, *Vospominaniya o moem Otse P. A. Stolypine*, New York 1953, pp 329-35.

other members of the royal family attended, as did Stolypin and other ministers.

On the evening of 1 September, during the interval of a performance in the Kiev Opera House, Stolypin was standing talking near the front of the stalls, when Dmitri Bogrov, who was known to the police both as one of their agents and as a Socialist Revolutionary, walked up to him, took out his revolver and shot him point-blank. He was immediately taken to hospital and died within a few days.

I will not here analyse in detail the circumstances surrounding the assassination of Stolypin.[114] One or two points, however, seem worth noting. Bogrov was given the ticket by which he was admitted to the Kiev Opera House by N. N. Kulyabko, head of the Kiev Okhrana, with the approval of P. G. Kurlov, Assistant Minister of the Interior (appointed against Stolypin's wishes) and head of the Department of Police. After the murder, the criminal investigation was carried out very hastily, and Bogrov was hanged without any public trial. Later, a Senatorial investigation, under M. I. Trusevich, produced material for charges of criminal negligence to be brought against Kurlov, Kulyabko and two other officials. However, in spite of the protests of the new Premier, Kokovtsev, the Emperor decided that the case was not to be pursued.[115] The evidence, in fact, strongly suggests, though it does not conclusively demonstrate, that Bogrov, whatever his personal motives may have been, murdered Stolypin with the connivance of high police officials. If so, this was not the first time that a Minister of the Interior had been murdered by a police agent working under him. The same had happened to Pleve in July 1904, whose murder was organised by the notorious double agent Azef. The case of Bogrov was somewhat different: he had not been active either as a police agent or as a revolutionary for some years before his act, and it looks as if Kurlov and Kulyabko improvised at the last moment, using Bogrov to eliminate a Premier who was hated in palace circles, but who had proved difficult to remove in other ways. At the very least, they cannot be said to have striven officiously to save him.

The Department of Police was an institution whose chief features Stolypin had inherited from his predecessors. He never had very

114 The best summary of the evidence, in my view, is that of Avrekh, *Stolypin i Tret'ya Duma*, pp 367-406.
115 Report of M. I. Trusevich's inquiry, *TsGIAL*, f 1276, op 7, d 31; see also Kokovtsev, *Iz Moego Proshlogo*, vol 2, pp 116-18.

much control over it, leaving the detailed conduct of its affairs to his subordinates, but he was compelled to rely on it to a very large extent indeed, especially for information on the revolutionary parties. The use of double agents was one which he had himself defended before the Duma when Azef's activities were at last brought to light. Whilst revolution and political terrorism were still a threat, perhaps he could not do otherwise. But it was this prop to his infirmity which eventually turned on him and removed him from the scene.

6

Social and political reform

Stolypin himself would have wished his government to be judged by the results of its reform programme. In the circular which he sent to provincial governors shortly after taking office, he categorically affirmed, ' the old order will be renewed '.[1] And in his ministerial speech to the Second Duma, rejecting the methods of the revolutionaries, and asserting, in a famous phrase, that the government was ' not afraid ' of them, he also outlined his vision of the future Russia:

Our fatherland, reformed by the will of the Monarch, must become a state ruled by law, since, until the written law defines the obligations and protects the rights of individual Russian citizens, then those rights and obligations will depend on the interpretations and whims of private persons . . . That is why the government has made it its main task to lay before the State Duma and State Council a whole series of legislative bills which will establish firm norms for the newly forming state life of Russia.[2]

The content of this reform programme was substantially that which Witte had laid before the Emperor in April 1906. Stolypin sought and found allies in society as much in the pursuance of this reform as in the suppression of revolution, and he began to implement the programme in the interval between the First and Second Dumas.

The heart of the reform programme was the establishment of peasant smallholdings. This was also the only reform which was passed fully in accordance with the intentions of the government. For in drawing independent social groups into the work of legislation. Stolypin was creating hostages to fortune. He was ensuring (and this was an essential part of the new system) that the government would in future no longer be able to compel the acceptance

---

[1] See above, pp. 23-4.   [2] *GDSO*, ii, pt 1, cols 107-8.

of reforms which it considered desirable. No longer would it be able simply to override interest groups which felt themselves threatened.

The case of local self-government institutions is particularly instructive, because here Stolypin was attempting a reform which directly affected the groups with whom he was working most closely in the 3rd June alliance: those whose political background was in the zemstvos and the nobility. His failure in this field was therefore particularly damaging to the prospects of the overall reform pro-gramme; whilst to us, looking back on it now, this failure also does imply that the prospects for social reform of all kinds were not good in Tsarist Russia, even had there been no World War. Those who have defended Stolypin's record have usually done so with the argument that, had he not been murdered in 1911, or had the First World War never taken place, then his reforms would have saved the old Russia. When we look at his actual attempts to pass his reforms, however, the evidence is not so impressive.

I shall therefore examine the attempts to reform the zemstvos and the local court particularly closely, whilst glancing at efforts in the reform of education, religious freedom and the workers' question, to show that the zemstvo experience was not an isolated or fortuitous one.

Local self-government: the background

In autocratic Russia, local government institutions were almost like foreign bodies. That, indeed, is why the Russians talked of local *self*-government (*mestnoe samoupravlenie*) – to distinguish it from the soulless machinery of the central bureaucracy, which also had its local agencies. The word *zemstvo*, and its adjective, *zemsky*, came to carry attributes of humanity, co-operative effort, closeness to the soil, love of the people, which, for good or ill, are almost completely foreign to the British popular image of local government.

As set up by Alexander II in the 1860s, the institutions of local self-government did indeed hang rather in mid-air, lacking either a floor or a ceiling. The zemstvos had been established at pro-vincial and district level, but not in the smaller administrative unit, the canton (*volost*) (nor of course were there elective bodies at the centre). Whereas the provincial and district zemstvos contained delegates elected by the entire population of the areas they served (though retaining social distinctions which usually gave a dominant

6

position to the landed nobility), the canton was a segregated peasant institution, limited to the conduct of peasant administration and justice, and not representing other inhabitants in its area. The canton was moreover quite largely dependent on police and other officials appointed by the Minister of the Interior.

The weaknesses of all three institutions reflected the high financial and military needs of the state in relation to the economic development of the countryside, as well as the suspicious attitude of the central bureaucracy towards independent initiatives and independent socio-political institutions. The first was a problem which for the moment could not be wished away by any amount of reform. The second, however, it was Stolypin's stated objective to overcome.

Before plunging into the politics of local government reform, we must consider in some detail the nature of the bodies which were to be changed. By the legislation of 1864 the district zemstvo was elected in three *soslovny*[3] curiae: landowners, townsmen and peasants, the last voting indirectly (from 1890 peasant deputies were appointed by the governor of the province from lists submitted by the cantonal assemblies). The assembly thus chosen elected delegates to the provincial zemstvo assembly from among its own members. The district and provincial Marshals of the Nobility occupied ex officio the posts of chairman of their respective zemstvo assemblies. The zemstvos also elected, from their own members or from outside, an executive board (*uprava*), which carried on their everyday work. Because of their comparative wealth and their influence in the countryside, as well as because of their strength in the electoral curiae (reinforced by the new electoral laws of 1890 and 1892), the nobles dominated the work of the zemstvos, especially at provincial level. In a sense this was a compensation to them for their loss of direct administrative power over a large section of the peasantry in 1861. The donkey work in the schools and hospitals run by the zemstvos was done by the professional men of the ' third element ', as they were known, men of often humble background

---

[3] The word *soslovny* is the adjective from *soslovie*, meaning an ' estate ', in the sense of an ascribed position in a hierarchical society, as in medieval Europe, or Russia till the early twentieth century. Since the word ' estate ' no longer carries this meaning in English, and the word ' class ' is not strictly accurate, I shall generally use the Russian word. Similarly, *vsesoslovny* means ' all-estate ', and *bessoslovny* means ' non-estate '.

but good education who brought a Westernised, usually oppositional outlook to their specialised work in the small towns and
villages. It was the alliance between the nobles and the 'third
element' which gave the zemstvos their characteristic moral and
political atmosphere – and which also provided much of the backbone of both the Kadet and the Octobrist parties, at the opposite
ends of Russian liberalism. Their oppositional attitude had often
been learnt in the practical experience of friction with a jealous
bureaucracy, for the legislation of 1864 had given the zemstvos wide
but poorly defined functions (often without abolishing the government departments which had previously exercised those functions),
and had strictly limited their right to tax the local population.
Furthermore, many zemstvo decisions required the approval of the
provincial governor, or even of the Minister of the Interior; from
1890 the governor also acquired the right of veto over the appointment of any official of the executive board.[4]

The canton was set up mainly in order to maintain the weak link
between the central government and the life of the peasant commune which played such an important role in the Emancipation
settlement. The canton consisted of a number of village communes,
whose members were represented in its assembly at the rate of one
delegate per ten households. The canton had both judicial and
administrative functions. Its judicial functions were discharged by
the cantonal court, consisting of three peasant judges elected by the
cantonal assembly: it was intended that these judges should be
trustworthy members of the community, steeped in local custom
rather than acquainted with written law, and hence able to interpret
the peasants' legal feeling. The cantonal administrative board
(*pravlenie*) consisted of the cantonal elder (*starshina*), together with
the elders (*starosty*) of all the constituent village communes. In
both judicial and administrative matters the canton's decisions were,
from 1890, subject to the veto of the land commandant (*zemsky
nachalnik*), who was the key mediator between the government and
the peasant institutions. He was appointed by the provincial governor in consultation with the district Marshal of the Nobility; in
theory he was supposed to be chosen from among the local nobility,

[4] For a full description of the zemstvos' composition and functions, see
A. Leroy-Beaulieu, *L'Empire des Tsars et des Russes* (3rd ed), Paris 1893,
vol 2, pp 164-216; Eroshkin, *Ocherki Istorii*, pp 233-5.

but in practice there were not enough nobles able and willing to carry out these functions for each canton in the Empire, and others, often retired army officers, were frequently chosen instead.[5]

The canton could be and was much criticised as a local government unit. In its defects it reflected, even more markedly than other local institutions, the cost of trying to maintain the military and financial status of a European great power on a backward and overextended rural economy. Perhaps its principal weakness was that it was artificial and largely an instrument of governmental control: it had no roots in the past, as the village commune had, but had been set up for administrative convenience in the Emancipation period.[6] Its officials were ignorant and often illiterate, and depended greatly on the clerk (*pisar*) who, by the nature of his job, had to be minimally literate, on the police, appointed by the Ministry of the Interior, and of course on the land commandant. Furthermore, being a segregated peasant *soslovny* institution, it had no authority over non-peasant inhabitants living in its area (nor the right to tax them); nor was it integrated into the imperial network of courts (through the local circuit court) and local government bodies (through the local district zemstvo). In both these functions it was subordinated through separate channels to the Ministry of the Interior. This segregation of the peasants, and the poor quality, venality and servility of peasant judges and officials led to much criticism both from the intelligentsia and even from inside the governmental bureaucracy itself. In 1884 a special commission under Senator Kakhanov recommended that the canton should be desegregated. In 1904-5 the Special Commission on the Needs of the Agricultural Industry recommended the abolition of the cantonal court and its replacement by a *vsesoslovny,* independent court forming the lowest unit in the imperial judicial network. N. V. Muravyev, then Minister of Justice, declared at one of its sessions that ' the cantonal court in the sphere of civil law creates complete confusion and bewilderment in the juridical ideas of the population ', and Witte called the court ' essentially . . . not a system of justice . . . but a crude form of settling accounts '.[7]

The rapid evolution of the government's ideas on the peasant

[5] H. Seton-Watson, *The Russian Empire, 1801-1917*, Oxford 1967, p 466.
[6] The Emperor Paul had established it, for state peasants alone, in 1797.   [7] Seton-Watson, *The Russian Empire*, p. 515.

question during 1905-6 naturally entailed a reappraisal of the question of local government and justice. To encourage the peasant to leave the commune and set up as a private smallholder meant making him a full citizen of the Empire, not subject to closed courts or administrative offices. In the Ministry of the Interior, V. I. Gurko chaired a committee which examined the implications of the proposed agrarian reforms for local administration and justice. The committee concluded that the peasant must enjoy all the rights of person and property laid down in the imperial civil and criminal law codes, and for that reason all segregated peasant agencies (including the canton, its administration and its court, and the office of land commandant) should be abolished. In their place new institutions of the zemstvo type should be set up representing all groups of the population, and ' the necessary consistency should be introduced into the organisation of the judicial affairs of the Empire '. Existing zemstvos should be ' reorganised '.[8]

Thus by the time of the convocation of the First Duma, the government was working out a programme of reforms in local administration and justice which would have gone far towards satisfying the radical parties in the Duma. But in its attempts to carry through these reforms, the government was to be increasingly hampered by the very class with which it was seeking a rapprochement in the existing zemstvos, the nobility.

The provincial and district zemstvo

In December 1906 Stolypin brought the Ministry of the Interior's proposals concerning the provincial and district zemstvos before the Council of Ministers. His report recommended broadening the franchise somewhat by repealing the restrictions on the peasant and urban vote established in the laws of 1890 and 1892, and also by making the franchise dependent on the amount of tax paid rather than the amount of property owned. On the other hand, it left untouched the division of electoral curiae into landowners, town dwellers, and

[8] *TsGIAL*, f 408, op 1, d 38, pp 4-5 (conclusions of an interdepartmental committee, 10 March 1906); ibid, pp 38-40 (letter of Gurko to A.P. Nikol'skii, Minister of Agriculture, 4 April 1906). These schemes even mention the possibility of a new zemstvo at the level *below* the canton, the *poselok*, or settlement, corresponding roughly to a village, or *uchastok*, corresponding to several of them.

rural inhabitants. It aimed to increase the zemstvos' effective powers by rescinding many of the restrictions which had been placed on their power of taxation, and by confining administrative supervision over them to the legality, no longer the expediency, of their decisions.[9]

To sort out the confusion of government and zemstvo offices operating at local level, the report proposed the establishment of a new body on the district level, the District Council (*uyezdny sovet*), which would have the task of co-ordinating them all. Representatives of the zemstvos, the municipalities and the nobility would sit on it, and its chairman, the District Commandant (*uyezdny nachalnik*), would be appointed by the Minister of the Interior. This District Commandant would clearly in practice have very wide powers over the life of the district, including the work of the zemstvos. The report stated openly that this would diminish the role of the nobility:

With the appointment of the District Commandant as chairman of the District Council, the office of district Marshal of the Nobility takes on a completely different complexion: his role will thereafter simply be that of representative of the noble *soslovie* . . . Of his social duties, the intention is to leave him only the guardianship of primary schools, the chairmanship of the district zemstvo assembly and of the district land-settlement committee.[10]

In short, the government was trying to democratise somewhat the composition of the zemstvo, extend its powers, improve its organisation, and counterbalance the nobles' domination by the appointment of a strongly placed governmental official. It would weaken, without entirely abolishing, the *soslovny* principle in local government.

Protests were not long in coming from the United Nobility. As early as 14 February 1907 a meeting of its Permanent Council decided to petition the President of the Council of Ministers, asking him to submit the new proposals to the nobles' and zemstvo assemblies for discussion before bringing them before the Duma.[11] A. A. Naryshkin, of Orel province, one of the leading figures in the United Nobility, had an interview with Stolypin, at which he told him that to pass through the present (Second) Duma a set of local reforms

[9] *TsGIAL*, f 1291, op 50, d 34, pp 47-48; M. S. Conroy, ' Stolypin's Attitude towards Local Self-Government, *SEER*, vol 46 (1968), pp 450-4.
[10] *TsGIAL*, f 1291, op 50, d 34, pp 48-9.
[11] *TsGAOR*, f 434 (Council of the United Nobility), op 1, d 76, p 75.

based on what he called 'democratic' principles would only un-
leash passions by attracting the politically unreliable ' third element '
to zemstvo work at the expense of those deeply attached to local
life. The virtual replacement of the Marshal of the Nobility by a
bureaucrat would weaken the standing of the nobility, a class which
had given forty years of outstanding work to local institutions, and
had deservedly won the predominant influence in local life. Stolypin
at first refused the nobles' request. He told Naryshkin that the
soslovny principle was out of date and must be eliminated from
local government. The third element, he said, presented no danger,
since the good sense of the peasantry would enable them to distinguish those capable of running local affairs. To submit the bill to
the zemstvos would be fruitless, since all that would result would be
a purposeless flood of written materials.[12] Shortly afterwards, however, when Count A. A. Bobrinsky repeated the petition to him,
Stolypin gave way, probably sobered by the unco-operative nature
of the Second Duma, which had met in the meanwhile. He said that
the noble and zemstvo assemblies were free to discuss the bill, and
that the Ministry would make copies of it available to them.[13]

The Third Congress of the United Nobility, held from 27 March to
2 April 1907, passed no detailed resolutions on the subject, but it
made its general disapproval very plain. Even the usually sober
A. B. Neidgart, Stolypin's brother-in-law and leader of the Centre
group in the State Council which usually supported the government,
mounted a vehement attack on the government's policy and called on
the nobility to defend themselves:

The nobility is not a political party, it is true, and it never has been
one: it is a historical estate of the Russian Empire. But once the vital
roots of that estate are touched, we have not only the right but the
duty to make our voice heard . . . We love Russia, and we will declare
that the elimination of the nobility from local life is not the elimination
of just any social group, but of the estate which forms one of the main
pillars of the idea dearest to Russia – that of monarchy.[14]

This speech conveys something essential about the corporate
spirit of the United Nobility. As a group of people not yet used
to having to defend themselves, they tended, partly by mutual

[12] ibid, p 90 (Naryshkin's report to the Permanent Council).
[13] ibid, p 104; *Trudy 3-ego S*ⁱⁱ*ezda Upolnomochennykh Dvoryanskikh*
    Obshchestv 32-kh Gubernii, SPB 1907, pp 13-14.   [14] *Trudy 3-ego*, p 20.

suggestion, to exaggerate the dangers facing them in rather panic-stricken fashion (there was, after all, in the government's proposals, no suggestion that the nobility should be 'eliminated' from local government, only that their influence be somewhat diluted). Haunted by memories of the burning ricks and of the government's near sell-out of 1905-6, they appealed hysterically to the symbols and watchwords of the past. Their over-reaction to change was itself a symptom of the depth of social and ideological conflict in post-1905 Russia.

It was the Fourth Congress (9-12 March 1908) which examined the proposed local government reforms in greatest detail. Reporting on the projected District Council and its chairman, F. D. Samarin said:

The fact that at present the first person [in the district] is a man chosen by one single estate gives him great value, and, above all, guarantees that the mode of election will be independent. This must unquestionably be considered preferable to the appointment by the government which is proposed . . . The District Commandant cannot have the moral standing which the Marshal of the Nobility possesses . . . He will serve for a salary, and will be appointed by the government, while the Marshal of the Nobility is elected and serves without remuneration.[15]

Many saw the new District Commandants as *préfets* on the pattern of revolutionary France. S. M. Prutchenko protested that all the government's plans were imbued with the mechanical rationalism of the Encyclopédie and the French Revolution. E. A. Isaev also warned that reforms must be gradual and evolutionary in their nature, otherwise the hydra of revolution would raise its head once again.[16]

The Congress resolved that the district Marshal of the Nobility must retain his numerous social duties, aided perhaps by a deputy, to be appointed by the provincial governor in consultation with the Marshal of the Nobility. The assembled nobles also sent a delegation with an address to the Emperor, the main point of which was a defence of the *soslovny* principle in local government:

The complete abolition of the *soslovny* principle, the disdain for institutions which have evolved organically, the dispersal of corporate bodies with deep roots, the insistently applied democratisation – all this, at a time when so much in Russia is already tottering, obliges the nobility,

[15] *Trudy 4-ogo*, SPB 1908, pp 232-3.   [16] ibid, pp 237, 261-2.

as a matter of conscience, to affirm for the sake of the state, that this fascination with the historical example of France in the reform of local life can scarcely be reconciled with due concern for the conservation and development of the monarchical principle, so near to the heart of the Russian people and so tightly bound up with its history.[17]

The zemstvos were also not long in expressing opposition to important elements in Stolypin's proposals. There was immediate disquiet in some of the provincial zemstvos. In May 1907 the Saratov provincial zemstvo drew up a petition for the 'preliminary examination by the zemstvos of all government bills concerning the future organisation of the zemstvo institutions, before their final presentation to the legislative chambers'. Counts D. A. Olsufyev and A. A. Uvarov (the latter a member of the Octobrist fraction in the Third Duma, though he later left it) sent a circular letter to all provincial zemstvos, asking them to support this petition and declaring:

If the government, in its reorganisation of zemstvo life, hopes that the knowledge of local life of members of the State Duma will make up fully for the broad experience which local zemstvo folk have . . . then it is making a great mistake. The huge majority of the State Duma, at least in this respect, is poorly qualified: carried away by all kinds of extreme projects and plans for wholesale reorganisation, they have never paid attention to the much more modest everyday needs of zemstvo life, have never taken any interest in them, and therefore know nothing about them.[18]

Of course, Olsufyev and Uvarov were here referring to the Second Duma. When a zemstvo congress met in July-August 1907, after the dissolution of that body, the atmosphere was somewhat less anxious. It did not express much concern about the position of the nobility in the reorganised district administration, but did object to the replacement of the electoral property qualification by a tax qualification. It approved the principles of *bessoslovnost* and democratisation of the franchise, but reiterated the demand that the government consult the zemstvos before tabling its local government reforms in the Duma.[19]

To this last request Stolypin decided to accede after the experience of the Second Duma. After all, if, in the next Duma, he was

[17] ibid, p. 267; Chernyshev–Bezobrazov, *Kratkii Obzor Deyatel'nosti Upolnomochennykh Dvoryanskikh Obshchestv*, SPB 1909, pp 19-21.
[18] B. B. Veselovskii, *Istoriya Zemstva*, vol 4, pp 80-1.   [19] ibid, pp 167-8.

going to put his trust in the men from the zemstvos, then he must be prepared to consult them. What he did was to revive the so-called Council for Affairs of the Local Economy, first set up by Pleve in 1903 and attached to the Ministry of the Interior. He invited representatives of the zemstvos to it, aiming to make it a forum for local opinion, a kind of ' pre-Duma ', with a purely consultative voice, in which ' zemstvo Russia ' would give its views on legislation which touched local interests particularly closely.[20]

A. N. Naumov, from a right-wing viewpoint, has left us a vivid picture of the work of the Council in 1908-9, when it was considering the local government reforms. It was flooded, he says, with ' the latest products of the bureaucratic imagination ', most of which was ' radical, chaotic, abnormal and cliche-ridden ' and completely ignored the variations in local conditions over the Empire. He also makes the interesting criticism that most of the reforms were framed as though the numerous class of private peasant smallholders envisaged in the agrarian reforms had already been created.[21] When the Council discussed the reform of the district zemstvo, in March 1909, the nobles were there in force, and a number of them (A. D. Samarin, Prince N. B. Shcherbatov, Prince P. P. Golitsyn, Prince I. A. Kurakin, and of course Naumov) warned against the ' bureaucratisation ' of the zemstvo which they saw as inherent in the appointment of a paid official of the Ministry of the Interior to take a leading position in local life. Their views found great sympathy, and in fact the Council rejected the government's proposals for the reform of the district zemstvo, as being based on a false understanding of zemstvo life. Stolypin was present in the Council throughout the discussion, and when the decisive vote was announced he stormed furiously out of the chamber.[22] He reacted thus, we may surmise, not just out of irritability, but because a cardinal element in his fragile political alliance was being undermined: he had failed to gain the support of zemstvo delegates for the reform which concerned them most closely.

After this defeat, the reform of the provincial and district zemstvos was dropped. In May 1909, the government got on with its Western Zemstvo project without waiting for a general zemstvo re-

[20] ibid, vol 3, p 583; vol 4, p 169.
[21] Naumov, *Iz Utselevshikh Vospominanii*, vol 2, pp 133-5.
[22] ibid, pp 135-8.

form.[23] Of all the local reform proposals of 1906, in fact, only those concerning cantonal administration and the cantonal court actually came before the Duma and State Council.[24]

The cantonal administration

In his memorandum of December 1906, Stolypin made the following main proposals for the reform of the canton:

(i) it would become a *vsesoslovny* institution, representing all property-owners in its territory, as well as the communal peasantry;

(ii) the main administrative body in the canton would be an assembly elected by all members of the canton (on a franchise weighted somewhat in favour of large property);

(iii) the executive tasks would be entrusted to the cantonal elder, aided where necessary, in the more populous cantons, by an executive board;

(iv) the post of land commandant would be abolished, and he would be replaced by a new government official operating over several cantons under the District Commandant; his authority would be administrative only (the judicial powers of the land commandant would go to a Justice of the Peace), and his supervision of cantonal decisions would extend only to their legality.[25]

In this memorandum, Stolypin did not call the new cantonal body a ' zemstvo '. But its structure, as he described it, has all the characteristics of a zemstvo, and Stolypin referred to it as such in his ministerial declaration to the Second Duma.[26]

However, the proposals came under heavy fire from the Fourth Congress of the United Nobility in March 1908. The Congress attacked the abandonment of the *soslovny* structure and also the projected cantonal administration, which they said would be impossibly expensive and too complicated for the peasant to

[23] See above, p 120.
[24] The *poselok* reform actually got as far as a committee of the Duma, but then was withdrawn for reconsideration by the Ministry of the Interior (letter of N. A. Maklakov to M. V. Rodzyanko, 7 March 1913, *TsGIAL*, f 1291, op 50, d 1, part 3, p 243). It was re-worked by the Ministry, and was due to be considered by the Council of Ministers when the war broke out.   [25] *TsGIAL*, f 1291, op 50, d 34, p 47.
[26] *GDSO*, ii, vol 1, col 111.

understand: the present cantonal elder, for all his faults, was accessible and did fulfil the role of intermediary between the peasant population and the government. All that was needed was to increase financial aid to the present canton.[27]

The Congress also stoutly defended the institution of the land commandant. Many speakers spoke of how the land commandants, universally abused by press and intelligentsia, had proved their worth in the upheavals of 1905-6. Thus, for example, Yu. V. Arsenyev:

All the pressure of the recent troubles was contained by the land commandants. Many of them, as you know, sacrificed not only their health, but their life, in that sacred cause. But thanks they got from no one. And now that an attempt is being made on them, we, as the estate which has borne this duty on its shoulders, we should declare for all to hear that this valuable institution has not been enough appreciated, and that the population must not be deprived of its benefits, which have been so apparent in these years of disarray and turmoil.[28]

A resolution was passed which affirmed that to abolish the land commandant was 'unnecessary and inexpedient', and 'in view of the prevailing political circumstances and the economic crisis . . . untimely and harmful'. The land commandant should remain and should retain the combined administrative and judicial powers which he held at present, as these were essential to his office.[29]

The bill which the government eventually submitted to the Third Duma was therefore considerably changed. The land commandant reappeared, though without his judicial functions, while the whole projected apparatus of the District Commandant, in his supervisory role, vanished.[30]

The Duma Local Government Committee accepted these changes, but stuck to the idea that the new cantonal administration should be called a *zemstvo,* and should look like one. The main features of the committee's proposals were as follows:

1 *Composition and functions of the cantonal zemstvo*

The new body would combine functions divided at a higher level between the governmental bureaucracy and the zemstvos: these

[27] *Trudy 4-ogo,* pp 127-48; Chernyshev–Bezobrazov, *Kratkii Obzor,* pp 18-19.   [28] *Trudy 4-ogo,* pp 83-4.

[29] ibid, p 322; Chernyshev–Bezobrazov, *Kratkii Obzor,* pp 17-21.

[30] *Obzor Deyatel'nosti Gosudarstvennoi Dumy 3-ego Sozyva,* SPB 1912, vol 2, pp 67-71.

would include the preservation of public order and the security of property, and the promotion of local welfare and amenities. It would have authority over all inhabitants of its area, regardless of *soslovie*. Its revenue would come from tax on all property in the area, fixed as a proportion of the district zemstvo tax. Deputies to the cantonal zemstvo assembly were to be elected by all owners of immovable property, grouped in four curiae, one of communal peasantry, the other three according to the amount of taxable property owned. Distribution of deputies between these curiae would be proportional to the share of taxation paid by each.

2 *The cantonal executive board*

All cantons were to have a full executive board, which would consist of a chairman and two members, elected by the cantonal zemstvo assembly for three years. To help them with their duties, they would have a secretary, village policemen (*sotskie*), and such other auxiliary personnel as were needed.

3 *Supervision*

To ensure the legality (and only the legality) of the canton's decisions, supervisory functions would be given to (i) the land commandant, (ii) a new body, the Special Office of the District Conference, to be attached to the district conference of land commandants. All financial dealings of the cantonal zemstvo outside those permitted by its statutes were to be subject to the approval of the district zemstvo.[31]

When the bill at last came before the house, in February 1911, the various groups which had fought over it since its inception reappeared to try and edge it in their particular directions. As usual, the Octobrists, being the most diverse party, suffered the greatest dissensions from this process.

Yu. N. Glebov (himself a district Marshal of the Nobility from Chernigov province) made the opening speech for the Local Government Committee. The key to his speech was an appeal to the ' zemstvo ' sympathies which, he knew, were strong in the centre of the house.

Members of the State Duma! The question to whose discussion we are turning today is for all of you an old acquaintance, and for some – I

[31] *GDSO*, III, 4, *Prilozheniya*, item 122, pp 30-63.

should like to think, a majority – a good friend . . . Gentlemen, most of you are active in the public sphere. I think you will understand me and not blame me if I say how much I should like to see this question discussed in a truly zemstvo spirit – a spirit characterised by involvement in the matter in hand, but at the same time by reticence in the exposition of ideas and by tolerance of the opinions of others.[32]

The invocation of a specifically ' zemstvo ' approach to problems was repeated by other speakers of the centre. Equally striking, throughout the debate, was the assumption that ' zemstvo ' activity is in nature different from governmental activity, and that to marry the two was a bold and delicate operation. Glebov, indeed, found it necessary to spend a considerable part of his speech arguing that they were not utterly incompatible.

In the main part of his speech, Glebov drew attention to the defects of the present canton. Its taxes were both inadequate and inequitable, since they were drawn entirely from the peasantry, while the proceeds financed improvements which benefited other classes as well. There was no precise indication in law of the territory the canton was supposed to cover, and by the juxtaposition of separate pieces of legislation one might come to the conclusion that the canton consisted of isolated chunks of communal territory. The cantonal assembly, theoretically the organ of peasant democracy at the cantonal level, had lost whatever living reality it might once have had, and met only occasionally, while the elder managed affairs at the bidding of local officials rather than of the peasants. Furthermore, in the absence of a zemstvo at the cantonal level, matters which should be dealt with, such as the upkeep of roads, the provision of primary schools, fire protection, welfare activities and the encouragement of local industries, were neglected, since the district unit was too big and the zemstvo at that level had not the time, resources or personnel to devote attention to them. The new body would be able to combine these functions, attract more revenue from the government and from non-peasants, and take the zemstvo idea closer to the peasant population.[33]

For the Kadets, A. I. Shingarev welcomed the bill, as rectifying a fundamental mistake of the 1860s. The effect of the legislation of those years, he declared, had been to turn the canton into ' a police, not a zemstvo unit ', and as a result

[32] *GDSO*, III, 4, pt 2, cols 1952-3.   [33] ibid, cols 1952-63.

The village, freed from slavery, has remained forgotten, neglected by culture, without equal rights, burdened by unjust discriminatory tax levies, and cut off from the cultured elements in the country. The zemstvo has had no point of support in the population, no bearer of its cultural ideas, has been deprived of contact with the real people of the soil, and thus the age-old divide between the cultured elements of the state and its foundation, the broad masses, has been artificially prolonged by a whole half-century.

But the bill before them, he indicated, had a number of serious defects. He called for a completely democratic franchise, and objected to the notion of curiae based on property. Zemstvo work, he said, ' is not the affair of the property-owner . . . it is the affair of the whole people, and those who do not own property are interested in it no less, perhaps indeed more '. He also objected to the lease of life given to the land commandant, and argued that the new small zemstvo was not being guaranteed enough finance.[34] The Kadets, somewhat differently from the Octobrists, looked on the zemstvos as the seed-bed of a radical, nation-wide and genuinely democratic liberalism uninfluenced by the bureaucracy. It was natural, therefore, that they should wish to see a grass-roots zemstvo established on an independent and socially egalitarian basis.

The main opposition to the committee's bill came from the Rights and Nationalists. They feared that the innovations proposed by the government in 1906, and supported in somewhat attenuated form by the Duma now, would break down existing traditions, and both bureaucratise and revolutionise the countryside. The Rightist deputy I. P. Sozonovich, from Mogilev, warned against the interest which the Kadets and Progressists were taking in the creation of a small zemstvo in the canton:

Deputies Shingarev and Efremov . . . have said that this bill is the pledge of a future Russian constitution, that the Duma constitution is insufficient for them, so let's set up a constitution in the canton, a real Russian constitution. (*Shingarev,* from his seat: 'And are you afraid of that?') I am not only afraid of it, I profoundly detest the idea, because I see falsehood in it, the very falsehood of which the zemstvo constitutionalists were guilty.[35]

The establishment of a zemstvo apparatus with its dangerous cargo of 'third element' intellectuals, the broadening of the franchise,

[34] ibid, cols 1968-87.   [35] ibid, col 2131.

the weakening of the powers of the land commandant, would all, they feared, contribute to this process. Not only this, but the zemstvo organisation, with all its trappings borrowed indiscriminately from Western Europe, was far too cumbersome and costly a thing to introduce in the Russian village. P. V. Sinadino, official spokesman for the Nationalists, even argued that a cantonal zemstvo would corrupt the heritage for which the zemstvos were valued: uncouth and illiterate peasants would become ' zemstvo men '.[36]

A. I. Lykoshin, Assistant Minister of the Interior, enumerated the government's objections to the changes the Duma committee had made in the bill. There was too much of the zemstvo in it for his liking, and it was not clear that the body the committee would create would always be capable of fulfilling the local functions of the government. In particular, he wanted better control by the government over the appointment of cantonal personnel, over the determination of the canton's territory, and over the financial decisions of the canton. He thought that, as a zemstvo, the canton would lose so much of its independence to the district zemstvo as to forfeit its significance as a unit of local self-government.[37]

The amendments proposed during the second reading reflected the parties' attitudes: the Progressists, the Kadets and the Labour group tried to limit the influence of the government administration and broaden the franchise, while the Rights and Nationalists tried to maintain the authority of the administration. The Octobrists wavered between the two, often split, and thus did not preserve a recognisable core of principle to the bill.

The Nationalists tried at the outset to have the word ' zemstvo ' deleted altogether from the bill. Having failed in this, they concentrated their efforts on cutting down the proposed cantonal zemstvo executive board to something like the existing cantonal board, essentially a one-man affair. Some Octobrists were also concerned at the complication and expense of introducing a full zemstvo executive structure: V. I. Stempkovsky proposed that a single-man executive (i.e. more or less the old elder) be facultative, while D. A. Leonov wanted this made permissible in a canton of less than 10,000 inhabitants.[38] Glebov, speaking for the committee, rejected these amendments. The government, he said, would find it much

---

[36] ibid, cols 2107-21.   [37] *GDSO*, III, 4, pt 3, cols 1391-3.
[38] ibid, cols 1941-5, 1950-4.

easier to bring pressure on a one-man institution. Indeed, if any of
these amendments were passed, the present elder would in many
cases simply be re-elected and continue to act primarily as a government agent. A full collegiate executive body would also be in a
better position to maintain absolute legality.[39] Nevertheless, many
Octobrists were attracted by Leonov's amendment, and it was
passed on second reading by 108 votes to 100, by the Rights,
Nationalists and a majority of Octobrists.[40] On third reading, however, it was rejected by 135 to 96, a figure which suggests that many
Octobrists either come out of abstention or changed their views.[41]

The Progressists, Kadets and Labour group made various
attempts to broaden the franchise. Shingarev maintained that intelli-
gent and cultured people living on the territory of the canton might
be excluded from participation in it simply because they lived on
rented property.[42] Glebov rejected these amendments on the grounds
that self-taxation was fundamental to the theory of self-government.
The house followed his lead and turned them all down.[43]

The left wing were more successful in their attempts to limit
administrative tutelage over the cantonal zemstvo, especially that
exercised by the land commandant. Here they could and did appeal
to the experience that many Octobrists had of working with stupid,
repressive or lawless commandants, and of having their initiatives
stifled by unimaginative bureaucratic supervision. M. I. Grodzinsky
(Progressist) declared that the land commandants consistently sowed
lawlessness among the masses, and wanted them kept out of the new
canton altogether: supervision should be laid directly on the District
Conference, which contained other figures besides land commandants.[44] Shingarev felt that the supervision of legality could only
be entrusted to men both independent and well acquainted with
the law. Land commandants were neither. He proposed to replace
them in their supervisory capacity by the district member of the
circuit court, and hence attach the new zemstvo to the judicial
network, until such time as a proper system of administrative courts
was established for the Empire.[45]

---

[39] ibid, cols 1966-72.   [40] ibid, col 1974; *Rech¹*, 31 March 1911.
[41] ibid, col 3703.   [42] ibid, cols 1629-30.   [43] ibid, cols 1635-6, 1641, 1686.
[44] ibid, cols 1488-1501; for this purpose the District Conference would include
the district Marshal of the Nobility, the chairman of the district zemstvo's
executive board and two members of its assembly, the district member of
the circuit court, and the latter's assistant procurator.   [45] ibid, cols 1501-6.

Glebov, answering for the committee, pointed out that the District Conference was intended to be the main organ of supervision, and that the land commandant was merely the most convenient channel of communication with it.[46] Markov 2, also defending the land commandants, took an altogether different line: pointing left, he shouted: 'They are hateful to you, who want to stir up revolution, for the very reason that they hinder the fulfilment of your base, criminal plans.'[47]

Trivialities could arouse mighty passions. In the event, both amendments were rejected on second reading, but in the third reading, Glebov gave the committee's support to the progressists' proposal, which was duly accepted.[48] This change of attitude was perhaps due to the success meanwhile of the left wing in cutting down some of the land commandant's other powers, that of verifying cantonal elections and that of conducting inspections of the canton.[49]

When it got to the State Council, the bill was held up there almost as long as it had been in the Duma by the complications of the attempt to introduce the relatively sophisticated zemstvo structure at canton level, as well as by the huge differences of principle it raised among the parties. The committee responsible for its preliminary examination took two-and-a-half years over the job, from 28 October 1911 to 21 April 1914.[50] Party differences were perhaps less, since there was no equivalent of the Duma's left wing, but the Rights' opposition to the bill was correspondingly more effective. Even more important, Stolypin had gone, and with the eventual appointment of N. A. Maklakov as Minister of the Interior, the government more or less lost interest in the bill.[51] That, at any rate, seems a reasonable interpretation of the words of N. A. Zinoviev, the bill's reporter in the State Council:

Not more than three years ago this bill was energetically defended in the State Duma by our respected colleague, A. I. Lykoshin. We then heard declarations in its favour in our committee as well, but, it is true, only during the first year of its work. Then somehow we heard

---

[46] ibid, cols 1521-4.   [47] ibid, col 1517.
[48] ibid, cols 1528, 3595-6; *Rech'*, 24 March 1911.
[49] ibid, cols 2557, 2560, 3760-1.   [50] *TsGIAL*, f 1276, op 4, d 86, p 312.
[51] For the significance of the appointment of N. A. Maklakov, see below, p 199.

no more of these views. The Ministry of the Interior began to be some-what colder towards the bill.[52]

In addition to all this, the United Nobility, at its Eighth Congress in 1912, called the bill, as passed by the Duma, ' unacceptable in its entirety '.[53]

Eventually the members of the committee agreed to disagree, worked out a version of the bill, and approved it by the barest of majorities, 14 to 13. This version was substantially different from that which the Duma had passed. The term ' zemstvo ' was once again removed, and the notion of a full executive board scorned: the old canton elder was once again to head the administration, unless the government specifically decided the canton was large enough to justify a full executive board. The electoral system was modified once more to give greater influence to large landowners. Supervisory powers were more firmly concentrated in the hands of the govern-mental bureaucracy.

These modifications were not enough for the State Council as a whole. In fact, without any more ado, the upper house rejected the entire bill on first reading. Most of those who spoke were generally in favour, so one must conclude that the silent members of the house voted against it. Probably the attitude of the government was decisive for them: now that Stolypin had gone, the right wing of the State Council was often decisively influenced by the government, especially when the Emperor was in agreement with it, as was now usually the case. The opinions with which their silence was re-plete were probably well expressed by Stishinsky and Durnovo. Stishinsky argued that for the creation of any broadly based local government body two conditions were necessary:

A number of enlightened and wealthy people, who, by entering the executive organ of that small zemstvo unit, could take on themselves unselfishly and without payment the guidance of work in it; and a level of economic well-being among the population such as would enable the small zemstvo unit to find the means to satisfy its cultural and economic needs by itself, through the material prosperity of its inhabitants. Gentlemen, it is no secret to anyone that at the present time neither condition is fulfilled in rural Russia.[54]

[52] *GSSO*, Sessiya 9 (1913-14), col 2156; see also Gurko, *Features and Figures of the Past*, pp 532-3.   [53] *Trudy 8-ogo*, SPB 1912, p 277-8.
[54] *GSSO*, Sessiya 9 (1913-14), cols 2203-4.

The nobility was too sparse, the new independent smallholders not yet numerous enough. Until the results of the agrarian reform could be clearly felt, it would be rash to set up a cantonal zemstvo.

Durnovo was even more fundamentalist. Not only was it premature, he declared, it was playing with fire. Those who wanted a cantonal zemstvo wanted it for purely political reasons:

> For a long time there has been insistent propaganda for a *vsesoslovny* cantonal zemstvo. This propaganda comes from liberal books, from liberal journals, and from liberal discussion circles. To politicians of that kind it is all the same what kind of canton we finish up with. What they want is the political education of the people in a certain tendency, the eradication in the people of all traditional beliefs, and the inculcation of denial and criticism. The new law hands over all local administration and local economic affairs to the peasants – those same peasants, who only eight years ago were robbing and burning the landowners, and who to this day covet the land at the expense of the nobles . . . The result of this will be the upheaval of the economy, which has scarcely returned to normal after the upheavals of 1905-6.

He specifically compared the situation with the creation of hospital funds for the workers: since they were administered by the propertyless poor, they were being used for irresponsible and ugly political aims.[55]

Durnovo's fears were symptomatic of a nation still deeply socially and ideologically divided. The State Council's rejection of the bill was its end. The government did announce its intention to bring in amendments in order to make the bill acceptable to the upper house, but the war intervened before anything could be done. That was the last that was heard of the cantonal zemstvo till just before the February revolution. The land commandants and the peasant elders held their sway.[56]

The canton court

The bill which the Ministry of Justice drew up in 1906 accepted the criticisms made by the Kakhanov Commission back in 1884. It adumbrated the following general principles for the reform of the local court system:

[55] ibid, cols 2297-2302.
[56] *GM*, 22 May 1914; Dubrovskii, *Stolypinskaya Zemel'naya Reforma*, p 161.

The local court should be formed on the basis of *vsesoslovnost,* of the equality of persons of all conditions before the law, and the independence of the judiciary. With these aims in mind, it is proposed to abolish the canton court, annul the judicial powers conferred on land commandants, District Conferences and Provincial Offices, and to restore for all minor judicial matters the elective Justice's court, in the person of Justices of the Peace, elected by the population, in general on the same principles as were laid down for them in the judicial code of 20 November 1864.[57]

Unlike the land commandants (and also unlike the English Justices of the Peace from whom their name was borrowed), the Justices were to be strictly confined to judicial functions, having no administrative powers whatever; and they were to be elected by the district zemstvo, not appointed by the crown. Russian doctrinaire liberalism, when adopted by a government department, was nothing if not thorough. The place of the J.P. in the judicial hierarchy was to be slightly different from 1864. Then the Justices were completely separate from the courts: their immediate organ of appeal had been the district Assembly of Justices, with, as a final court of cassation above them, only the First Department of the Senate.[58] Now, however, in the Ministry's bill, the verdicts of Justices were to be subject to appeal in the regular courts, with their hierarchy ascending through the circuit (*okrug*) court and the Palais de Justice (*sudebnaya palata*) to the Senate.

In this form, the bill was brought before the First Duma, which, however, was dissolved before having a chance to discuss it. The Second Duma actually got as far as the first reading, on which it spent the last day of its brief life.[59]

It was not, therefore, till the Third Duma that the legislative passage of the local court bill was seriously begun, and then in political circumstances much less favourable to it. The Fourth Congress of the United Nobility, as we have already seen, roundly condemned the proposal to abolish the office of land commandant. It also made very specific criticisms of the projected abolition of the canton court. The new Justice of the Peace, the Congress

[57] *TsGIAL,* f 1276, op 2, d 77, p 819 (Journal of the Council of Ministers, 19 and 23 January 1907); the Provincial Office mentioned was a chancellery attached to the provincial governor to supervise the District Conferences of Land Commandants.   [58] Eroshkin, *Ocherki Istorii,* p 242.
[59] *Rech[1],* 1 June 1906; *GDSO,* II, vol 2, cols 1323-58, 1574-1606.

resolution declared, would be far more distant from the peasantry than their own elected cantonal judges, and could never know peasant life as peasant judges did. The government's aims could better be achieved by reforming the cantonal court through (i) regulating the penalties that could be imposed by cantonal judges, (ii) improving the quality of the cantonal judges, (iii) improving the mechanism of appeal against the verdict of the cantonal court. In a speech at the Congress, the Rightist Duma deputy, G. G. Zamyslovsky, himself Assistant Procurator of the Vilna circuit court, insinuated that the Justices of the Peace would be used by the radical parties to 'politicise' the countryside and could well be a subversive force.[60]

Furthermore, when the bill came up for debate in the Duma in October 1909, the centre majority in the house was beginning to disintegrate, as a result of the Naval Staffs crisis, in a way which imperilled the bill's passage by allowing chance majorities of right and left to defeat the centre over important points.

At the committee stage, the Octobrists, most of whom still looked for a complete return to the principles of the great reform era, gained from the government the concession of a separate hierarchy of Justices, independent of the regular courts.[61] Reporting this in the house, the committee's spokesman, N. P. Shubinskoi, described the whole bill as being the product of co-operation between government and Duma. The new institution of the Justice of the Peace rested, he said, on three main principles. First, its independence, to be guaranteed by its autonomous position within the judiciary, by the election of Justices in the district zemstvo, and also by a property qualification. Secondly, the new system would function without the old *soslovny* distinctions: all classes of the population would appear before the Justice in minor civil and criminal cases. Thirdly, the law would ensure that the Justices were educated men, not primarily in legal learning, but in broad culture and sensitivity of conscience, such as were necessary to the correct expedition of justice.[62]

The Minister of Justice, I. G. Shcheglovitov, likewise evoked the reforms of the 1860s, whose principles, he said, made the continued existence of segregated *soslovny* courts 'a major anomaly'. The cantonal court had been a temporary necessity in order not to intro-

[60] *Trudy 4-ogo*, pp 151-226; Chernyshev–Bezobrazov, *Kratkii Obzor*, p 19.
[61] *TsGIAL*, f 1278, op 2, d 3471, p 23 (Journal of the Duma Committee on Judicial Reforms, 31 January 1908).   [62] *GDSO*, III, 3, pt 1, cols 1030-1.

duce friction into peasants' affairs at a time when their obligations to the landlords had not been fully liquidated. The ignorance and venality of the peasant judges had then forced the government to appoint land commandants to supervise them. This mixture of administrative and judicial powers could no longer be tolerated: the promise of civil freedoms in the October Manifesto demanded a wholly independent judiciary. That was why the cantonal court must be abolished, not just reformed or 'improved'. The government was, however, he went on, anxious to ensure that the J.P.'s independence did not lead to irresponsibility, and for that reason was proposing two safeguards not envisaged in the Duma committee's bill:

(i) that the chairman of the district Assembly of Justices should be appointed by the crown;

(ii) that the district Assembly should be subordinated to the hierarchy of regular courts for appeal purposes.[63]

Opposition to the bill among the Rights and Nationalists was based on the same premises as that of the United Nobility: that the government, in pursuit of aims that were at best bureaucratic, at worst revolutionary, was unnecessarily destroying a time-honoured institution in which the peasantry had long successfully settled their disputes. G. A. Shechkov, of Kursk province, professed no surprise that the legislation of Witte should have been full of the spirit of *égalité* of the French Revolution, but, he said, he was astonished that the present government had not learnt its lesson. The cantonal court, he declared, was not set up 'by the paper work of some St Petersburg chancellery', but was a court 'with its roots in life'.[64] Bishop Evlogy, Russian Orthodox prelate in the eastern regions of Poland, maintained that the peasantry was much superior to the intelligentsia in deciding practical judicial questions in the Russian village:

It is true that our peasantry is still ignorant, uneducated, unenlightened, cannot understand subtle legal concepts, but he possesses a great gift – the sound Russian capacity for sizing up a situation (*krepkaya russkaya smetka*). He knows profoundly, from experience, our folk life, the conditions in which it is formed, he understands closely the people's psychology . . .

[63] ibid, cols 1041-59; also pt 2, cols 488-92 (speech of the Assistant Minister of Justice, A. N. Verevkin).   [64] ibid, pt 1, cols 1152-4.

Then, gentlemen, one must after all speak the truth – what is the Russian intelligentsia? . . . There are exceptions, of course, but one must unfortunately admit that our life has not yet given birth to a proper national intelligentsia, an intelligentsia living the same life, through the same faith and the same ideals as the people.[65]

Both of these speakers, in the highly coloured language of the Right, raised a serious objection, not to be lightly dismissed, as it lay in the very nature of Russia's local institutions: that is, the distance of both government officials and intelligentsia from the peasants for whose sake they claimed to be working. The idea of the Justice of the Peace was in many ways an élitist one, and this implication did not escape the peasants, of all fractions. For the Rights, Zamyslovsky proposed that the cantonal court should not be abolished, but should become a collegiate body, like the *gmin* court in Poland, in which three local men would form the bench, one of whom, the chairman, would be required to have at least secondary education.[66] Very similar proposals were advanced by A. A. Bulat, of the Labour group, and they appeared as a minority recommendation in the committee's report.[67] At least one Octobrist, A. E. Favorsky, supported them in his speech.[68]

Left wing attacks on the bill concentrated on three main points: (i) Article 17, the appointment of the chairman of the district Assembly of Justices by the government; (ii) Article 19, on the level of property qualification required by a candidate for the post of Justice; (iii) Article 64, the subordination of the district Assembly of Justices to the regular court hierarchy.

Article 19 was radically changed. M. S. Adzhemov, speaking for the Kadets, argued that property was a guarantee neither of independence (since so much of it was mortgaged), nor of moral worth, nor even of knowledge of local life. A better judge of all three would be the district zemstvo, whose choice should therefore not be artificially restricted by property qualifications.[69] Some members of all parties, especially the peasants, supported this proposal. M. S. Andreichuk (Nationalist) suggested that the property qualification be lowered to one-sixth of the level envisaged by the committee: this would give some peasants, including, on his own estimation, himself, the right to become J.P.s.[70] N. N. Opochinin, for the Octobrists,

[65] ibid, cols 1268-71. [66] ibid, col 1178. [67] ibid, cols 1080, 1411-29.
[68] ibid, cols 1674-86. [69] ibid, pt 2, cols 93-8. [70] ibid, cols 120-3.

put forward an amendment allowing the district zemstvo by a three-quarters majority to waive the property qualification altogether when they felt a worthy candidate had presented himself.[71]

The curious result of the voting on this article was that Andrei-chuk's and Opochinin's amendments were both passed, by a majority which included the Rights, the Poles, most of the peasants and some clergy, as well as the traditional opposition.[72] This anomaly reveals the chance majorities to which important details became subject when issues were complicated and party discipline did not hold. The peasants and village clergy felt strongly about the cantonal court, and were not prepared to support proposals which would set up outsiders as judges over them. The result of the haphazard passing of amendments was that paragraph 3 of Article 19, containing both these amendments, was unacceptable in toto when it came up for the vote, and was rejected. The effect of this would have been to delete all mention of any property qualification whatsoever, but at the third reading a compromise was adopted, by which half the qualification recommended by the committee was passed.[73]

Articles 17 and 64 were both finally passed in versions put forward by the left. A Labour amendment was passed to the effect that the district Assembly of Justices should elect its own chairman. In the majority were not only the whole opposition, but also the Rights and some Octobrists.[74] Finally, in Article 64, the government's version was defeated and that recommended by the committee was passed, supported by the opposition.[75]

Why the Rights supported these amendments is not clear, unless they wished to see the bill pass the Duma in a form as unacceptable as possible to the State Council. On the other hand, that the Octobrists voted in such a haphazard manner may be attributed both to the genuine complication of the issues and to the disarray within the fraction in the early months of 1910, especially at the time of Guchkov's second resignation from the leadership.

The bill now went before the judicial committee of the State Council. Here the government suddenly and unexpectedly made a

---

[71] ibid, cols 104-5.   [72] *Rech*[1], 26 January 1910.
[73] *NV*, 30 March 1910; *GDSO*, III, 3, pt 2, cols 249-53; pt 3, cols 2140-1.
[74] ibid, pt 3, cols 2067-9; *Rech*[1], 28 March 1910, specifically mentions Leonov, Opochinin, N. A. Khomyakov, A. N. Boratynsky and N. L. Markov.   [75] *GDSO*, III, 3, pt 3, col 2216.

complete volte-face. Shcheglovitov had defended the bill against attack from many members of the committee, when Stolypin, also attending the sessions, suddenly declared that he did not want to see the cantonal court abolished at all. According to Neidgart, this had always been his view, and one that he had defended in the Council of Ministers.[76] This is almost certainly not the case: everything indicates that the abolition of the cantonal court was an integral part of the government's reform programme, nor is there any indication of serious disagreement in the relevant Journals of the Council of Ministers.[77] Much more likely is that Stolypin had been swayed by the persistent opposition of the United Nobility, and was dismayed now to find it repeated in the State Council's committee.

So the partisans of the cantonal court triumphed in the upper house. It was not to be abolished, but reformed. The main reforms recommended by Neidgart and Manukhin for the committee were aimed to meet specific frequently repeated criticisms of the court.

(i) That peasant judges were ignorant and venial. The committee proposed to raise the judges' honorarium, being convinced that better candidates were available among the peasants, and would come forward, for many peasants already carried out jury service excellently.

(ii) That peasant judges were dependent on the government administration. To counter this, they should be elected directly by the population (rather than, as at present, appointed by the land commandant from a list submitted by the canton). Also a ' higher village court ' should be set up above them, consisting of a Justice of the Peace (here was a role for them!) and two elected peasant judges: this court would consider appeals from the cantonal court. The judicial powers of the land commandant would, as both government and Duma agreed, be abolished.

(iii) That the court was a segregated one. This was inherent in its nature, and could not be remedied. However, the competence of the court could be lowered from cases involving 300 rubles to a maximum of 100 rubles.[78]

Stishinsky made an attempt on behalf of the Rights to get the land commandant restored in all his powers,[79] but this was defeated.

[76] Naumov, *Iz Utselevshikh Vospominanii*, vol 2, pp 161-2.
[77] *TsGIAL*, f 1276, op 2, d 77.   [78] *GSSO*, Sessiya 7 (1911-12), cols 1756-60.
[79] ibid, cols 1774, 1779-80.

The whole bill passed the State Council in the form recommended by the committee. Apart from the above changes some other details were modified. The Justices were left with a much more modest role, of course, and their property qualifications were once again raised, though with provision for waiving them in case of special judicial qualifications. The chairman of the Assembly of Justices was once again to be appointed by the government, and the Assembly was to be subordinated for appeal purposes to the Palais de Justice. Jews were debarred from the post of Justice.

The joint conciliatory committee which met to reconcile the Duma and State Council versions of the bill had stormy meetings. The Kadets K. K. Chernosvitov and N. A. Zakharyev protested that what was before them was not an amended version of the bill which had passed the Duma, but a completely new bill, on the reform of the cantonal court, and therefore it ought to go through the whole Duma procedure again from the start. In this they were supported by the Rights. The majority of the committee rejected this view and then proceeded to approve, article by article, the State Council's version of the bill. The Octobrists, at a fraction meeting, had decided to cut their losses and accept this in order to achieve some reform, however imperfect, of the local court system.[80] Kutler accused the Octobrists of going back on their principles and giving way to the upper house simply in order to pass the bill somehow and thus ' increase the Third Duma's baggage and have something to show off to the electors '. K. N. Lomonosov, an Octobrist peasant from Tambov province, agreed with him: ' I, as a representative of the people, cannot accept third-class justice for the peasants; I want peasants to have first-class justice.'[81]

The Duma, however, passed the State Council's version virtually unaltered. In this way the cantonal court was retained and the original intentions of both the government and the Octobrists were thwarted.

Other reforms

If we look at other elements in the Witte-Stolypin reform programme of 1906, we find that their fate was not very different. Interest groups, having a certain modicum of independence thanks

[80] *Rech¹*, 18, 19 April 1912; *GM*, 15 May 1912; G. Yurskii, *Pravye v 3-ei Gosudarstvennoi Dume*, Khar¹kov 1912, pp 196-9.
[81] *GDSO*, III, 5, pt 4, col 1580; *GM*, 15 May 1912.

to the new state system, would make their appearance to resist them; the government would become discouraged and decide the projected reform was too complicated, expensive or dangerous; whilst in the legislative chambers, relatively trivial details would be found to raise insurmountable difficulties of principle. In the end the reform would be seriously emasculated or dropped altogether.

Primary education is a good example. Nearly all Russians, of whatever party, agreed on the need for the general introduction of primary education as soon as possible. Yet the Duma and State Council failed to pass a bill codifying the general principles on which this should be done. The bill drawn up for the purpose by the Duma Education Committee fell down because:

(i) It proposed the establishment of District School Boards, to which all primary schools, including those of the Orthodox church, were to be subordinated. The Holy Synod, the priests and the United Nobility protested energetically against this weakening of the church's influence over the young in a period of social turmoil: the people, they warned, would turn to sectarianism or unbelief, and the result would be a repeat of the ' illuminations ' of 1905. The State Council accordingly exempted church schools from the bill.

(ii) It proposed in minority areas, to allow instruction to be conducted in a language other than Russian. The State Council insisted that all instruction (except, significantly, in religion) should be in Russian from the second year of schooling onward. Any other solution, they warned, would lead to the fragmentation of the Empire.

The conciliatory committee of the two houses could not compose these disagreements, and so the bill as a whole was rejected.

Perhaps the ultimate irony is that the Ministry of Education proceeded anyway with plans for the introduction of universal primary education. By 1917 virtually every district zemstvo in the country had submitted plans to the Ministry and started on the construction of the required network of schools. Without having agreed on the fundamental principles, the Duma and State Council voted the necessary funds. Not only could the new legislative institutions not pass a primary education bill, but their failure to do so was seen to be irrelevant.[82]

[82] *GDSO*, III, 4, pt 1, cols 108-14, 130-1, 1275-6, 1279; *GSSO*, Sessiya 7 (1911-12), cols 2712, 2714-21, 4675, 4701-2; *Trudy 6-ogo*, SPB 1910,

The bills granting freedom of religious belief and worship were no more successful. These grew out of promises the Emperor had made in 1905. The Ministry of the Interior drafted bills regulating the conditions of religious freedom in two areas, in conversion from one faith to another, and in the civil status of Old Believers. The Duma passed both these bills in a somewhat liberalised version. But again the Holy Synod and the priests warned that the Orthodox church would be exposed to competition from the sectarians and from the Old Believers, and that the very foundations of the state would be undermined. The State Council hedged the bills with restrictions designed to prevent sectarians and Old Believers publicly proclaiming their faith, and to make organisation and registration more difficult. Once again, no compromise between the two houses could be reached, and both bills were dropped.[83]

In the field of factory legislation, the Duma and State Council were somewhat more successful, though even here their achievements fell far short of what the government had originally intended in 1905. In that year Kokovtsev had drawn up a programme of reforms whose chief features were:

(i) a reduction of the working day from $11\frac{1}{2}$ to 10 hours, and 8 where any night work was involved;

(ii) the legalisation of trade unions and arbitration bodies, representing workers and employers, for the settlement of industrial disputes; the legalisation of economic strikes;

(iii) insurance schemes to cover workers against sickness, accident, loss of working capacity, old age and death; compulsory provision of medical attention by employers.

The Russian industrialists reacted much like the nobility when they discovered that their interests were no longer going to receive automatic protection. They wriggled out of the first committee which discussed these reforms (in May 1905) by claiming that they were too ' shocked and agitated ' at the naval defeat of Tsushima. They then circulated memoranda arguing that in the competition with foreign manufacturers the Russians suffered all kinds of disadvantages: their costs were higher, because of long-distance transport and the severe climate, their work force was inconstant and

p 458; *Trudy 7-ogo*, SPB 1911, pp 4-23; N. Hans, *History of Russian Educational Policy*, New York 1964 edition, pp 214-15.

[83] J. S. Curtiss, *Church and State in Russia*, New York 1965 edition, pp 322-6.

illiterate, and their home market small and uncertain. For these reasons, they claimed, they needed special protection and most of the proposed reforms would be impossibly expensive for them.

The government took a cautious line. It legalised economic strikes and trade unions by Ukazes of 2 December 1905 and 4 March 1906, but in both cases with restrictions, while the continued operation of emergency laws over most of the country made it very difficult for workers to take advantage of either of these laws.

The shortening of the working day was dropped altogether, but the various insurance schemes did come before the Third Duma. Here they were thoroughly (and slowly) reworked by the Committee on the Workers' Question, headed by Baron E. E. Tizengauzen, director of the Konshin textile factory at Serpukhov, near Moscow. The committee did everything possible to ensure that the employers' financial responsibility was minimised and their influence maximised. The Ministry of the Interior, meanwhile, was becoming concerned about setting up ' strong workers' organisations, in whose hands there will be large sums of money ', and was trying to ensure that police control over the various sick funds and insurance associations was as great as possible. Thus the insurance schemes which became law in 1912, though they were a genuine legislative achievement, cost the workers more, and were more subject to both employer and government control, than Kokovtsev had envisaged in 1905.[84]

As a postscript, it should be noted that the government's fears were well founded. During the World War, the workers' sick funds, and their newspaper *Voprosy Strakhovaniya* became the major centres of working-class and especially Bolshevik organisation in Petrograd. Such was the depth of social and ideological conflict in Russia, that those who feared the effects of reform very often had excellent reasons for doing so.[85]

[84] *Rabochii Vopros v Kommissii V. N. Kokovtseva*, Moscow 1926, passim; *PSZ*, 3rd Series, Nos 26987 and 27749; *A. Ya. Avrekh*, Tret'eiyunskaya Monarkhiya i Rabochii Vopros, *Ist. SSSR*, no 1, 1966, pp 42-69; *S. M. Shvarts*, Sotsial'noe Strakhovanie v Rossii v 1917-19gg, New York 1968, pp 15-17.
[85] See Sandra Milligan, ' The Petrograd Bolsheviks and Social Insurance, 1914-17 ', *Soviet Studies*, vol 20 (1968-9), pp 369-74.

The record of Stolypin's government in reform legislation was, then, disappointing. The 3rd June system was one in which independent pressure groups, the nobility, the zemstvos, the industrialists, even (through the Holy Synod) the clergy, could mount effective resistance to reform initiatives which threatened their position. In doing so, they were able to make use of the complications inherent in trying to introduce new institutions, often based on Western experience, in backward Russia. But, more important, social and ideological conflict remained so strong (if for the moment latent), that relatively trivial issues could raise insurmountable differences of principle. It was never difficult for the Rights in the State Council, if a bill got as far as them, to use these objections and fears to emasculate or kill the reform.

In short, there is not much evidence for supposing that, through the system which he set up on 3 June 1907, Stolypin (or any successor) could ever have effected radical reform by parliamentary means.

7

The breakdown of the 3rd June system

The political defeat and then murder of Stolypin were blows from which the 3rd June system never recovered. The alliance at whose centre he had stood broke down. The Council of Ministers fragmented into feuding factions and lost much of its authority. The Octobrists and Nationalists likewise split and moved towards political impotence. Furthermore, the last years before the outbreak of the World War were the years of the Beilis trial and the rise of Rasputin, as well as of growing labour unrest at home and a sharpening of international relations abroad. The political system was facing new challenges at a time when it was under severe internal stress and was being increasingly discredited.

The break-up of the Octobrist fraction

By the end of the Third Duma's natural term, the Octobrists were in a state of disarray and, what was worse, apathy. The Western Zemstvo affair had driven them into an oppositional stance which many of them found distasteful. As Khomyakov complained in May 1911, not only did many Octobrists fail to turn up at fraction meetings, but they actually sat in the next room playing cards.[1]

The problem was that the party had nothing more to offer them. It had compromised its original principles for the sake of co-operation with a government which had promised reform and seemed capable of effecting it. That government had now proved a broken reed, and as a result the party could offer its faithful supporters neither place, principle nor any prospect of influence on events. Meanwhile Guchkov, nominally their leader, dashed unpredictably from one scheme to another, seeking an outlet for his personal ambition.

Two bad splits came in the year after the Western Zemstvo crisis. The first was over the election of a successor to Guchkov as

[1] *TsGIAL*, f 669, op 1, d 8, p 25.

President of the Duma. Rodzyanko was the fraction's candidate, and was duly elected. But several leading left-wingers among the Octobrists voted against him, and the possibility of forming a breakaway group was openly discussed. However, the initiative came to nothing.[2]

The second split separated Guchkov from most of the fraction on the very issue which he had always regarded as peculiarly his own: naval and military affairs. When the Duma gave way in 1911 on the Naval Ministry's original battleship construction programme, the Ministry worked out an enlarged programme, designed to equip the Baltic Fleet with the latest Dreadnoughts. The credits requested for this amounted to 502 million rubles. Guchkov argued that the army's needs were more urgent, and that the navy should play a secondary and purely defensive role. However, his two closest colleagues in the Duma Imperial Defence Committee, A. I. Zvegintsev and N. V. Savich, felt that Russia should have a battle fleet capable of aggressive action in the Baltic, and refused to support him. Guchkov gave in. Together with some like-minded Octobrists, G. G. Lerkhe, I. V. Godnev and A. V. Eropkin, he left the Imperial Defence Committee and declined to oppose the credits inside the fraction. Most of the fraction followed Zvegintsev, and the credits were passed.[3]

The elections to the Fourth Duma took a heavy toll of the Octobrists. The indifference and disorganisation of their followers combined with active administrative pressure by the government against their known left-wingers to ensure this. In some of the provinces, governors and police chiefs closed down Octobrist electoral meetings and disqualified their candidates. The Holy Synod mobilised the clergy in support of the Rights and Nationalists and warned against voting for the Octobrists: Archbishop Agapit of Ekaterinoslav went so far as to call them ' those who sold Christ '.[4] In the major cities, on the other hand, they had to contend with the Kadets and

---

[2] *TsGIAL*, f 669, op 1, d 7, pp 45-58.

[3] *Rech¹*, 10, 20, 21, 22, May 1912; Kokovtsev, *Iz Moego Proshlogo*, vol 2, p 7; Shatsillo, *Russkii Imperialism i Razvitie Flota*, pp 186-7; *TsGIAL*, f 669, op 1, d 10, pp 43-8. Guchkov was still smarting from the dismissal of the Assistant War Minister, Polivanov, whose fall was generally attributed to his intimacy with the Duma.

[4] M. V. Rodzyanko, 'Krushenie Imperii: Zapiski Predsedatelya Russkoi Gosudarstvennoi Dumy', *Arkhiv Russkoi Revolyutsii*, vol 17, Berlin 1926, p 69; Shidlovskii, *Vospominaniya*, vol 1, pp 205-7.

7

Progressists, who were better organised and had a cleaner record of opposition to the government. Their most spectacular defeat was in the Moscow first curia, where Guchkov was unseated by a Kadet; but they also lost the urban first curia vote in fifteen other provinces.[5] The Octobrists were officially listed as having 95 deputies (still narrowly the largest single fraction) in the Fourth Duma, as against the 150 with which they were credited at the beginning of the Third Duma.

The Rights, Nationalists, Kadets and Progressists had all gained at their expense. But the right wing was now much more fragmented than in the Third Duma. A new, so-called Centre fraction had been formed to the right of the Octobrists. Headed by P. N. Krupensky and V. N. Lvov, it had its origin among those Nationalists who considered their fraction too servile at the time of the Western Zemstvo crisis: they had amalgamated with the Right Octobrists.[6] Even the surviving Nationalists had split, a breakaway group having been formed under Vasily Shulgin. The motives for this split seem to have been purely personal, the dissidents wishing to escape from the uninspired leadership of the mediocre, though undeniably wealthy, Balashov.[7]

The final split in the Octobrist ranks came at the beginning of the Fourth Duma's second session. In November 1913 the fraction organised a conference in St Petersburg, to which representatives of local branches of the Union of 17 October were invited; its purpose was to discuss the possibility of entering an opposition bloc. Guchkov, now operating from outside the fraction, wanted it to shed its right wingers and join such a bloc. On the eve of the conference *Golos Moskvy* stated with some retrospective idealisation of Stolypin:

What was an exception in his time has since become the general rule, and in the last session of the Third Duma the chasm which separated

---

[5] E. D. *Chermenskii*, 'Vybory v 4-uyu Gosudarstvennuyu Dumu', *Vop. Ist.*, 1947, no 4, pp 21-40; the same scholar provides more information in his unpublished doctoral dissertation, 'Bor'ba Klassov i Partii v 4-oi Gosudarstvennoi Dume', pp 44-138. The Octobrists who failed to be re-elected included, apart from Guchkov, Anrep, Boratynsky, Glebov, Golitsyn, Iskritsky, Kamensky, Kapustin, Leonov, Lerkhe, Tizengauzen, Favorsky: this was a substantial proportion of the fraction's left-wing.

[6] *GM*, 18 November 1912; *Ezhegodnik Gazety Rech'*, 1913, p 234.

[7] Shidlovskii, *Vospominaniya*, vol 1, p 311.

the Duma's central fraction from the government became clearly evident . . . Finally, the government's policy in the last year, its attitude to the Duma and its stubborn unwillingness to set about the passage of major reforms, have made co-operation with it quite impossible.

For the same reasons, co-operation with the Rights and Nationalists was impossible, *Golos Moskvy* argued, but an arrangement with the opposition might be concluded, if it could be to some extent weaned from the doctrinaire leadership of Milyukov. This move might cause a split in the fraction:

It is of course no secret that the change in the Duma's tactics does not meet with unanimous approval in the Union of 17 October. Its right wing is is not happy about what is commonly called the 'leftward move', but it can hardly be doubted that the majority of the forthcoming St Petersburg conference will disagree with them. The minority will then either have to submit or leave the party – and that will be the salutary turning-point which the Union of 17 October has long needed.[8]

Guchkov tried to get the Union's Central Committee to agree on proposals to put before the conference, but the committee found itself completely divided and did not pass any resolution.[9] The brunt of the split thus fell, without any disguise, on the conference itself.

Guchkov's speech at the conference was the dominating one, and set the tone for the whole proceedings. It was also a verdict, by its own leader, on the party which was at the centre of the Russian constitutional experiment. It is therefore worth quoting at length.

Looking back on the path we have trodden, we must admit that the attempt made by Russian society in the form of our party to achieve a rapprochement with the government, the attempt at a peaceful, painless transition from the old order to the new, has failed . . . The attempt of Octobrism to reconcile government and society has failed.

Was Octobrism a historical mistake? Are we to blame for having taken promises seriously? . . . No, Octobrism was not a historical mistake. Russian society would have acted inexcusably if it had refused support to a government which to all appearance had embarked on reform with conviction and determination. A government deprived of any support would have had too easy a justification for a return to the old order . . . But it would be a totally inexcusable mistake to

[8] *GM*, 6 November 1913.
[9] *Otchet Tsentral'nogo Komiteta Soyuza 17-ogo oktyabrya o ego deyatel'-nosti s 1-ogo oktyabrya 1913g po 1-oe sentyabrya 1914g*, Moscow 1914, pp 6-7.

continue the experiment in the present changed circumstances . . . The agreement has been broken and torn up. If earlier the country could afford not to worry about its parliament, with which all Russia's future is bound up, then now, with the existing governmental course, we must recognise that there exists a direct threat to the constitutional principle.

And, looking towards the future, he urged that the Octobrists should now undertake relentless opposition, by all parliamentary means, in defence of the constitutional system, and he warned that failure would lead Russia to disaster.

Before a State Duma which is loyal to its duty, both to the Emperor and to the Empire, there lies but one path. It must take into its own hands the defence of Russia's freedom and of the inviolability of our state system. In the name of long-awaited political liberty, in defence of the constitutional principle, in the fight for reform, all legal means of parliamentary struggle must be applied . . . It is time to declare that our patience is exhausted, together with our trust. We cannot leave to the professional opposition, to the radical and socialist parties, a monopoly of opposition to the government and to the fateful course it has taken. That would foster the dangerous illusion that the government is fighting against radical utopias and socialist experiments, whereas in actual fact it is resisting the fulfilment of the most moderate and elementary demands of society, such as once drew approbation from the government itself . . .

This is the last chance for a peaceful outcome to the crisis. Let no one mistake the mood of the nation, let no one be lulled by external signs of tranquillity . . . Never have Russian society and the Russian people been so profoundly revolutionised as by the present policies . . . And the historical irony lies in the fact that we are compelled to defend the monarchy against those who are the natural protagonists of the monarchical principle, we must defend the government's authority against the very holders of office.[10]

Most speakers at the conference endorsed Guchkov's call for unequivocal opposition, and the tactical resolution which was adopted reflected entirely the spirit of his speech:

The parliamentary fraction of the Union of 17 October . . . should undertake unrelenting struggle with the harmful and dangerous direction of government policy and with the manifestations of arbitrariness and lawlessness from which Russian life suffers so much today . . . The parliamentary fraction should use to the full all legal means of parlia-

[10] *GM*, 9 November 1913.

mentary struggle, such as the freedom of the parliamentary tribune, the right of interpellation, the rejection of legislative proposals, and the refusal of credits.

The responsible work and the onerous struggle which await the parliamentary fraction demands from it the maximum exertion of energy, complete solidarity in its actions, and the firm closing of its ranks.[11]

This resolution received the explicit endorsement of the Central Committee. But the Octobrists' Duma fraction proved less pliable than the Union's leadership had hoped. The fraction meeting of 29 November 1913, which considered the conference resolution, was far from unanimous in accepting it. Nor were the recalcitrant ones in a minority: in fact, the majority of the fraction expressed reservations about the resolution by voting merely to ' draw support ' (*pocherpnut podderzhku*) from it, and asserting that the fraction had not, in any case, deviated from the principles formulated in it. Only a relatively small group of left-wingers, twenty-two in number, led by Opochinin, voted unreservedly to be guided (*rukovodstvo-vatsya*) by the conference resolution; they also called for strict voting discipline in the fraction. A small right-wing group, led by G. V. Skoropadsky, recommended that the fraction should do no more than ' take cognisance of ' (*prinyat k svedeniyu*) the resolution.[12]

When the majority carried its wording, Opochinin's group threatened to leave the fraction and form an independent group of Left Octobrists. A further meeting of the fraction was therefore called, which tried to stave off the split by adding two further points to the previous meeting's resolution; one was to ' take as guidance (*prinyat k rukovodstvu*) the decision of the conference ', the other was to stiffen the voting discipline of the fraction by allowing only abstention, not contrary voting, in case of disagreement with the fraction decision.[13]

But this semantic quibbling failed to mend matters. Guchkov, alarmed to find the majority of the fraction against him, called a meeting of the Central Committee to discuss the differences, whilst *Golos Moskvy* changed its line and called now for a reconciliation: ' The crisis which has broken out in the fraction . . . removes the

[11] *Rech*[1], 10, 11 November 1913; *GM*, 12 November 1913; *Otchet*, pp 9-11.   [12] *GM*, 30 November, 1 December 1913; *Otchet*, pp 11-12.
[13] *GM*, 3 December 1913; *Otchet*, p 13.

last hope that work might be possible, and merely strengthens the right wing of the Duma. This fact . . . should move both sides to reconsider the decisions they have taken and should compel them to find common ground.'[14]

The Central Committee meeting, however, was a failure. Only seven members attended and no resolution was passed.[15]

With the failure of this meeting the breach became final, and during the Christmas recess the various groups inside the fraction went their own way. The twenty-two formed a group of Left Octobrists under Shidlovsky, with Opochinin as vice-chairman; among its other members were Godnev, Klyuzhev, Zvegintsev, Khomyakov and Meyendorf, who thus resumed the ties with his colleagues which he had broken over the Finnish affair. The majority of the fraction formed a group of 'Zemstvo Octobrists' under Rodzyanko, numbering sixty-five, and agreeing not to be bound by the conference resolution. The remainder (according to the Central Committee report 'about fifteen', though this seems too many) did not seek admission to either group, and called themselves 'non-party' deputies. The Central Committee resolved to remain in touch with all three groups.[16]

This split was the final enfeeblement of the party which had been the keystone of the government's attempt to work with the Duma. The Octobrists ceased to play any significant independent role, and the political influence of the party's members only revived as part of other alliances.

The attempt to form an opposition bloc

Throughout the Third Duma the leading party of constitutional opposition had been the Kadets. Unlike the Octobrists, they had not compromised with the government on matters of principle, and had retained their doctrinal purity – which, however, condemned them to impotence in the 3rd June system. For what it was worth, they had been proved correct in supposing that long-term co-operation between a constitutionalist party and Stolypin's government would be impossible. But this perspicacity had not brought them any greater influence on events. Under the firm and patient, though

[14] *GM*, 5 December 1913.   [15] *Rech¹*, 7 December 1913; *Otchet*, p 14.
[16] *GM*, 16, 17, 18 January 1914; *Otchet*, pp 14-15.

somewhat doctrinaire, leadership of Milyukov, they forswore alliances, power and place, but remained tightly disciplined and retained the prestige which they commanded in educated society.

The breakdown of the tacit alliance between the government and the Octobrists opened new possibilities for the opposition. Here the Kadets' isolationist devotion to principle was a less certain asset. What was needed was an opposition more amenable to compromise and to co-operation with others, especially after the elections to the Fourth Duma, when the left wing was strengthened and the opportunity presented itself for the first time of forming a working opposition nucleus on which an eventual majority might be constructed.

It was not the Kadets, but their neighbours, the Progressists, who set themselves this aim in 1912. The Progressists originated in the Party of Peaceful Renewal (Partiya Mirnogo Obnovleniya), which was set up in the summer of 1906 by three disillusioned Kadets, P. A. Geiden, N. N. Lvov and M. A. Stakhovich. Among its members were Moscow zemstvo activists and industrialists who had left the Octobrists, such as D. N. Shipov, S. I. Chetverikov, A. S. Vishnyakov and P. P. Ryabushinsky.[17] Their leader in the Third Duma was I. N. Efremov, a Don Cossack landowner. In the Third Duma the Progressists played a modest role. Most of their deputies came from the Urals and the eastern part of European Russia. They sat just to the right of the Kadets in the chamber and voted with them on most issues.

In the last two years or so of the Third Duma, however, the Progressists took on a new lease of life. As the Octobrists' failures became more manifest, those who had earlier left them began to seem more than mere voices of conscience crying in the wilderness. The Moscow industrialists also felt that the interests of trade and industry, whose future was so important for Russia, were not being adequately represented in the Duma. In November 1909 a group of them founded a newspaper *Utro Rossii* (Russia's Morning), aimed against the conservative industrialists of the Tizengauzen ilk, and in favour of a broad programme of reform which, among other things,

[17]E. D. Chermenskii, *Burzhuaziya i Tsarizm v Revolyutsiyu 1905-7gg*, Moscow–Leningrad 1939, pp 318-19; F. Dan and N. Cherevanin, 'Soyuz 17-ogo oktyabrya', in *Obshchestvennoe Dvizhenie*, vol 2, pt 1, p 205; Laverychev, *Po tu Storonu Barrikad*, pp 51-2; also see above, p. 40.

would create the right atmosphere for a flourishing industry. Among those who financed the new paper were the brothers P. P. and V. P. Ryabushinsky, A. I. Konovalov, N. D. Morozov, S. N. Tretyakov and S. I. Chetverikov.[18]

As the elections to the Fourth Duma approached, this paper and its financiers, together with the existing Progressist fraction, became the centre of an attempt to form a new, broader and more flexible opposition. At a meeting of the Society of Peaceful Renewal in St Petersburg in November 1911, Efremov spoke of the resistance shown in the State Council to reforms passed by the Duma, which, he said, must make clear to the electors ' the necessity of electing definitely progressive politicians, firm fighters for the rights of the people's representative assembly and for essential reforms '. The meeting accepted the idea of a broadly based platform which could unite ' progressive elements ' of different parties.[19] At the initiative of V. P. Ryabushinsky, informal talks were held with some Kadets and a few Octobrists known to be on the left wing of their party, on the possibility of forming a non-party opposition bloc for the elections to the Fourth Duma. In March 1912, Efremov, with the help of the Progressists' principal ally in the State Council, M. M. Kovalevsky, organised a bureau of ' non-party progressives '. A similar bureau was set up in Moscow soon after, supported by the industrialists of *Utro Rossii* and headed by N. N. Lvov.[20] They deliberately refrained from drawing up a definite programme, but made known their intention to act ' in defence of the constitution ', and in ' concern for the internal unity and might of Russia ' against the ' false nationalism ' of the Nationalists and Rights which had grown ' under orders from above '.[21] These concepts were also intended as weapons of the commercial bourgeoisie against the still lingering, though decrepit, hegemony of the nobility, as well as the rigid supervision of the bureaucracy. At a banquet in April 1912, at which the Moscow industrialists received Kokovtsev, P. Ryabushinsky proclaimed:

---

[18] Laverychev, ibid, pp 62-6.

[19] V. N. Seletskii, ' Obrazovanie Partii Progressistov ', *Vestnik Moskovskogo Gosudarstvennogo Universiteta* (Istoricheskaya Seriya), 1970, no 5, pp 34-5.

[20] ibid, pp 35-6; Laverychev, *Po tu Storonu Barrikad*, pp 86-9; *GM*, 24, 29 April 1912; *Utro Rossii*, 24 April, 1 May 1912.

[21] Seletskii, ' Obrazovanie Partii Progressistov ', p 37.

We are constantly seeking new ways to develop industry and trade, we are constantly improving our productive processes and techniques, and so by the very nature of our activity we are convinced men of progress. But to fulfil these aims we need other general favourable conditions, we need elbow-room, we need to be spared superfluous formalities and the various obstacles which should be removed from the paths on which life itself is advancing.[22]

Utro Rossii made a very similar declaration:

It is high time for the merchant class to step into the political arena: it is already such an advanced economic force that it not only can but should possess commensurate political influence. The merchantry will be a force which, in its political demands, rests not only on certain ideals of justice, but – what is most important of all – on a certain economic strength . . . Considering furthermore that the Russian merchantry has always been inspired by and has always shown liberal political tendencies, and has not become bogged down in its own narrow ' parish-pump ' interests, then one can only welcome its wholely timely appearance on the political scene . . .

Hitherto, the task of liberalism has lain wholly on the Kadet party. No one will think of reproaching them with betraying their ideals. But by its very nature the party has a weakness. It is a party of the intelligentsia, shorn therefore of any economic strength, and consequently does not have any real weight in the eyes of the government . . . Once the intelligentsia has played the part, which always falls to its lot and to which it is suited, of the political avant-garde, its work in parliament is more fruitful if alongside it there stands another party – also one of justice, but in addition possessing strength.[23]

The new Progressists took care not to set themselves up in opposition to the Kadets, but to act as a complement to them, drawing new and powerful elements into the struggle they had long been conducting. As Efremov emphasised in a circular to local organisers:

The aim of the organisers is not dissension and strife, and it is not at all our intention to direct the present election campaign against the existing constitutional parties – the Kadets and Octobrists – or in exclusive support of the Progressists. On the contrary, it is desirable to go into the elections in close co-operation with the Kadets and the genuine Octobrists.[24]

---

[22] ibid, p 39; Kokovtsev, *Iz Moego Proshlogo*, vol 2, p 71.
[23] *Utro Rossii*, 4 April 1912.
[24] Laverychev, *Po tu Storonu Barrikad*, p 87.

The Kadet party on the whole took a slightly distant attitude, hoping to use the opportunity for widening their support without losing their doctrinal independence. A Central Committee meeting on 18 March recommended that members of the party should not take seats on the various non-party progressive bureaux, but should take part in electoral meetings organised by them, striving always to *guide* those meetings.[25] The Kadets, in fact, saw the non-party progressive alliance as a purely electoral arrangement, and were suspicious of attempts to extend it beyond that, whereas the Ryabushinsky group, *Utro Rossii* and the Duma Progressists aimed at making it the germ of a future large and integrated opposition party.

As an electoral arrangement, it was certainly a success. Together the Progressists and Kadets, by combining their forces in the first urban curia, took sixteen seats from the Octobrists. The most spectacular success was that of the Kadet M. V. Chelnokov, who defeated Guchkov with Progressist support in Moskow.[26]

Inside the Fourth Duma, the Progressists continued to try to unite the opposition. They held a congress from 11-13 November 1912, which worked out a programme and laid the basis for a nation-wide organisation. Amongst the aims mentioned in the programme were the abolition of the electoral law of 3rd June, reform of the State Council, the guarantee of all civil liberties, the abolition of all national and *soslovny* distinctions, the introduction of universal primary education, and active defence of the interests of agriculture, trade and industry. To achieve these aims, the programme said, it was essential to establish ministerial responsibility to the Duma. Until this was attained, the party should use all available means of parliamentary struggle, including the systematic refusal of budgetary credits:

Progressists should cherish and defend the rights, dignity and significance of the State Duma as an institution. They should value in it the embryo of a national parliament, the only means of transforming Russia peacefully. But there is no necessity to cherish the Fourth Duma as such. We should not, of course, thoughtlessly provoke its dissolution, but neither should we be afraid of it; circumstances may arise when

[25] *Utro Rossii*, 21 March 1912.
[26] Laverychev, *Po tu Storonu Barrikad*, pp 91-2; Seletskii, ' Obrazovanie Partii Progressistov ', pp 45-6.

it will be necessary consciously to reckon with dissolution and even hasten it, if that lies within our power.[27]

The Kadets in the Fourth Duma were divided in their reactions. Milyukov was still for conserving the strict independence of the party. He stated his case at a party conference of 2-3 February 1913. If the Duma was to have any influence as a political factor, he maintained, then three conditions must first be fulfilled: the democratisation of the electoral law, reform of the State Council, and the establishment of ministerial responsibility to the Duma. To achieve these conditions was the basic task of the Kadet party. To join a united opposition would, he said, mean limiting oneself to more easily attainable purposes, without any guarantee that they would be achieved either (the opposition, even when united, being still in a minority). Therefore, co-operation by the combined opposition should never take precedence over the party's basic task.[28]

Since the three basic conditions named by Milyukov also figured prominently in the Progressists' programme, and most of their other aims were common to both parties, one suspects that years of defending his principles in an entrenched position had disinclined Milyukov to working in a wider framework. And in fact he was opposed by some Kadets at the conference, notably N. A. Gredeskul, Maklakov and Chelnokov. They claimed that the achievement of Milyukov's ' basic conditions ' would require a revolution in present circumstances; the party should do what it could for the moment by co-operating with the other opposition parties over limited aims.[29] The conference amended somewhat Milyukov's theses, in obeisance towards oppositional co-operation, and raised the question (leaving it, however, unanswered) of ' more active means of parliamentary struggle '.[30] In retrospect, there is an air of unreality about these conference debates. Both Milyukov and critics assumed that the Kadets were somehow more ' left ' than the Progressists. But there is no indication of why they thought this. It is true that the ' compulsory expropriation ' of landowners had never been officially dropped from the Kadet programme, but it was no longer ever mentioned, and it is difficult to see much else that divided them from the Progressists. In effect, personal differences, the past and the

---

[27] S''ezd Progressistov: 11, 12 i 13 noyabrya 1912g, SPB 1913, pp 6, 22-3.
[28] TsGAOR, f 523, op 1, d 14, p 68.   [29] ibid, pp 15-18, 20-30.
[30] ibid, pp 46-55.

time-worn formulae of 1905-7 were keeping the opposition parties apart.

Discontent with Milyukov's leadership continued inside the Kadet party. In March Maklakov sharply criticised him for tabling bills for the reform of the State Council, the introduction of universal suffrage and the guarantee of all civil liberties. These, he said, were purely demonstrative bills, and stood no chance whatever of being passed; ' leftward aberrations ' simply alienated the Progressists and Left Octobrists. By the autumn of 1913 a majority of members were reported to be dissatisfied with the failure to form any kind of alliance with the rest of the opposition. Many, too, felt that the Kadets should pursue a more active foreign policy and express open sympathy for the peoples of the Balkans in their struggles against Turkey and Austria. In October, indeed, there was a rumour that Maklakov intended to break with the Kadets and set up his own National Liberal party.[31]

By the spring of 1914 voices were also being heard on the left of the party, worried by the lack of any contact between the Kadets and the rapidly growing workers' movement. ' Why did none of our St Petersburg deputies appear in the factories when the widespread poisoning started there?' asked A. M. Kolyubakin: ' the Social Democrats went along. We must not only speak from the platform, but also plunge into the thick of things '. N. V. Nekrasov argued that all possible means must be used of isolating the government, and this meant going outside parliament: the Kadets must strengthen their influence in the country, go over to the attack against anti-Semitism, review their policy towards the army, and conduct propaganda among the workers. He warned that young people were no longer looking to the Kadets, and added: ' there are professors belonging to the Kadet party, and if they, in the name of the party, call on young people to show restraint by frightening them with revolutionary horror stories, then that will be a great mistake '.[32]

The Progressists were also looking over their shoulders at the

[31] *TsGAOR*, f 102 (Department of Police), op 14, d 27 (1913g), pp 25, 27-8, 60-1; f 63 (Moskovskoe Okhrannoe Otdelenie), op 50, d 40, p 30.
[32] *TsGAOR*, f 523, op 1, d 31, pp 103-5, 116 (K. D. Central Committee meeting of 17 February 1914). The poisoning to which Kolyubakin refers seems to have been caused by fumes from poor quality polish used in making galoshes. See A. E. Badaev, *Bol'sheviki v Gosudarstvennoi Dume*, M 1935 edition, p 148.

workers' movement threatening to outbid them on the streets.
Konovalov was particularly energetic in trying to get all the Duma
fractions of the left together for common action, if possible in
co-ordination with the workers. His first attempt, in January 1914,
was confined to the Kadets, Progressists and Left Octobrists. It
came to nothing because the Zemstvo Octobrists, whose participation was thought to be essential, would not agree to form any bloc.[33]
At the beginning of March 1914 Konovalov called a wider group,
including Social Democrats and Socialist Revolutionaries as well.
To them he announced his disillusionment with attempts to unite the
Duma opposition, and argued that even if such unity were achieved,
it would not do much good, as the Duma was impotent in the
country as a whole. It was necessary, therefore, he said, to co-
ordinate the activities of the Duma opposition with those of the
revolutionary parties both in and outside the Duma, to organise
workers' demonstrations and strikes, peasant disorders, and campaigns by newspapers and professional associations, such as would
alarm the government, and force it to make concessions. The immediate aim would be the realisation of the October Manifesto, on
which all oppositional and revolutionary parties could agree, whatever their differences on ultimate goals. As a first step in this campaign of co-operation, Konovalov proposed the establishment of
an ' Information Committee ', which was apparently indeed set up.[34]
Through its Bolshevik member I. I. Skvortsov-Stepanov, Konovalov
even made a tentative offer of 20,000 rubles to Bolshevik funds for
the convocation of a party congress, which Lenin considered essential at this time. It seems that in the end nothing came of this offer;
certainly the Bolsheviks eventually broke with the Information Committee.[35] Nor is there any evidence that the Information Committee
achieved anything much in the way of contact with the workers: the
July 1914 disturbances certainly had no connection with it.

[33] GM, 30, 31 January 1914; Rech¹, 28 January, 4 February 1914; TsGAOR,
    f 1467, d 576, p 14 (Department of Police report of 28 January 1914);
    f DP, d 307A (1914g), pp 18-19 (report of 7 February 1914); f 102, op 14,
    d 27 (1913g), pp 25-6.
[34] TsGAOR, f 63, 1913g, op 47, d 408, pp 62-4 (report of 17 April 1914).
[35] ' Otvet V. I. Lenina I. I. Skvortsovu-Stepanovu ', Istoricheskii Arkhiv,
    1959, no 2, pp 11-18; see also the Department of Police reports in the
    same journal, 1958, no 6, pp 8-13; see also L. Haimson, ' Social Stability
    in Urban Russia, 1905-1917 ', pt 2, SR, vol 24 (1965), pp 4-8.

In forming the Information Committee, Konovalov was probably seeking to draw on the resources of another potentially important binding force in the radical politics of these years, namely the Masonic movement. There has been quite a surge of interest among historians in recent years in this aspect of pre-revolutionary politics, especially since the Masonic oath required members of the movement to observe strict secrecy about it. We are now in a position to describe the main features of the movement, if not to name the members. It seems that Russian Freemasonry, dormant since the days of the Decembrists, revived sharply in a new form after 1905, with Maxim Kovalevsky playing a leading role. The new Freemasonry in some ways scarcely deserves the name: it had virtually no ties with foreign Masons, the complex ritual and hierarchy were absent, and (horror of Masonic horrors!) women were admitted. On the other hand, lodges existed, with their own oath of admittance and internal discipline. Their chief role was that of bringing together from various political movements people divided by the events of 1905, but having opposition to the government in common. Members ranged from Octobrists to Bolsheviks and included Konovalov and Efremov of the Progressists, Nekrasov and Tereshchenko of the left Kadets, Kerensky of the Labour group, and Skvortsov-Stepanov of the Bolsheviks, as well as a number of Georgian Mensheviks. Existing evidence does not permit us to say much about the activity of these lodges: probably continuing contact and mutual solidarity across increasingly irrelevant party divisions was their main achievement, and one which certainly paved the way for the formation of the Provisional Government of 1917.[36] For the

---

[36] B. Elkin, 'Attempts to revive Freemasonry in Russia', *SEER*, vol 44 (1966), pp 454-72; G. Aronson, *Rossiya nakanune Revolyutsii*, New York 1962, pp 109-42; I. V. Gessen, 'V Dvukh Vekakh', *Arkhiv Russkoi Revolyutsii*, vol 22, Berlin 1937, pp 216-18; Haimson, 'Social Stability in Urban Russia', pt 2, pp 13-17; A. F. Kerensky, *The Kerensky Memoirs: Russia and History's Turning Point*, London 1966, pp 87-90; S. P. Mel'gunov, *Vospominaniya i Dnevniki*, vol 1, Paris 1964, pp 144-5. It is a curious fact that, as far as I have been able to ascertain, none of the very detailed police reports on the opposition parties mentions Freemasonry, though Nicholas II was known to be anxious to keep trace of the movement (see A. Gerasimov, *Der Kampf gegen die erste russische Revolution*, Leipzig 1934, pp 146-7). Perhaps this is because the main police agent in the Kadet party, Prince Bebutov, was himself a Freemason.

moment, however, the apparent importance of Freemasonry does no more than illustrate the generally felt lack of any other common arena for opposition politicians.

By 1914, then, the political parties formed in 1905-7 were proving difficult to hold intact: they were all splitting. But as yet there was no crisis powerful enough to break through the personal and ideological barriers erected in those earlier revolutionary years. The basis, however, had been laid for a more co-ordinated opposition such as was to emerge in the war years in the form of the Progressive Bloc.

The Council of Ministers

Not even Stolypin had always succeeded in maintaining the principle that all ministers were responsible to the cabinet as a whole. But in general, under his premiership, the Council of Ministers kept up a united front. This was a fact which was used by reactionaries to insinuate that he was eclipsing the Emperor and becoming some kind of dictator. Nicholas was sensitive to such insinuations, and Alexandra deeply so. When she first met Kokovtsev, she begged him not to mention his predecessor, who had ' overshadowed his sovereign ', and went on: ' We hope that you will never go along with those terrible political parties, which dream only of seizing power or of subjecting the government to their will . . . Remain yourself; do not seek support in political parties. They are so insignificant in Russia. Rely upon the confidence of the Emperor.'

The Octobrists and Nationalists were in any case splitting apart at the seams, so that Kokovtsev was scarcely in a position to rely on the parties. The Emperor, like his wife, regarded this as an advantage. When Kokovtsev wrote to him, complaining of the absence of a ' disciplined moderate conservative majority ', Nicholas replied: ' Your relationship to the Duma, peaceful and non-party, is the only correct one, in my opinion. It is already showing its beneficial effect on the internal life of the country in a general calming down and decline of " politicking ".'[37]

These warnings set the tone of Kokovtsev's tenure of office. He had no ready-made Duma majority to rest on, and he did not attempt to create one. He was certainly not the man to revive a bold reform

[37] Kokovtsev, *Iz Moego Proshlogo*, vol 2, pp 7-8; *TsGIAL*, f 966 (V. N. Kokovtsev), op 2, d 11, p 6 (letter of Nicholas II to Kokovtsev, 18 November 1911).

programme in the face of the Duma's impotence and the State Council's hostility. All his instincts were those of the highly competent, efficient and correct official (the characteristic mixture of conscientiousness and complacency is well revealed in his memoirs). His strength was punctilious day-to-day work. Co-operation with the Duma to him meant detailed consultation on budgetary niceties in Alexeyenko's Duma Budget Committee, whose work gave him so much pleasure. It certainly did not mean the active cultivation of party support, nor even the forceful statement of principles, at which his predecessor had been such an adept. He alienated the Rights as soon as he was appointed by refusing to increase their subsidy, as well as by his close ties with the commercial world; he alienated the Nationalists by telling them bluntly that he was not willing to become the plaything of any political party; and he alienated the Empress by his dislike of Rasputin.[38] In fact he never had the sources of support or authority which Stolypin had enjoyed for a long period, and the dispersion of authority which had begun in the last years of Stolypin's premiership was deepened under him. As he stated to the Provisional Government Investigatory Commission, ' it is easy to be decisive when one stands on firm ground, but when one is on shaky ground then one must permit compromise and one must manoeuvre in order to avoid sharp conflicts for the sake of conserving what is most important '.[39]

What he thought ' most important ' was budgetary consolidation and the maintenance of peace in the Balkans. Further than that he rarely looked. But even these aims brought him into frequent conflict with the War Minister Sukhomlinov, who wanted to spend more money on the army and was impressed by the growing strength of Pan-Slavism in public opinion. In such conflicts, Kokovtsev often felt the lack of any support from the Emperor, from any political party, or even from any significant section of public opinion (the most vocal of the merchants were joining the Pan-Slav chorus at this time). As he later wrote,

All such arguments in the Council of Ministers were extremely distasteful to me. They clearly demonstrated my isolation and even

[38] Kokovtsev, *Iz Moego Proshlogo*, vol 1, pp 313, 483-6; vol 2, pp 89-90, 111-13.
[39] A. L. Sidorov (ed), ' Interesnaya Nakhodka : Delo Kokovtseva ', *Vop. Ist.*, 1964, no 4, p 108.

complete helplessness. Nominally I was considered the head of the government, directing its activities, and responsible for it to public opinion. But in reality one part of the ministers was totally indifferent to what was going on around them, whilst the other part was conducting a policy clearly hostile to me and gradually weakening my position.[40]

The leader of this ' hostile ' fraction was N. A. Maklakov, Minister of the Interior from December 1912. He was appointed in place of Makarov, whose manipulation of the Fourth Duma elections had not been very successful, and who, in the Emperor's view, was not firm enough with the press. The appointment was the Emperor's own personal choice, and he pushed it through against the objections of Kokovtsev, who came to protest personally to him about it, but did not take his objections as far as resignation.[41] Maklakov, brother of the Kadet deputy and former governor of Chernigov province, was probably recommended to the Emperor by Prince V. P. Meshchersky, an influential adviser in the past, who had been for some years eclipsed by the Duma and Stolypin. An associate of Alexander III and Pobedonostsev, dilettante writer of high-society novels, and editor of the weekly paper *Grazhdanin* (The Citizen), Meshchersky was accustomed to a certain influence on the course of politics, and with the removal of Stolypin saw a promising vacuum. Maklakov, for his part, was a convinced monarchist who held that ' the legislative institutions do not limit autocracy as a whole, but represent a certain delegation of the supreme powers of the Emperor to the people in the field of legislation and supervision '.[42]

Maklakov and Meshchersky set out to play on Nicholas's remorse about renouncing his autocratic power, in order to reduce the powers of the Duma and of the Council of Ministers, the bodies which they felt did most to limit the Emperor's power. During the years 1913-14, they were able to profit by the patent impotence of the legislative institutions, as well as by various ' scandals '.

They had a fine opportunity in the summer of 1913. The occasion was a dispute which had broken out between the Council of Ministers and the Duma. In the general debate on the budget, Markov 2, attacking the Ministry of Finance in a very heated speech, talked of

[40] Kokovtsev, *Iz Moego Proshlogo*, vol 2, p 109.   [41] ibid, pp 84-9.
[42] Testimony of N. A. Maklakov, in *Padenie Tsarskogo Rezhima*, vol 3, pp 86-7; on Meshchersky, see Kokovtsev, *Iz Moego Proshlogo*, vol 2, pp 311-20, and M. A. Taube, *La Politique Russe d'Avant-guerre et la Fin de l'Empire des Tsars*, Paris 1928, pp 297-8.

' bribery ' and even ' theft '.[43] Normally such language would have led to a sharp reprimand from the President of the Duma, some kind of disciplinary action against the speaker, and an apology to the Minister. For some reason, however, Prince Volkonsky, presiding for the day, did no more than mildly rebuke Markov. Kokovtsev, in his punctilious way, rang Volkonsky and reproached him for allowing insults to be uttered from the tribune of the house. Volkonsky, Rodzyanko and the Duma Council of Elders (which dealt with questions of protocol) decided rather touchily that they could not in any way associate themselves, even by apology, with a conflict which was between two persons, one of whom had insulted the other.[44] The Council of Ministers, equally petulantly, resolved that, until a public apology was made in the Duma, no Minister would attend its sessions, though they would send their assistants to replace them. In effect, they declared a ministerial strike. The Emperor heartily approved their decision, remarking that he thought Ministers should not visit the Duma anyway. It appears to have been at the cabinet meeting which took this decision that Maklakov first suggested that the best way out of the crisis might be to dissolve the Duma.[45]

No settlement was reached before the summer recess, and so the ' ministerial crisis ' continued until the Duma reassembled in November 1913. Meshchersky and Maklakov used the recess to mount a campaign designed to bring about Kokovtsev's resignation, the abolition of the Council of Ministers, and the dissolution of the Duma, accompanied by a change in the Fundamental Laws reducing the Duma to a purely advisory status. In June Maklakov brought a draft press law before the Council of Ministers, which would have reimposed preliminary censorship. In particular, he proposed to prevent the reporting of Duma speeches in what he called a ' tendentious manner '– meaning the practice of quoting at length, and with italics, from oppositional speeches, while ignoring or curtailing loyal speeches. The Council of Ministers approved the general principles, but did not proceed immediately with it, for which Meshchersky upbraided them in his rag.[46]

[43] *GDSO*, iv, 1, pt 3, cols 65-6.
[44] Kokovtsev, *Iz Moego Proshlogo*. vol 2, pp 164-5; testimony of Prince V. M. Volkonskii, in *Padenie Tsarskogo Rezhima*, vol 6, pp 133-4.
[45] *GM*, 31 May, 2 June 1913; Kokovtsev, *Iz Moego Proshlogo*, vol 2, p 166; Chermenskii, ' Bor'ba Klassov ', p 218.
[46] *GM*, 13, 16 June 1913; Kokovtsev, *Iz Moego Proshlogo*, vol 2, p 199.

During September and October, while Kokovtsev was abroad, Meshchersky wrote a series of articles in *Grazhdanin* accusing him of becoming a kind of Grand Vizier and encroaching on the autocratic power of the Emperor. He was bolstering his own independent position, Meshchersky said, by seeking support in the Duma, and hence in effect he was trying to introduce ' parliamentarism '. It was time to end these ' West European innovations ', for which there was no place in autocratic Russia, abolish the Council of Ministers and replace it with the old Committee of Ministers, bound by no collective responsibility to anyone but the Emperor. He suggested Goremykin as a suitable man to take the (nominal) chair in such a body. Kokovtsev wrote angrily from abroad to Maklakov, saying that he held him morally responsible for these calumnies by his patron. Maklakov returned him a very cool reply.[47]

The Emperor was widely reputed to read only *Grazhdanin* as a source of information and comment on internal affairs. Maklakov tried to draw him into the campaign. In October 1913, when the Duma deputies were beginning to return to St Petersburg in a strongly oppositional frame of mind he wrote to Nicholas warning that the workers and intelligentsia of the capital were restless and that the Duma would ' raise the temperature of public opinion '. He asked permission to make a declaration threatening the Duma with dissolution if it did not show a more co-operative spirit and work with the government for the welfare of Russia. In case the Duma should react by making a public protest to such a threat, Maklakov further asked for two blank Ukazes for use if necessary, one ordering dissolution of the Duma, the other placing St Petersburg under ' extraordinary protection '.[48]

In his reply Nicholas went even further:

I also consider it necessary and proper that the Council of Ministers should immediately discuss the idea, which I have long pondered, of

[47] Kokovtsev, ibid, pp 199-201; according to S. E. Kryzhanovskii (*Vospominaniya*, pp 158-9), Kokovtsev had threatened during Stolypin's premiership to stop the government subsidy to Grazhdanin because of its attacks on Izvol'skii.

[48] V. P. Semennikov (ed), *Monarkhiya pered Krusheniem*, Moscow–Leningrad 1927, pp 93-4; testimony of N. A. Maklakov, *Padenie Tsarskogo Rezhima*, vol 5, pp 193-5. The Journal of the Council of Ministers for 17 October 1913 suggests that the Council as a body proposed dissolution (*TsGIAL*, f 1276, op 2, d 158, p 19). However, Maklakov's letter was written earlier (14 October), and it seems clear that the initiative was his.

changing the article of the Duma statutes by virtue of which, if the Duma does not accept amendments made by the State Council and will not ratify them, the bill lapses. Since we have no constitution in our country, that is completely senseless. If instead the opinions of the majority and of the minority are presented to the Emperor for his choice, that will be a good way of returning to the previous tranquil course of legislation, and moreover in the Russian spirit.[49]

However, the Council of Ministers, in the absence of Kokovtsev, did not take any decisive steps. By the time Kokovtsev returned, the Markov incident had been settled through the intermediacy of Shcheglovitov, who persuaded Markov to apologise before the house. In this way, the immediate occasion of the conflict was removed, and the initiative of Maklakov and the Emperor petered out.[50] It is evident that the reactionaries, like everyone else, were not sure of their ground.

In any case, Kokovtsev mounted a counter-offensive on his return from abroad. He went to see the Emperor at his summer resort of Livadia, on the Black Sea. The immediate occasion of his visit was a proposal by Maklakov to appoint as Mayor of Moscow a well-known reactionary, B. V. Sturmer, who would clearly be unacceptable to the lively Moscow public. The Emperor agreed to drop his support for this proposal. But Kokovtsev went further. He asked the Emperor to remind Maklakov that collective responsibility was binding on him as a member of the Council of Ministers. Maklakov, he said, had repeatedly tried to take major decisions without the approval of the cabinet, and was being encouraged by Meshchersky's articles in *Grazhdanin,* some of which he showed to Nicholas, with the warning that they were undermining the prestige not only of the government but of the monarchy as a whole. If this kind of intrigue was not stopped, he said, he would resign. Nicholas was noncommittal, remarking that he thought Kokovtsev attributed too much importance to the articles: he claimed he never read them himself. Returning to St Petersburg, Kokovtsev warned his colleagues that he had offered his resignation, and that he would not tolerate intrigues against himself from inside the cabinet. All ministers were to observe the law, and must submit to the Council of

---

[49] Semennikov, *Monarkhiya pered Krusheniem,* p 92; *Padenie Tsarskogo Rezhima,* vol 5, pp 195-6.

[50] Kokovtsev, *Iz Moego Proshlogo,* vol 2, pp 167-8; Rodzyanko, ' Krushenie Imperii ', p 70; *GDSO,* iv, 2, pt 1, cols 540-1.

Ministers all decisions which concerned departments other than their own, or were of general political significance.[51]

Kokovtsev survived for the moment, but his position was clearly weakened. His downfall came over a somewhat different issue. The Emperor had long been troubled about the high rate of drunkenness among the Russian peasants and workers and the fact that it rested on a state liquor monopoly which brought in about a quarter of the treasury's revenue. He had long pondered, with the support and advice of Krivoshein, who thought it an essential supplement to the agrarian reforms, a project for restricting the sale of alcohol, reorganising state finances on the basis of an income tax, and then mounting a temperance campaign. Kokovtsev had always opposed this scheme because of the financial dislocation it would cause and because he feared that to restrict the sale of alcohol would encourage a clandestine trade. But Witte, who had first proposed the introduction of income tax in 1906, spoke for a temperance bill in the State Council, to the accompaniment of bitter attacks on the Ministry of Finance for balancing the budget by encouraging popular debauchery (though it was Witte himself who had originally initiated the state liquor monopoly). What Witte proposed was that the revenue from the sale of spirits should be fixed at a certain level, say 700 million rubles, and that any excess above that should be spent in measures for combating drunkenness. If the revenue should actually decline, then, Witte said, ' dig out the new tax proposals which have been lying peacefully in the bowels of the Tauride Palace for eight years '. Krivoshein groomed a successor at the Finance Ministry in the person of P. L. Bark, who was duly appointed on 30 January 1914. Among the most prominent supporters of this temperance campaign, as Akimov admitted to Kokovtsev, were Meshchersky and Rasputin.[52]

Kokovtsev also lost his job as President of the Council of Ministers. His dismissal must be seen as another stage in the dispersal of authority. In his letter to Kokovtsev, Nicholas said he had become convinced by experience that the office of President of the Council of Ministers should not be combined with that of Minister of the Interior or Finance (a tacit criticism of both Stolypin and Kokovtsev,

[51] Kokovtsev, *Iz Moego Proshlogo*, vol 2, pp 243-51.
[52] ibid, pp 269, 320-37; P. L. Bark, ' Vospominaniya ', *Vozrozhdenie*, vol 48 (December 1955), pp 73-5; vol 157 (January 1965), pp 59-62; *GSSO*, Sessiya 9 (1913-14), cols 341-8.

and a confirmation of Meshchersky's 'Grand Vizier' thesis).[53]
To avoid any such similar concentration of power, he appointed the
aged and flaccid Goremykin as President of the Council of Ministers, without any other portfolio. Under him, relations between
government and Duma deteriorated to the kind of direct confrontation which had characterised them in the First Duma. Maklakov
had not got any further with his press law, but he was still determined to reduce the effect of the Duma speeches on the population.
After a fiery speech by the Social Democrat N. S. Chkheidze, in April
1914, Maklakov recommended to the Council of Ministers that
Chkheidze should be indicted under Article 129 of the Criminal
Code for attempting to subvert the existing order and extol the
virtues of a republic. Although this step plainly contradicted the
Duma statutes, which forbade prosecution for a speech from the
tribune, the Ministers gave their preliminary consent to it. Again,
however, the reactionaries lost their nerve: after some months the
Emperor ruled that the case could not be proceeded with[54]

The budget debates of 1914 gave rise to concerted opposition
attacks on the government's whole course, and for the first time the
Kadets and the Progressists joined the far left in voting against the
budget as a whole, applying a tactic they had long anxiously discussed and finding an ad hoc unity which, however, was never
formalised.[55] The Social Democrats and Labour group, for their
part, obstructed the debate as a protest against the proposed indict-
ment of Chkheidze. They refused to submit to the President, and
had to be removed from the chamber by force, Skobelev shouting
' for seven years you have crawled to the government – it is enough! '
All the Social Democrats and Labour deputies were suspended for
fifteen sessions.[56]

After the end of the Duma's second session, on 18 June 1914, the
Emperor called a special conference of all ministers to discuss the
lack of co-operation between the government and the Duma. He
complained that laws which the country badly needed were being
buried in the Duma or rejected because of disagreement between

[53] Kokovtsev, *Iz Moego Proshlogo*, vol 2, pp 278-9.
[54] *Rech'*, 15 April 1914; *GM*, 16, 17 April, 9 July 1914; Badaev, *Bol'sheviki
v Gosudarstvennoi Dume*, pp 162-4.
[55] *Rech'*, 27 April, 3 June 1914; *GDSO*, IV, 2, pt 3, cols 1196-7.
[56] *Rech'*, 23 April 1914; Badaev, *Bol'sheviki v Gosudarstvennoi Dume*,
pp 164-6.

the Duma and the State Council. He reintroduced his proposal to reduce the Duma and State Council to consultative status. This time all the Ministers, including Maklakov, advised against the step. Shcheglovitov even declared that he would consider himself a traitor to the Emperor if he advised him to do such a thing.[57] Did the assassination of the Archduke Franz Ferdinand (which had taken place in Sarajevo three days before) perhaps overshadow their discussion with the foreboding that before long all the Duma's support might well be needed?

We do not know. All that seems clear is that on the eve of the war the government and the Duma were hovering round one another like indecisive wrestlers, neither side able to make a definite move.

The difficult years

The breakdown of the 3rd June system in St Petersburg was accompanied by a revival of social unrest in the country at large. The reawakening of a revolutionary spirit began in the universities. In November 1910 Leo Tolstoy died his strange death at the remote country railway station of Astapovo, and the Holy Synod, regarding his anarchist politics and his personalist Christianity as a heresy, refused a church burial to the man who for many was the ' conscience of Russia '. No issue could have been better calculated to remind the youth of the ideals of 1905, and of the stand Tolstoy had taken against the death penalty. In St Petersburg, Moscow, Kiev, Odessa, Kharkov, Warsaw and elsewhere students came out on the streets, boycotted classes and held meetings calling for the abolition of the death penalty. When the Minister of Education, L. A. Kasso, responded by banning student associations and meetings, the students declared a general strike in February 1911. Kasso retaliated with numerous expulsions and arrests, and in the end a distinguished body of Moscow University professors, headed by Russia's leading historian, V. O. Klyuchevsky, resigned from the faculty in protest against what amounted to the abolition of the autonomy the universities had won in 1905.

There is no record of serious working-class unrest to support these student demonstrations. From 1912 to 1914, however, it was the urban workers, particularly those of St. Petersburg, who took the

[57] Testimonies of I. G. Shcheglivitov and N. A. Maklakov, *Padenie Tsarskogo Rezhima*, vol 2, pp 435-8; vol 3, p 133.

lead in protest against the regime, and this time almost without the support of the intelligentsia. In April 1912 a strike at the Lena gold mines in eastern Siberia led to a clash with troops in which some two hundred workers were killed. The result was a wave of protest strikes which brought half a million out on May Day. It is interesting to observe, however, that these strikes and demonstrations did not really gather momentum until after the Duma's first debate on the subject, in which the Minister of the Interior, A. A. Makarov, made a tactless speech that received a fiery rebuttal from the Social Democrats. It seems that at this stage the Duma tribune and the Social Democrat newspapers, with their ' workers' correspondents ', were the most important channels of agitation and even of organisation for the urban working class.[58] Makarov's successor, Maklakov, certainly thought so, and, as we have seen, was sufficiently worried by their influence to try to restrict the deputies' freedom of speech and the newspapers' right to report them.

The wave of strikes, many of them now politically motivated, did not abate after Lena, but continued for more than two years, and culminated in the St Petersburg general strike of July 1914, which brought barricades and street fighting to parts of the capital during the official visit of President Poincaré. Of course, one should not imagine that working-class protest and even violence was peculiar to Russia at this time. On the contrary, these were the years of miners' and railway workers' strikes in France, and of the creation in Britain of a so-called ' Triple Alliance ', to prepare for a nation-wide general strike. Russia was not the only country in which the outbreak of war halted a very threatening workers' movement. Yet there were peculiarly ominous signs in Russia. Those who hoped for a peaceful and legal development of the Russian labour movement could not but be struck by the way the Bolsheviks, with their exclusive commitment to revolution, were strengthening their hold on the workers. In the elections to the Fourth Duma, they had won six of the nine labour curiae seats in the Empire, including all six of those in the major industrial provinces. In 1913 they won control of the strongest trade union in St Petersburg, the Union of Metal-workers, and in 1914 of the Chief Insurance Council, set up as a result of the labour legislation of 1912. The rapid industrial growth

[58] *GDSO*, III, 5, pt 4, cols 1941-53, 1963-9; I am indebted to recent unpublished research by Professor Leopold Haimson for the link between the Duma debate and the growth of the workers' protest movement.

of 1910-14 much strengthened Russia's economy, but also brought new and disoriented elements from the village to the labour force, especially in the key cities of St Petersburg and Moscow, who were easily moved to revolt and sometimes went beyond what even the Bolsheviks expected or could cope with.[59]

On the extreme right wing of Russian politics, also, there was little to rejoice those who hoped for peaceful evolution, or indeed even protagonists of firm but responsible government. The constitutional years had not produced a level-headed conservative party. The monarchist parties, having proved electorally expendable, had broken into small groups squabbling for government subsidies. The Union of the Russian People had split into two factions: the followers of Dubrovin, who refused to accept the existence of the Duma, and the followers of Markov, who felt that the Russian parliament was an acceptable tribune from which to discredit parliaments in general and to extol autocracy, Orthodoxy and Russian nationalism. Even within Markov's group a further split took place, and Purishkevich set up his own extravagantly named Union of the Archangel Michael, divided from its parent by no very apparent programmatic differences.[60]

In February 1911, at a time when the monarchists' stock of prestige (and party funds) was extremely low, the Duma began looking at a bill, tabled by the opposition, for the abolition of the Jewish Pale of Settlement. It aroused the predictably vehement opposition of the Rights in the Duma, where Markov denounced the Jews as ' a criminal race and one that hates mankind ', and in the United Nobility, where there was even talk of ' clearing Russia of the Jews '.[61] The Rights, for all their indignation, must have known that the bill had no earthly chance of passing both the Duma and State Council. Equally, however, they can hardly have doubted that its rejection would be a prolonged and noisy affair, well covered in the liberal newspapers. So they decided to mount their own counter-publicity. In March 1911, a twelve-year-old boy was found murdered in Kiev, his body pierced by numerous stab wounds. The local monarchists immediately seized on the case as an opportunity for reviving the centuries-old accusation that Jews murdered Christian

[59] Haimson, ' Social Stability in Urban Russia ', pt 1, pp 619-42.
[60] Rogger, ' Was there a Russian Fascism?', p 412.
[61] GDSO, III, 4, pt 2, col 1556; A. S. Tager, *The Decay of Czarism: the Beilis Trial*, Philadelphia 1935, pp 18-20.

children at the Passover, in order to use their blood for ritual purposes. The horrifying aspect of this affair was not so much the lunacy of the Kiev monarchists as the fact that their initiative was upheld and encouraged by the Minister of Justice, I. G. Shcheglovitov, under whose direction the judicial authorities fabricated a case against a Jewish brickmaker, Mendel Beilis, whom they knew to be innocent of the murder. The fabrication of the fictitious evidence took over two years, during which time Russian educated society tensely debated the outcome. Comparisons were made with the Dreyfus case in France a few years previously, though one could hardly say the Russians were as divided as the French had been: the absurdity of the accusation was patent, and even a prominent monarchist, Vasily Shulgin, editor of the conservative newspaper *Kievlyanin* (The Kievan), wrote a leading article exposing the government's chicaneries and urging them to drop the whole corrupt and mismanaged business. The liberals sent a good team of lawyers to defend Beilis, headed by the well-known Jewish advocate O. O. Gruzenberg, and the Kadet parliamentarian V. A. Maklakov. Beilis was acquitted, though in circumstances which suggested that the carefully picked peasant jury did not altogether reject the possibility of ritual murder, even if not committed by the defendant. The Rights were defeated but not routed.[62]

As Hans Rogger has pointed out, the staging of the Beilis trial is hardly to be attributed to a sinister conspiracy alone. Nor is it conceivable that Stolypin would have allowed it to go ahead (the Ministry's interference started in earnest after his death). In retrospect, it looks like a desperate publicity stunt by monarchists worried about their low prestige, and profiting by the post-Stolypin disunity in the Council of Ministers. Shcheglovitov was able to go his own way, encouraged by the Emperor and unrestrained by his colleagues.[63]

The major scandal of these years, however, and the one which did more than anything else to discredit the monarchy, even in the eyes of many staunch monarchists, was that of the unorthodox ' holy man ', Grigory Rasputin. At first sight he looks like a symbol of decadence and obscurantism, of the complete corruption of the imperial court in which he was able to float to the top. And so he

[62] See Tager, ibid, and M. Samuel, *Blood Accusation*, New York 1966.
[63] H. Rogger, 'The Beilis Case: Anti-Semitism and Politics in the Reign of Nicholas II ', *SR*, vol 25 (1966), pp 615-29.

has usually been treated in the history books. The temptation to wallow in the rhetoric of the lower depths in describing him is almost irresistible. And yet the truth is somewhat simpler: Rasputin was only able to play the part he did because of the dispersal of authority which very much deepened after Stolypin's death, and because of the bewildered and unhappy isolation in which the royal couple found themselves.

Let us take the second point first. Nicholas and Alexandra, ever since their wedding in the shadow of Alexander III's death, had always been a retiring couple, happier in their private apartments than in the company of Grand Dukes and Duchesses. They did their duty and gave a certain obligatory minimum of receptions and balls, but they had no real desire to play a leading part in St Petersburg society, and much preferred a few simple but intimate companions like the dumpy Anna Vyrubova, victim of a brief and unhappy marriage with a naval officer. Court social occasions took place much less often than under their predecessors—to such an extent, indeed, that the life of the St Petersburg ' haut monde ' came to take place apart from them, even to some degree in hostility to them.[64] When one writes of the ' court ' during the reign of Nicholas II, one does not mean the high society of the capital, but rather the palace officialdom, whose responsibility was merely for the arrangements on state occasions, and also a few chosen advisers, those whom Nicholas found it easy to talk to, those who did not stand upon ceremony and did not overemphasise painful facts. Nicholas was not devoid of statesmanlike sense, otherwise he would never have supported through their various crises men like Witte and Stolypin, who did not spread butter on the truth. But on the whole such clear-headed asperity in his advisers exhausted him; he preferred the easygoing and the deferential.

Rasputin was not quite that, but then his *point de prise* was Alexandra and her son. Alexei's haemophilia deepened the rift between the imperial couple and St Petersburg society. In her anxious desire both to give him a healthy life and yet also to protect him, she sought recreations for him in the open air, at the seaside, in the

---

[64] Maurice Paléologue, the French ambassador, recalls how at St Petersburg tea-parties, even just after the outbreak of the war, society hostesses would criticise the Emperor and Empress in front of him (*La Russie des Tsars pendant la Guerre*, vol 1, Paris 1922, pp 190-1); see also V. N. Shakhovskoi, *Sic Transit Gloria Mundi*, Paris 1952, p 187.

forests, in the snow, away from the artificial and unhealthy life of the capital. When Rasputin proved able to staunch the painful and dangerous bleeding to which Alexei was liable, she clung to him as to a saviour.[65]

Nicholas seems, initially at least, to have been a little more sceptical about the ' man of God ' now ever more in their midst. But for him too Rasputin fulfilled important personal needs. In the painful dilemma which he had created for himself by granting a constitution, he was constantly looking for the path which would best accord with his own concept of his royal responsibility. The Duma, he felt, had not fulfilled its mission of keeping him in contact with his people. The first two Dumas had been rebellious, and the third, though better in many respects, gave political standing to insufferable power-seekers like Guchkov. And so he came to see in Rasputin a representative of the simple, devout Russian peasant folk from whom he felt aggrievedly the Duma and the bureacracy had cut him off. To Dedyulin, palace commandant, who once expressed doubts about Rasputin's character, Nicholas explained: ' He is just a good, religious, simple-minded Russian. When in trouble or assailed by doubts, I like to have a talk with him, and invariably feel at peace with myself afterwards.'[66]

Nevertheless, the continued presence in the Emperor's immediate entourage of a man who was reputed to be a sectarian caused grave offence to many. It was feared that his homely preaching of an evening might seduce the Tsarevich from the Holy Orthodox church. Even worse, the doctrine of redemption through sin which he had worked out for himself was not just a theory but a way of life, and he was prepared to put it into practice in the company of St Petersburg ladies in search of ' new sensations '. The newspapers began to carry ' confessions ' of women who had sought spiritual purification in his arms. Rasputin found, in fact, that his exclusive position at court laid before him the opportunity of money, of sexual conquest and even, in the circumstances of the time, of political influence. His growing influence, like the obscene dishonesty of the Beilis trial, was a symptom of the breakdown of responsible govern-

[65] In his very moving and usually reliable book, *Nicholas and Alexandra*, London 1968, R. K. Massie describes how haemophilia, and the constant anxiety caused by it, tends to isolate parents and children from society (see especially pp 145-8).

[66] Rodzyanko, ' Krushenie Imperii ', pp 37-8.

ment. Early in 1911, Stolypin, then still fairly firmly in the saddle, was sufficiently worried about Rasputin to have the Holy Synod prepare a report on his sectarian activities, which he submitted to the Emperor. Nicholas in reply merely asked Stolypin to see Rasputin personally, which he did. Rasputin made a passing attempt to hypnotise the Premier, who, however, resisted the force of his personality and told him to clear out back to his native village under pain of prosecution for illegal sectarian activities. It was always one of Rasputin's strengths that he could take a temporary defeat, so he went back to Pokrovskoe with his tail between his legs. But only a few months later, with Stolypin in a much weaker position, he turned up at the Kiev festivities, and from then on hovered around the royal family more or less continuously.[67]

Kokovtsev, once, in February 1912, repeated his predecessor's attempt to warn the Emperor about Rasputin's reputation. Nicholas avoided Kokovtsev's eye, muttered that the whole matter was extremely unpleasant, and promised to take ' decisive measures '. He did nothing, however, though the next week Rasputin came to see Kokovtsev and said he would leave St Petersburg. He actually did so, but this time stayed away for only about a month.[68]

The Duma also took notice of Rasputin's activities. On 26 February 1912 Rodzyanko, as President of the Duma, had a long audience with Nicholas and told him that Rasputin was a member of the Khlyst sect, which was reputed to worship God through erotic frenzy. ' Rasputin ', he declared, ' is a weapon in the hands of the enemies of Russia, who use him to undermine the Church and the Monarchy. No revolutionary propaganda could achieve as much as the presence of Rasputin.' Nicholas was shaken by this admonition, and after a restless night asked Dedyulin to entrust Rodzyanko with the task of examining and reporting on the Holy Synod's files concerning Rasputin.[69]

Meanwhile, however, others members of the Duma were tackling the question more publicly. For Guchkov, of course, this was the perfect issue. By exploiting it he could combine patriotism and outspokenness, and simultaneously vent his hatred of the royal family. Not all leading Octobrists felt the same way: some of them, indeed, were getting very exasperated by Guchkov's maverick activities and warned him that it was irresponsible to make major speeches based

[67] ibid, pp 33-5.   [68] Kokovtsev, *Iz Moego Proshlogo*, vol 2, pp 33-41, 53-4.
[69] Rodzyanko, ' Krushenie Imperii ', pp 42-8.

on gossip or, at any rate, unproven assertions.[70] Guchkov, however, went his own way. In January 1912 his paper, *Golos Moskvy,* had published a long letter by an authority on religious affairs, M. A. Novoselov, giving evidence that Rasputin had belonged to the Khlyst sect, and condemning the Holy Synod for tolerating his corrupting influence in the highest counsels of the Empire. This number of the paper was confiscated, but Guchkov got round that difficulty by submitting an interpellation to the Duma containing the full text of Novoselov's letter, which thus became available to the press in a form which could not be censored. Guchkov's name was even connected with hectographed copies of letters from the Empress to Rasputin, which were circulating in the capital; the letters were written in an exalted and intimate style which could easily be used to insinuate that the Empress herself was one of Rasputin's ardent female followers.[71]

In his speech on the Holy Synod estimates on 9 March, Guchkov brought his campaign to a climax:

I want to say to you, no, I want to shout to you, that the church is in danger, the state is in danger . . . You all know what a terrible drama Russia is living through . . . At the centre of that drama is a mysterious tragi-comic figure, like a shade of the underworld, or a survivor of the darkness of past centuries, a strange figure in the light of the twentieth century . . . How did that man rise to a central position and gain such influence that the supreme bearers of state and church authority bow before him? (Shout from left: Kiss the little hands!) Just think for yourselves, who commands in the highest spheres, who turns the wheel which brings changes in policy and personalities, raises some and casts down others?

Markov 2 shouted out, 'Old wives' tales!' – but the staunch, if mercurial monarchist, Purishkevich, seconded Guchkov: 'Not one revolutionary of the troubled years has perpetrated so much evil in Russia as the recent happenings in the Orthodox Church.'[72]

Such unwonted unanimity, of course, merely strengthened the Empress's conviction that all the politicians in the Duma were against her and were determined to persecute her saviour. Nicholas was also furious – and indeed, whatever the truth of the other accu-

[70] *TsGIAL,* f 669, op 1, d 8, p 166.
[71] S. S. Ol'denburg, *Tsarstvovanie Imperatora Nikolaya II,* Belgrade and Munich 1939-48, vol 2, pp 86-9.
[72] *GDSO,* III, 5, pt 1, cols 73, 583.

sations, there was very little in the charge that Rasputin was making major political appointments and decisions at this stage. At any rate, Nicholas dropped his intention of hearing Rodzyanko report on Rasputin's suspected sectarianism and wrote to Kokovtsev: ' The Duma's behaviour is absolutely outrageous. Guchkov's speech on the Holy Synod estimates was especially disgusting. I shall be very pleased if my displeasure is made known to those gentlemen, one can't always be bowing and smiling to them.'[73]

If then, the Emperor was ever disposed to ponder seriously on Rasputin's bad reputation, he was alienated by the exaggerated attacks in the Duma and by the scurrilous rumours circulating among the public. He retreated into the stone-faced defence of his family's honour and the crown's sacred aureole.

This was not the first time that the Russian royal court had fallen prey to a sectarian of dubious credentials. But it *was* the first time that it had happened before a press free from preliminary censorship (and well able to risk fines in the interest of publicity), before a parliament whose proceedings were public, and before demoralised liberal politicians eager for an issue to restore their prestige.

The mixture was a fateful one. Rasputin began as a symptom of the royal family's isolation from the public; he ended by deepening that isolation to an unbridgeable chasm.

Conclusion

The failure of the Stolypin–Octobrist alliance, the burial or emasculation of reform legislation, the conservative obstructionism of the State Council, the splits in the political parties, the dissensions in the Council of Ministers – all these phenomena brought Russian politics by the summer of 1914 to a point where the already ambiguous constitution of 1905-6 no longer meant very much. The Emperor, the various Ministers, the Duma parties, the nobles, the press and the public were all going their own way. As Rodzyanko reported to the Emperor in December 1913: ' Each minister has his own opinion. For the most part, the cabinet is divided into two parties. The State Council forms a third, the Duma a fourth, and of your own opinion the country remains ignorant. This cannot go on, your Majesty, this is not government, it is anarchy.'[74]

[73] Kokovtsev, *Iz Moego Proshlogo*, vol 2, p 50; Rodzyanko, ' Krushenie Imperii ', pp 52-4.
[74] Rodzyanko, ibid, pp 72-3.

The regular process of legislation through the Duma and State Council was being replaced by the formation of cliques close to the Emperor, intent on impending change and encouraged by the dissipation of authority to use their private advantages. At a lower level, every official felt more able to pursue his own personal interest or obsession. It was only in such circumstances that the rigged trial of Beilis could have been allowed to go ahead or that Rasputin and Meshchersky could have risen to positions of serious influence.

These disintegrative tendencies, already quite clear by 1914, deepened and accelerated during the war, when the dual threat of national defeat and of social revolution made the issues more urgent. After the Progressive Bloc had failed to stop the rot, these divisions led directly to the collapse of the monarchy.

8

Towards the First World War

Stolypin, as is well known, once said: 'Give us twenty years of peace, and you won't recognise today's Russia.' And many historians of early twentieth century, implicitly or explicitly, echo the message by portraying constitutional Russia as a political organism which might have flourished had it not been torn from its roots by the World War.

The earlier chapters have, I hope, shown that the new constitutional system had by 1914 already demonstrated its inability to induce long-term co-operation between government and society or to effect serious reforms. But even if that were not so, it would still not be possible to dismiss the war as an extraneous and fortuitous factor. For in fact it was the very parties most devoted to the constitutional experiment which were also the advocates of policies that helped to involve Russia in the war.

One must understand this as part of the transition to constitutional politics. The Octobrists, the Progressists, the Kadets, and often also the Moderate Rights/Nationalists were seeking a foundation for their own political standing, a foundation other than the autocracy and bureaucracy which they were attacking. And of course they found it in the Russian 'people', a source of authority to which they could always appeal. Persistent reference to the 'people' led them in foreign policy and nationality questions to take up attitudes which were (with the regular exception of certain Kadets) both Russian nationalist and Pan-Slav, and which helped to create the climate of opinion wherein war against Germany and Austria-Hungary appeared an acceptable and indeed necessary instrument of policy. In entering the war in July 1914, the Emperor was acceding to the declared wishes of the constitutionalist parties rather than to the views of the reactionary advisers who often determined his attitude to internal affairs.

The object of this concluding chapter is to show how the Duma parties, from the Nationalists to the Kadets, tried to gain greater influence (as against 'irresponsible' elements) in the conduct of foreign affairs, claiming to do so as a result of their mandate from the 'people'; and how their Russian nationalist and Pan-Slav interpretation of the concept of the 'people' led them into attitudes of hostility to Austria-Hungary and Germany and moved them to attacks on Tsarist diplomacy for being supine and inactive in the face of the Teutonic threat. It would clearly be false to contend that the Duma parties bear a major part of the responsibility for the outbreak of the war: the decisive causes lay elsewhere. But it *is* true that Russia's involvement in it was entirely of a piece with the policies the Duma parties were pursuing in foreign affairs, and with the ideology by which they justified their political existence.

To assert the importance of nationalism for the Duma parties between 1905 and 1914 is to invite comparison with German politics in the same period, especially since Fritz Fischer's work has shown us how the confluence of dynastic-militarist and bourgeois-liberal nationalism imparted the dynamic to German foreign policy which was a decisive factor in bringing about the war.[1] I shall maintain that a similar process had begun in Russia: that there were two types of nationalism, dynastic and constitutional – but that no synthesis of the two had been achieved, so that the two camps regarded each other with continued suspicion until the February revolution overthrew one of them altogether.

A number of similarities may be noted between German and Russian nationalism at this time. In both countries the concept of the 'nation' or 'people' (*Volk/narod*) played a key role in the uneasy transition from absolutism to constitutional politics, which in neither state was complete. It served as a reference point in the search for a firm basis of authority when the old certainties of autocracy were no longer valid. Further, the notion of the people's historical and organic unity was a powerful counter-slogan to the Socialist call to class struggle, which constantly appeared to threaten Germany, and had such devastating effect in Russia in 1905.

That which distinguishes Russian nationalism from German is no less important in analysing its nature.

(i) The large number of non-Russians within the Empire imposed on all who sought to define the term 'Russian nation' the duty of deciding their attitude to these. The Kadets wanted to allow them

[1] F. Fischer, *Germany's Aims in the First World War*, London 1967 (translated from the German), pp 3-20.

autonomy within a multi-national Empire; the Rights, at the other extreme, excluded all non-Russians (often all non-Great Russians) from the concept until such time as they had properly Russianised themselves: until then their national culture must be regarded with extreme suspicion and limited as far as possible. Either way, the Russian situation was completely different from that of the Germans, whose Empire was composed almost entirely of ethnic Germans, but saw many of their fellow countrymen living abroad under foreign rule. To this extent, German nationalism had a greater tendency to be expansive and absorptive.

(ii) For Russia the equivalent of the *Auslandsdeutschen* were the Slav nationalities living outside the Empire. They, however, offered a much less satisfactory occasion for aggressive nationalist propaganda. For one thing, they were not Russian: they had languages, cultures, religions and traditions that were often very different from Russia's (and from each other's). In particular, the Poles, undeniably Slav, but strongly attached to Roman Catholicism, were an irreducible embarrassment to the Pan-Slavs. These nations were hardly all to be assimiliated into one national community. For that reason Pan-Slavism has often been difficult to distinguish from simple Great Russian nationalism, and always tends to deteriorate into it.

(iii) Russia had recently been defeated in a major war, which had destroyed her navy and exposed the shortcomings of her army. Russian foreign policy for most of this period was therefore conducted from a position of weakness.

(iv) Russia's social structure gave Russian nationalism a different quality from the German. In Germany far more peasants were small property-owners, the proportion of urban population was much higher, and primary education had for some time been universal. For these reasons the consciousness of what nationality meant was much more widely diffused than in Russia. The life of the Russian peasant, oriented towards commune and village, and his lack of literacy, made his understanding of what a 'nation' meant very vague, unless he lived in the Jewish Pale or some other region where he would meet foreigners frequently. The politician, of whatever party, who claimed to be speaking for the 'Russian people' in national questions (and few did not, at one time or another), was ignoring or forgetting this. No member of the Provisional Government in 1917 really understood why the 'peasants in uniform' were abandoning the war and making for home.

The two poles in Russian nationalism can be represented by the Kadets, at one extreme, and by the Rights at the other.

The Kadets had worked with some of the non-Russian national revolutionary movements in 1904-5, and their party programme always envisaged a wide measure of autonomy for the constituent nationalities, especially the Poles and Finns.[2] This was the issue on which they first broke with the future Octobrists in 1905. Their interest in national questions did not go further than this in the years of revolution, but with the establishment of the 3rd June system, they met the challenge of an aggressive official nationalism by formulating their own constitutional brand. The man who enunciated it most clearly, though also provocatively, was P. B. Struve, in the January 1908 issue of the journal *Russkaya Mysl* (Russian Thought). Struve was always on the right wing of the Kadets, and is certainly not to be taken as a typical spokesman of the party: but he was the profoundest and perhaps the clearest thinker among them, and was not afraid to pursue his reflections through to their implications. That is why his statement of the new constitutional nationalism is of particular value to us.

Struve's main thesis was that the constitutionalists could no longer afford grandly to ignore the field of foreign affairs as irrelevant to the nation's real concerns. A future ' great Russia ' (he deliberately quoted Stolypin) would need to be a constitutional state, but certainly also a great world power.

Russia's true mission, the mission her people would recognise, was, Struve asserted, in the Balkans:

Our Far Eastern policy was the logical culmination of the whole foreign policy of Alexander III, when *reactionary* Russia, from lack of true statesmanship, turned away from the Near East. The main fallacy of the foreign policy which led us to Tsushima and Portsmouth was that it transferred its centre of gravity to a region inaccessible to the real influence of Russian culture.

. . . Now it is time to recognise that for the creation of a Great Russia there is only one road: to direct all our forces to the area which is genuinely open to the influence of Russian culture. That area is *the whole Black Sea basin*: that is, all the European and Asian countries bordering on the Black Sea.[3]

[2] Vodovozov, *Sbornik Programm Politicheskikh Partii*, vol 1, pp 43-4.
[3] *Russkaya Mysl'*, 1908, no 1, pp 144-6 (all italics in the original).

Austria, Struve warned, had just adopted universal suffrage, and was ready to expand into the Balkans on the more healthy basis this would afford. But Russia could forestall her. Russia had racial, religious, cultural and economic ties with the peoples around the Black Sea, such as made the area a natural one of expansion for her. She had a constitution, which would be a basis for her people's involvement, and an alliance with Britain and France, on which such expansion could rest internationally. But in order that Russia might fulfil her mission, her statesmen must sincerely strive to make the new constitutional system work; and also the radicals must abandon their old ' anti-state ' spirit, and learn the necessity of ' state discipline '.[4]

Even allowing for the provocative intent of Struve's article, its language is striking. In its basic preoccupations as in its repeated use of words such as ' healthy ', ' creative ', ' organism ', ' power ', ' might ', it reflects the projection of Darwinism on to international relations which played such a large part in German political thought in the late nineteenth century. His ideas have much in common with those of the German National Liberals from the unification of Germany to the First World War. It is no accident that he compares the contemporary Russian situation with the Prussian constitutional crisis of the 1860s, which was the road by which Bismarck came to power and began the unification of the German state. In Germany, Struve comments,

The victory of the government was neither a humiliation of the people nor a contravention of the rule of law. The greatness of Bismarck as a statesman was indeed that he never confused the state with individuals, whoever they were. Government and people were reconciled on the basis of the realisation of the national idea, and united Germany, affirming her external might, has been able to combine its historical traditions with its new state institutions on the democratic basis of universal suffrage.

Like Guchkov, Struve sometimes hoped that Stolypin might become the Russian Bismarck.

Internally, Struve felt the Russian Empire should become a free multi-national state like the U.S.A. Russia had the makings of such a state, as the original Slav nucleus had assimilated many other racial elements:

[4] ibid, pp 146-57; the whole article is reprinted in Struve's collections of essays published under the title *Patriotica*, SPB 1911.

Not only the national flesh, but the national soul and culture have with great nations always been composed of many strains, the fruit of a complex and protracted assimilatory process. The spirit and the policies of the introverted nationalism which is in the ascendant at the moment strive to hinder and curtail this process of assimilatory growth, by which the Russian nationality and Russian culture have been and are still being created. For the Russian nation, like the American, is still evolving. It is, as the Americans says of themselves, 'still in the making'.

The ideal to which the Russian nationality in Russia should aspire must, I am profoundly convinced, be the free and organic hegemony which the Anglo-Saxon element has secured for itself in the U.S.A. and in the British Empire.

This kind of national assimilation could not be applied to the Poles and Finns, fully formed nations in their own right, which must go their own way. But for all other nationalities in the Empire, communion with Russian culture would mean progress and hence would be quite acceptable. Official, narrow-minded, repressive nationalism, on the other hand, would only alienate them and hence weaken the Empire.[5]

The British Empire was a better analogy for what Struve had in mind than the U.S.A., where most of the assimilated nationalities had been voluntary immigrants. And, indeed, Struve's views sound like those of an enlightened colonial administrator in the era of Milner and Curzon. His strident, Darwinist language would not have been used, or even approved, by most Kadets, but they shared his viewpoint on essentials: on the necessity for a non-repressive policy towards the internal nationalities, encouraging them to develop their own culture within the framework of the Empire, and on the close link between the constitution and the possibility of a new and healthier type of Russian patriotism. Many Kadets would even have accepted his call for a more active Russian policy in the Balkans, though here official Kadet policy, expounded regularly by Milyukov in leading articles in *Rech,* made the maintenance of international peace an overriding aim.

At the opposite pole from the views of the Kadets stood those of the extreme Right. They were the inheritors of the official nationalism of Nicholas I and Alexander III, and for them nationalism was linked in an indissoluble trinity with autocracy and the Ortho-

[5] *Russkaya Mysl¹*, 1910, no 6, pp 168-78.

dox faith. For them, the ' people ' existed as a community only in
its relationship of devotion to the church and the Tsar. Autocracy
led, the church bound the people together: these were the forces
which had created Russia and would ensure her survival and greatness in the future. Europe might be more advanced and more
cultured, but lacked the spirit of brotherhood, faith and unity which
the Russians had preserved (and here the ideology of the Right
borrowed from the original Slavophiles of the 1830s and 1840s).
Foreigners were a threat, seeking to undermine this unity. This was
especially true of the Jews, who had long formed a fifth column
inside the Empire and had recently given birth to another poisonous
breed, the socialists. The aims of national policy must be to defeat
these threats and weaken non-Russian cultures, so that all inhabitants of the Empire might become good Russians. As far as foreign
policy was concerned, Russia must be very cautious, as unconsidered
military adventures would open the way to revolution at home.

     This ideology of the Right had no thinker as brilliant and per-
suasive as Struve to clarify it. Perhaps its most cogent exposition
in these years was the celebrated memorandum which Durnovo
submitted to the Tsar in February 1914, warning against involvement in a war with Germany. The people, he felt, unless bound
together by autocracy and Orthodoxy, were not at all inherently
patriotic, but on the contrary selfish and susceptible to socialist
propaganda:

The peasant dreams of obtaining a gratuitous share of somebody else's
land; the workman of getting hold of the entire capital and profits of
the manufacturer. Beyond this, they have no aspirations. If these
slogans are scattered among the populace, and the government permits
agitation on these lines, Russia will be flung into anarchy such as she
suffered in the unforgettable period of troubles in 1905-6.

     Durnovo believed that war between Britain and Germany was
inevitable, but that Russia had no need to be drawn in on Britain's
side, for she had no essential conflicts of interest with Germany.
Indeed a war between Russia and Germany would be profoundly
injurious to both, since it would undermine the ' conservative principle ', of which the two powers were ' the only two reliable bul-
warks '. It would lead to a social revolution in the defeated country
which would rapidly spread to the victor. Nor would such a

revolution in Russia long be led by the Duma parties, for they would soon lose control, and total anarchy would ensue:

The trouble will start with the blaming of the government for all misfortunes. In the legislative institutions a bitter campaign will begin against the government, followed by revolutionary agitation throughout the country, with socialist slogans, capable of arousing and rallying the masses. They will start with the division of the land, and follow it up with a division of all valuables and property. The defeated army, having lost all its dependable men, and carried away by the tide of primitive peasant desire for land, will find itself too demoralised to serve as a bulwark for law and order. The legislative institutions and the intellectual opposition parties, lacking real authority in the eyes of the people, will be powerless to stem the popular tide aroused by themselves, and Russia will be flung into hopeless anarchy, whose outcome cannot be foreseen.[6]

One cannot deny the perceptiveness of this analysis, and it shows up the thinking of the Duma majority parties in rather stark light.

Between these two poles of nationalist thinking there were many intermediate positions, consistent and inconsistent. The mass of nondescript deputies who became Octobrists and Moderate Rights at the opening of the Third Duma were capable of moods of Struvian optimism, and in particular most of them supported the idea of an active policy in the Balkans; on the other hand, they inclined towards the extreme Right on questions of policy towards the constituent nationalities of the Empire, as we have seen in examining the Finnish and Western Zemstvo issues. Stolypin's government was in much the same position: not of itself anti-Semitic, but supporting anti-Semitic movements where politically expedient, using Struvian patriotism for rhetorical purposes while pursuing a repressive policy towards the non-Russian nationalities.

Neo-Slavism

The constitutional nationalism of the Duma parties brought new wine to the old bottle of Pan-Slavism. The main difficulty of the old Pan-Slavs of the 1860s and 1870s had been to reconcile the Tsarist government with the democratic revolutionaries of the Balkans. But after 1905, with a parliament in Russia acting as the

[6] F. A. Golder, *Documents of Russian History, 1914-1917*, New York 1927, pp 20-2.

voice of public opinion in government affairs, the gap seemed not so difficult to bridge. Prince Evgeny Trubetskoi summed up the new mood in an article in the *Moskovsky Ezhenedelnik* (Moscow Weekly) in May 1908:

We must convince the Slav peoples that we have no intention of encroaching on their individuality, and that unlike the Slavophiles [*sic*] we are ready to respect their distinctive spiritual life. In the Balkans Russia has assumed the mission of emancipator of the brother races. At home she has been an oppressor, and has indeed become abhorrent to the Slav peoples whom she has freed. They have feared the fate of Poland and have turned away from us. That is the main reason for the mistrust towards us so deeply imbued in the Austrian nationalities. This abyss we must bridge, whatever the cost. That is essential for the security of our western frontiers.

The acid test, as he added, was Poland:

In the name of the feeling of national honour and love of country, we must be full of respect for the Poles and for every other nationality. We must make the Poles citizens of our great empire and grant them the same rights as Russian citizens, the right to be taught and administered in one's own language, the right of local self-government and freedom of religion.[7]

Even the Polish problem did not seem quite so formidable after 1905. Under Roman Dmowski, the Polish National Democrats worked for reconciliation with Russia, and, despite the Octobrists' coolness, hoped to achieve a measure of autonomy for Poland. The passage of a new law in Prussian Poland, simplifying the expropriation of Poles in favour of Germans in the provinces of Posen and West Prussia, also inclined the Poles to regard Germany as the number one enemy and to look with favour on the huge eastern empire which already brought them considerable economic advantages.[8]

At the same time, as we have seen from Struve's article, Pan-Slav ideals played an important part in the revival of foreign policy interests among Russian radicals. Furthermore, the interests of Russian trade, much of which left from the port of Odessa and sailed through the Black Sea and the Straits, required the right to

[7] A. Fischel, *Der Panslawismus bis zum Weltkrieg*, Stuttgart 1919, pp 516-17.
[8] E. Chmielewski, *The Polish Question in the Russian State Duma*, Knoxville 1970, passim.

send Russian warships through the Straits and a greater influence over the states commanding the Black Sea coast. The ultimate dream was to replace the half moon with the cross on Hagia Sophia in Constantinople, though few allowed their imaginations to run quite so far.

In the other Slav countries, too, conditions were favourable to a revival of Pan-Slavism. The accession of the Karadjordjević dynasty in Serbia had brought that country towards a pro-Russian stance. In the Austrian half of the Hapsburg monarchy, the introduction of universal suffrage in 1907 created a Slav majority (albeit a very small one) in the Reichsrat in Vienna, and seemed to bring nearer the day when the realm of the Hapsburgs might evolve into a Slav empire. At the same time, the rise of the Young Czechs in Bohemia and Moravia, under the leadership of Karel Kramář, meant that Czech politics were now dominated by a pro-Russian, anti-German party.[9]

There were many reasons, then, why new Pan-Slav initiatives should have been ripening as revolution died down in Russia after 1905. In April 1908 a Society for Slav Culture was opened in Moscow, and a Society for Slav Scholarship in St Petersburg. Their aim was an exchange of Slav literatures and scholarly activities such as would help the separate Slav stems to appreciate the full richness and variety of their common traditions. Among the founder members of these groups were Milyukov, Struve and Maklakov from the Kadets, Stakhovich, N. N. Lvov, M. M. Fedorov and Shipov form the Progressists, and Guchkov, Khomyakov and Kapustin from the Octobrists. A Society for Slav Mutuality (Obshchestvo Slavyanskoi Vzaimnosti) was founded in St Petersburg somewhat later, under the Rightist General V. I. Volodimerov.[10]

On the initiative of Volodimerov and Kramář, a Slav Congress was held in Prague in July 1908, with the encouragement of Stolypin's government. Its aim was to continue the work of the Moscow and St Petersburg Societies and popularise it among the other Slav nationalities. To distinguish the movement from the old Pan-Slavism, a new word was coined, Neo-Slavism. The attendance on

[9] A. J. May, *The Hapsburg Monarchy, 1867-1914*, Cambridge, Mass., 1960, pp 329, 415; Z. A. B. Zeman, *The Break-Up of the Habsburg Empire*, London 1961, pp 14-17.
[10] *Rech'*, 4 April 1908; *NV*, 4 April 1908; Fischel, *Der Panslawismus*, pp 515-16.

the Russian side was rather disappointing: neither Milyukov nor Guchkov attended, Milyukov because he feared, after meeting Kramář, that the whole movement was going to take on an overtly right-wing and semi-official character.[11] The Russian delegation was headed by Count V. A. Bobrinsky, of the Moderate Rights, and General Volodimerov, and included Maklakov from the Kadets and N. N. Lvov from the Progressists.[12]

The Congress concentrated on cultural and economic affairs, youth movements and tourism, and seemed inclined to accept that no single Slav state could ever be created. On the vital Polish-Russian issue the results achieved were rather ambiguous. On the one hand Dmowski declared: 'A regenerated Russia, based on the recognition of the rights of other nations and, at the same time, of the Poles, will be a state necessary not only for the Russian people, but also for the Polish people and for the whole of humanity.' On the other hand, he also wanted an explicit recognition by the Russians of Poland's right to a ' free national development ', while Bobrinsky in return exhorted him to recognise ' the principle of the Russian state and the single Russian nation '.[13]

Whatever may have been the hopes of a Russo-Polish reconciliation after the Prague Congress, they were very soon dashed by the Russian government's declared intention to create anti-Polish zemstvos in Lithuania, Belorussia and the Right-Bank Ukraine, and also to detach the region of Kholm (Chełm) from the Congress Kingdom and make it an additional province of Russia.[14] The Austrian annexation of Bosnia-Herzegovina in October 1908 was another bitter blow to Neo-Slavism, partly because of the Bulgarian declaration of independence, a twin breach of the Treaty of Berlin committed in complicity with Austria, and partly because most of the Austrian Slavs voted *for* the annexation (which increased the Slav majority in the Viennese parliament), but mainly because Russia was seen to be powerless to help her Slav brothers. Slav unity, in fact, showed itself to be strictly limited to certain fields, a doctrine only honoured when not overshadowed by other, more important

[11] Milyukov, *Vospominaniya*, vol 2, p 45.
[12] P. N. Korablev, *Slav¹yanskii S¹¹ezd v Prage 1908g*, SPB 1908, pp 4-5.
[13] Fischel, *Der Panslawismus*, pp 518-35; Korablev, *Slav¹yanskii S¹¹ezd*, pp 4-6, 26, 31-2, 38.
[14] Chmielewski, *The Polish Question*, pp 117-20.

interests. A further congress was held in Sofia (1910), but Neo-Slavism wilted until its revival in the First Balkan War.[15]

The importance of Neo-Slavism was neither in its organisation nor in its activities, which led almost to nothing. Rather it was in the confidence which it gave to Serb nationalism in the years leading up to 1914, and in the Slav sentiment which coloured the language of the Duma majority parties and of some members of the Russian diplomatic corps. These certainly helped to produce the Balkan crisis of July 1914, though they would not of themselves have turned it into a World War.

The Duma and foreign policy

It was always the aim of the Duma majority parties, and particularly the Octobrists, to gain greater influence over the conduct of foreign affairs. In a sense, it is paradoxical that this was so, since according to Article 12 of the Fundamental Laws, the conduct of foreign affairs remained the prerogative of the Emperor and of his appointed Ministers. But foreign affairs were analogous to the military field. The Duma had no special committee studying international relations, but used the annual Foreign Ministry credits to debate the government's foreign policy. They aimed to make it the accepted custom that the Duma should be informed and consulted over foreign affairs. This was an integral part of the 'constitutional offensive' which the Octobrists led. Behind their efforts, we sense, as in the military field, the anxious question: who has the power, and, above all, who bears the *responsibility* for the conduct of foreign affairs? Is it the cabinet, or the 'irresponsible' court camarilla? The Octobrists and Kadets took care, in their criticisms of Russian diplomacy, to make it clear that the weaknesses they were attacking sprang from the Foreign Ministry's anomalous position of being (like the War and Navy Ministries) not subordinate to the Council of Ministers, and hence open to irresponsible influences. Speaking in the debate following Izvolsky's first foreign policy statement in the Duma (on the establishment of a mission in Tokyo), Milyukov declared:

The fraction of the People's Freedom has listened with profound satisfaction to the words of the Foreign Minister and deems it fitting to

[15] Fischel, *Der Panslawismus*, pp 538-81; H. Kohn *Panslavism, its History and Ideology*, New York 1960 edition, pp 250-4.

welcome his first appearance before the country's representative body with an account of the problems of Russian foreign policy. There can be no doubt that at the present moment, after an unsuccessful war . . . the Government particularly needs to lean upon public opinion in its coming diplomatic measures, which will have to some extent to compensate for our temporary material weakness . . . We believe that further appearances of this kind by the Minister before this assembly will save the country in future from the interference of irresponsible diplomats in the regular activity of his department.[16]

The Duma centre parties and many newspapers (including *Novoe Vremya*) began to maintain that the Foreign Ministry was no longer capable of meeting the demands made on Russian diplomacy in the modern age, and demanded reforms in its structure. The distribution of representatives abroad was outdated: for example, while Ministers were still sent to all the individual royal courts of the German Empire, there was only one diplomatic mission in the whole of Latin America. Furthermore, the foreign service was in the habit of appointing ambassadors to overseas posts for very long periods, during which they lost touch with Russia and with public opinion at home, so that their world was bound by the social life of the capital to which they were accredited and by the despatches from the Pevchesky Most. In March 1909, after the Bosnian débâcle, *Novoe Vremya* attacked by name most of Russia's leading ambassadors abroad – Benkendorf (London), Nelidov (Paris), Osten-Zaken (Berlin), Urusov (Vienna), Dolgoruky (Rome), Zinoviev (Constantinople) – as ' anachronisms in the new Russia, with her representative system and her strong Slav consciousness '. By failing to make foreign powers conscious of the strength of Russian sentiment, they had materially contributed to their country's recent humiliations.[17]

Reform proposals widely discussed in the newspapers included:
(i) the closure of missions which had outlived their usefulness, and their replacement by new missions in places where Russia's interests urgently required to be represented;

---

[16] *GDSO*, III, 1, pt 2, cols 119-20.
[17] *NV*, 16 March 1909; *Novoe Vremya*, in its capacity as a semi-official (and widely quoted) St Petersburg daily, was giving hospitality to both constitutional and dynastic nationalists at this time. Cf. the article by Men'shikov of 7 October 1908, quoted below, p 231.

  (ii) the creation of a Foreign Office Press Department to keep the press better informed and to enlist its aid in new undertakings;

  (iii) adaptation of the consular services for regular help to Russian trade, for example, through reports on the state of local markets, help in advertising Russian goods, negotiating trade agreements, etc;

  (iv) regular and more frequent transfers of diplomatic personnel in home and overseas posts;

  (v) stricter educational requirements for entry into the diplomatic service.[18]

Izvolsky as Foreign Minister took rather an ambiguous stand towards the Duma. He had the reputation of being a liberal, and indeed an admirer of the British constitutional monarchy, and certainly he wanted the Duma's support. For this purpose he obtained the Emperor's permission to report substantively on foreign policy during the debate on the Foreign Ministry estimates in 1908 and 1909. However, it seems probable that he courted the Duma in order to strengthen his own position vis-à-vis Stolypin and the rest of the Council of Ministers. He wanted, in fact, to retain his semi-independence as a Minister. When the Council of Ministers asked him to explain what had happened at his conversation with the Austrian Foreign Minister, Aerenthal, at Buchlau, he declined to do so, saying that he could not give any account without first receiving permission from the Emperor ' as the Supreme and only authority over all our foreign policy '.[19] His successor, Sazonov, was Stolypin's son-in-law, and kept in much closer contact with the cabinet; he also abandoned the experiment of discussing foreign policy with the Duma until the tense atmosphere surrounding the Balkan Wars moved the government once again to seek the Duma's express support for its diplomacy.

The Bosnian crisis

The Russian defeat in the Japanese War was followed by a reorientation in her foreign policy, towards an entente with Britain

[18] I. V. Bestuzhev, *Bor'ba v Rossii po Voprosam Vneshnei Politiki, 1906-10gg*, M 1961, pp 60-1. This is an abstract made by Bestuzhev of the most important reform proposals formulated in *Rech'*, *Golos Moskvy* and *Novoe Vremya* between June 1907 and September 1910.

[19] *Kokovtsev, Iz Moego Proshlogo*, vol 1, pp 331-6.

and a renewed interest in the Balkans, which, as we have seen, met with the whole-hearted approval of the Duma majority parties. This reorientation was not, however, universally greeted in ruling circles. There were those, on the right wing of the Duma and State Council, in diplomatic and military circles, and among the royal family, who felt that closer ties with constitutional Britain and republican France would undermine monarchical solidarity. The right wing papers *Zemshchina, Russkoe Znamya* and *Grazhdanin* warned against too close an involvement in Balkan affairs, against sentimental attachments to Slav ' brothers ', who had too often in the past bit the hand that fed them. Among the most influential advocates of a rapprochement with Germany were, apart from Durnovo, Goremykin and Shvanebakh in the State Council, Krivoshein, Shcheglovitov, Rukhlov and Kasso in the Council of Ministers, most of the ambassadors attacked in *Novoe Vremya,* many of the Grand Dukes, some of the General Staff, and of course the Empress and Rasputin.[20] The Emperor was naturally susceptible to these influences, and indeed they momentarily took the upper hand when he met the Kaiser Wilhelm at Björkö in 1905, but the agreement signed there was speedily repudiated by the Foreign Ministers of both countries.

Up to the autumn of 1908, the Duma parties, from the Moderate Rights to the Kadets, shared the aims of Izvolsky: to strengthen ties with the Balkan nations, prepare for the collapse of the Ottoman Empire, and try to improve Russia's position on the Black Sea and in the Straits without alienating Austria, indeed if possible in cooperation with her. Izvolsky's meeting with Aerenthal at Buchlau, at which he probably agreed to an Austrian annexation of Bosnia and Herzegovina in return for Austrian support in seeking an international agreement that Russia should send warships through the Straits, was an attempt in just this direction. However, Aerenthal's ruthless shrewdness and the undocumented confusion of the conversations combined to convert what should have been mutual backscratching into a provocative unilateral step by Austria. On 23 September/6 October 1908 the Austrian government announced that

[20] *Bestuzhev, Bor'ba v Rossii*, p 45; *The Memoirs of Alexander Izvolsky,* London 1920, p 285; G. Louis, *Les Carnets,* Paris 1926, vol 1, pp 30-1, 62; W. M. Carlgren, *Iswolski und Aerenthal vor bosnischen Annexionskrise: Russische und Österreichisch-Ungarische Balkanpolitik,* Uppsala 1955, pp 89-91.

it was annexing the provinces of Bosnia and Herzegovina, which hitherto it had only administered provisionally.

The effect in Russia was sensational. Not only had Izvolsky been tricked, but he had not informed anyone in St Petersburg of the kind of negotiations he was conducting. Stolypin was furious and had a long and anxious interview with the Emperor, who claimed *not* to have approved Izvolsky's step.[21] Newspaper comment was at first rather restrained, since it was clear Russia could not go to war over the matter, and anyway Izvolsky, after his own fashion, had been attempting exactly what the majority parties thought right. As time went by, however, and Austria's determination became clearer, the tone of press comment became more unequivocally anti-Austrian. It also began to take up the theme of the ' irresponsibility ' of Russian diplomacy. Izvolsky, who had earlier been something of a hero to the Duma, now suddenly became a symbol of the old-fashioned Russian diplomats who refused to take the public into their confidence and thereby forfeited the weight which public opinion could give to their démarches. In the debate on the Foreign Ministry estimates on 12 December 1908, Guchkov protested:

It is to be regretted that the State Duma is the last of the European parliaments to which representatives of the executive have reported on their activities in the sphere of foreign policy . . . After all, the worth of all your diplomatic démarches, notes, circulars and ultimata depends on how much the people's consciousness, the people's will, stands behind them. And when you have to raise your demands and have recourse to ultimata, to the final sanction – it is to us you will come for your war credits, you will need our blood and that of our brothers and sons, you will come for money and manpower, and we shall give you them. But we can give you yet more: the pledge of victory, the enthusiasm without which struggle and victory are impossible. And it is for this reason that you should from the outset initiate us into the complex of problems which you are dealing with . . . Fear of the free expression of public opinion, of the free manifestation of popular feeling, fear of the independent word, remains as a relic of the old order.[22]

Here, for the first time, the shadow looms up, at any rate in Guchkov's imagination, of the ' dark forces ' which eight years later so many felt were undermining Russia's war effort.

[21] Kokovtsev, *Iz Moego Proshlogo*, vol 1, pp 331-6. The events in Europe are here given in both Old Style and New Style dates.
[22] *GDSO*, iii, 2, pt 1, cols 2763-7.

The parties differed on the best way out of the Bosnian situation. For the Kadets, *Rech* (which represented Milyukov rather than the party as a whole) rejected the idea of compensation in the Straits as unworthy and irrelevant. The states which really needed compensation were the Balkan Slav states and Turkey herself. The paper laid emphasis on the need to get the European powers to agree on revision of the Berlin Treaty such as would restore equilibrium to the Balkans. In the Duma, Milyukov said that the most Russia could achieve was autonomous status for Bosnia-Herzegovina inside the Hapsburg Empire, guaranteed by a European conference. To refuse to recognise the annexation would be a grave mistake, as Russia could not back up such a refusal by military means.[23]

Novoe Vremya, more inclined to Pan-Slav sentiment, felt that the Austrian provocation should be used as an opportunity to forge the South Slavs into an alliance: ' Russia could not receive better and fuller compensation than by using the Bosnian incident for the final rallying of all the South Slavs.'[24]

The Rights, on the other hand, took the view that Russia must concentrate first of all on suppressing revolution at home, and could not afford to pursue any kind of enterprising foreign policy. In the Duma Purishkevich attacked those who tagged along with public opinion, especially as preached by the Kadets, who, he said, had now discovered that their revolutionary tactics had failed and were hastily donning the mask of Neo-Slavism. He warned against being led into embroilments with Germany by tempting slogans while Russia still had so much to do at home. He did, however, feel that a war against Austria was inevitable sooner or later – which, of course, made it all the more important to strengthen the country internally before it came.[25] Menshikov in *Novoe Vremya* took up a similar stand. While Russia was weakened by revolutionaries at home and by Jews abroad, he said, her foreign policy ' could not be anything other than distasteful '. ' Russia is not ready for war. But even if she were, she would not in the least be obliged to fight for Serbia. That we once helped Serbia to free herself does not oblige us to assume an indefinite responsibility for her fate.'[26]

Nearly six months passed before the crisis was settled, during

[23] ibid, col 2691; *Rech*[1], 24, 27 September, 15 October, 30 November, 5 December 1908.
[24] *NV*, 26 September 1908.   [25] *GDSO*, iii, 2, pt 1, cols 2652-8.
[26] *NV*, 7 October 1908.

which time both the Austrians and the Serbs took a very truculent attitude and mobilised their armies. The end of the crisis was brought about by a sharp German note to Russia, of 8/21 March 1909. The Russians capitulated and recognised the annexation, without any compensation.

For Russian public opinion and the Duma majority parties the course of the crisis showed that Austria was now determined to pursue an aggressive policy in the Balkans, which was both a threat to the Slavs and a danger to European peace. Solidarity with the Slavs was therefore not just a matter of Slav sentiment but essential to the preservation of peace. *Rech* called for a strengthening of ties with Britain and France and accused Austria of ' a crime before all Europe '.[27] *Novoe Vremya* drew attention to Germany's role, suspecting that the Austrian belligerence was only part of a larger German scheme.

Germany aims to advance in the Balkans right up to the Aegean, and then into Asia Minor and Persia. Russia has the choice either to submit to this advance or to resist it. In the first eventuality she will be surrounded by Germany from the west and south. In the second, she must strengthen and broaden her agreements with Britain and France. The choice is clear. There can be no two opinions about our final decision.[28]

This was the first time the Russian press had written in such a tone about Germany, though it was to become familiar four to five years later.

The Duma was also bitter about the conduct of Russian diplomacy. Milyukov characterised Izvolsky's foreign policy as ' a series of impressive gestures, regularly followed by exceedingly unimpressive retreats '.[29] *Novoe Vremya* drew the parallel with the Naval Ministry in an article entitled 'A Diplomatic Tsushima ',[30] while *Golos Moskvy,* in a philippic which bore the imprint of Guchkov's style, considered the wider implications of the Foreign Ministry's failure:

The basic reason for the persistent degradation and external dishonour of Russia is to be found, of course, in what remained unchanged after the radical reforms carried out in the aftermath of the Manchurian disaster. In that time Russia has been transformed from an absolutist

[27] *Rech*[1], 8 March 1909.   [28] *NV*, 18 March 1909.
[29] *GDSO,* III, 3, pt 2, col 2761.   [30] *NV*, 16 March 1909.

state into a constitutional one. But the reforms of her internal administration have not had the slightest effect on the War, Naval and diplomatic departments, whose disorganisation and whose failures had most clearly demonstrated to public opinion the historical necessity of general reforms. The War, Naval and Foreign Ministries were not included in the unified cabinet which was supposed to co-ordinate as far as possible the government's general policy with the needs of Russia and with the demands of patriotic public opinion. The reforms proclaimed from the throne bypassed these spheres, where under the new constitutional flag the old pre-reform regime continues in force. What else could it conceivably produce but a repetition of the Manchurian 'triumphs'? . . .

Yes, we are going through new humiliations, but let Russia's enemies not hasten to celebrate their victory . . . It is not the flabby indolence of official Russia, but the indignant patriotism of the whole Russian people, its readiness to lay down its life for its friends, that foreign, and indeed our own diplomats must reckon with. Taking our stand on this disregarded spiritual strength of the Russian people, we may boldly cry in our enemies' faces: ' Russia has not yet fallen, she will rise again!'[31]

What the Bosnian crisis crystallised for Russian public opinion and for the Duma parties was
  (i) that Austria was determined to humiliate or absorb the Slavs of the Balkans;
  (ii) that Germany was prepared to give her more or less a blank cheque to pursue this policy;
  (iii) that Russian diplomacy, still influenced by ' irresponsible ' circles, could only be furtive and vacillating, and was bound to lead the country to international humiliation.

The Balkan wars

With some hesitations, the Russian Foreign Ministry began to prepare the way for an alliance of the Balkan states. Two diplomats in particular, Gartvig in Belgrade, and Neklyudov in Sofia, worked for such an alliance with a Pan-Slav zeal which exceeded their instructions: for, though anxious to strengthen the Balkan states, neither Izvolsky nor his successor, Sazonov, wished to provoke Austria into any step which might endanger European peace.[32]

[31] *GM*, 17 March 1909.
[32] Bestuzhev, *Bor'ba v Rossii*, pp 336-54; E. C. Thaden, *Russia and the Balkan Alliance, 1911-12*, Pennsylvania 1965, pp 1925.

The outbreak of a war between Turkey and Italy in September 1911 much increased the military prospects of an alliance of the Balkan states directed against Turkey. And in fact, in the following twelve months, with the energetic help of Gartvig and Neklyudov, a military alliance was pieced together between Serbia, Bulgaria, Greece and Montenegro. In the summer of 1912 Guchkov visited Sofia and Belgrade as a representative of public opinion, and encouraged the ripening plans for the alliance: one can imagine him confirming the impression nourished by Gartvig that the caution of official Russia was not to be taken too seriously, and that the mass of the Russian people would be behind their Slav brothers in a war against Turkey.[33] The four powers mobilised their armies in September 1912 and declared war on Turkey in the following month.

The Balkan War produced much more serious rifts than the Bosnian crisis between public opinion and the government. Many social organisations immediately declared their support for the cause of Slavdom. The Russian Red Cross, of which Guchkov was the chairman, announced on 18 September 1912, even before the declarations of war, that it would establish field hospitals in Serbia, Bulgaria, Montenegro and Greece, manned by Russian volunteers. The Slav Philanthropic Society in St Petersburg, one of the old Pan-Slav organisations, began collections in aid of the Balkan nations. The National Club (organised by the Duma Nationalist fraction), the Slav Philanthropic Society and other groups held meetings at which members of the Duma (especially Octobrists and Nationalists) spoke. Some of the gatherings ended with calls to ' put the cross on St Sophia '. The government, alarmed at these unlicensed Pan-Slav outbursts, began to impose restrictions on such meetings, even when addressed by the most respectable public figures, requiring that no attacks should be permitted on the Austrian government, nor any appeals for warlike action.[34] The Foreign Ministry, for its own part,

[33] Thaden, ibid, p 112; E. C. Helmreich, *The Diplomacy of the Balkan Wars, 1912-13*, Cambridge, Mass., 1938, pp 106-7.
[34] I. V. Bestuzhev, ' Bor'ba v Rossii po Voprosam Vneshnei Politiki nakanune Pervoi Mirovoi Voiny, 1910-1914gg ', *Ist. Zap.*, vol 75, p 60; *Rech'*, 5, 23, 28 October, 15 November 1912; *GM*, 28, 29 October 1912; The Emperor wrote on this agitation: ' In Russia no decent person wants war for the sake of the Slavs; only the wretched Jewish newspapers, with Guchkov and his " Novoe Vremya " [sic] at their head, write that public opinion is stirred – it is a lie and a calumny.' (*Letters of Tsar Nicholas and Empress Marie*, p 279.)

was preparing a joint note with Austria, warning the Balkan states to observe the status quo and keep the peace.[35]

Somewhat unexpectedly, the Balkan states carried everything before them. By late November (December, N.S.) the Turks sued for peace, and a Conference of Ambassadors opened in London, representing all the great powers of Europe, to re-draw the map of the Balkans. The Austrians were most anxious that their number one bogey, Serbia, should not benefit from Turkey's defeat to the extent of gaining a port on the Adriatic. She proposed the establishment of a wholly new state, Albania, between Serbia and the sea. When it was announced that the London Conference, with the participation of the Russian government, had agreed to this, there were storms of protest in the Russian press. *Novoe Vremya* called the decision ' a terrible blow to Slavdom ' and an ' ignominious retreat ' on the part of the Russian government. It echoed its earlier article on the Bosnian crisis with one entitled this time 'A Diplomatic Mukden ', and predicted that Austria's appetite would grow with success.[36] The Progressists' organ, *Utro Rossii,* forecast that Austria's next step would be to deal with Serbia, encouraged by her ' latest, once more bloodless victory over Russian diplomacy '. More surprisingly, the paper also struck a note which did not become general till the World War by attacking the German influence inside the Tsarist bureaucracy, which, it said, ' is standing at the moment on our path to the hearts of South Slavdom, is paralysing our political will and our national energy '.[37]

The only major public newspaper to defend the Foreign Ministry was *Rech.* It took the line that Russian solidarity with the Slav powers in the Balkans was mainly for the purpose of deterring the Austrians from unconsidered adventures, and should be restricted to the extent necessary to preserve peace. Once war had broken out in the Balkans, Russian diplomacy must strive to isolate the war and prevent it from involving the major European powers. The paper welcomed the London Conference's decision on Albania as an acceptable compromise, noting that Albania would be subject to the supervision of the powers, and that Serbia would be guaranteed the use of a port there.[38]

[35] Thaden, *Russia and the Baltic Alliance,* pp 128-9.
[36] *NV,* 9, 10 November 1912.   [37] *Utro Rossii,* 7, 25 December 1912.
[38] *Rech*[1], 4, 5, 7 October, 11 December 1912; Milyukov, *Vospominaniya,* vol 2, pp 140, 144-8.

Another incident which prompted furious protests from the public was the international intervention in the Montenegrin siege of Scutari. Lying just to the south of Montenegro, the port town of Scutari was to form the northern extremity of the new state of Albania. The Turks holding it, however, refused to surrender, and the Montenegrins besieging it did not enter the town till 10/23 April 1913. Having taken it at considerable cost, they refused to part with it again. Both before and after the final success of the siege, Montenegro was under pressure from the London Conference to give up all hope of the town and transfer it to Albania. The Conference organised, first, an international naval demonstration before the town, and then an international landing force to compel the recent victors to evacuate it. The Russian Foreign Ministry gave its support to both moves.

Already by the middle of March, when it became clear how things were going at Scutari, the Neo-Slavs were agitating. In St Petersburg a crowd demonstrated and tried to break into the Austrian embassy; it had to be dispersed by police using horse-whips.[39] A meeting of ' progressive public men ' at Maxim Kovalevsky's flat declared that the government's decision to let Albania have Scutari showed ' an insulting lack of faith in the strength of the Russian people and the Russian army '. Slav banquets were held to condemn the government's betrayal of Slavdom. One of them received a telegram of greeting from the Grand Duke Nikolai Nikolayevich, always the leader of the anti-German party in the royal family, and something of an odd man out in that respect. At another banquet, speakers from different Duma parties demonstratively drowned their differences in support of the common Slav struggle; they were Bobrinsky for the Nationalists, Guchkov for the Octobrists, N. N. Lvov for the Progressists, and Bryanchaninov for the Kadets.[40] As an example of the kind of resolution passed by these banquets, we may take the one sent to Kokovtsev by the ' Fourth Slav Banquet ' on 28 March 1913:

We express the deep sorrow of the Russian people that Russian diplomacy should have found it possible

[39] *GM*, 19 March 1913; S. D. Sazonov, *Vospominaniya*, Paris 1927, pp 104-5.

[40] *NV*, 24, 25, 28, 29 March 1913; *Rech'*, 26, 28, 30 March 1913; *GM*, 22 March 1913; E. D. Chermenskii, ' Bor'ba Klassov in Partii v 4-oi Gosudarstvennoi Duma ' (unpublished doctoral dissertation), p 431.

(i) to intervene in the Balkan war to the advantage of Austria, and against the Balkan allies;

(ii) to violate their indubitable right to conduct the siege of Scutari without interference to its desired end;

(iii) by an actual blockade of the Montenegrin shore to violate our neutrality on the side of Turkey against the Slavs.[41]

And when the Montenegrins finally took Scutari, *Golos Moskvy* greeted the occasion with a article of rare truculence:

All the resolutions of the London Conference were composed at a time when Scutari was considered an Albanian town. Now it has become by right of conquest Montenegrin, and the diplomats' decisions have thereby been nullified. We must now reckon with the altered situation and insist on a new delineation of Albania's frontiers.

Europe, of course, will not be slow to charge Montenegro with disobedience to her will. But there is a more powerful and lasting principle than all the resolutions of diplomats; victors are answerable to no court.[42]

Once again, the only public newspaper to defend the Foreign Ministry's action was *Rech*. There was much impatience by now, however, inside the Kadet party at Milyukov's pacific stance. Already at a Central Committee meeting of 12 October 1912, Gredeskul had called Milyukov's position ' undesirable and dangerous ', as it encouraged Austria to bellicose actions; to prevent war, he said, it was necessary not to be afraid of it. Struve went even further: the Russian people, he claimed, were thoroughly roused by the Slav movement, and only the intelligentsia, ' worm-eaten with introspection ', could fail to notice it. ' We must set the people alight with our slogans ', he exclaimed.[43] At a further Central Committee meeting of 16 March 1913, Maklakov, Bryanchaninov, Karaulov, Petrazhitsky, Gredeskul and Struve all attacked Milyukov and the editorial policy of *Rech*. I. V. Gessen threatened to resign from the editorship of *Rech*, and Milyukov seems to have considered resigning the party leadership; but a final breach was avoided, and afterwards *Rech* took a somewhat more aggressive line in its foreign policy editorials.[44]

[41] *GM*, 29 March 1913.   [42] *GM*, 11 April 1913.
[43] *TsGAOR*, f 523, op 1, d 30, pp 225-8.
[44] *TsGAOR*, f 102, op 14, d 27 (1913g), pp 27-8; Chermenskii, ' Bor'ba Klassov ', p 430.

Alas for the fire-eating Pan-Slavs, the course of the Second Balkan War amply justified Milyukov's scepticism. Disputes over Macedonia led to a sudden Bulgarian attack on Serbia in June 1913. Greece, Rumania, and even the old enemy, Turkey, saw their opportunity, and joined with Serbia. Bulgaria was speedily crushed. Any coherent Pan-Slav ideology hereupon collapsed in ruins, but not before it had stoked a lasting glow of resentment, given Serbia new power and prestige, and created major international collisions which made further retreat by Russia very difficult.

Sarajevo

The course of the Balkan Wars increased the anti-Austrian feelings of the Duma parties and their press. It also increased their resentment at the feebleness of Russian diplomacy. The impression became fixed that Russian tractability had gone to the absolute limit which national dignity or the interests of international peace would allow: at the next challenge from Austria Russia must take up an unyielding stance and be ready to back it by military means.

The conviction had also taken root that the real villain behind Austria's rapacious policy was Germany. In the Duma on 6 June 1913 Bobrinsky warned of the German *Drang nach Osten*: Germany, he said, was merely using Austria to draw an iron ring round Russia by forcing her influence through the Balkans to Asia Minor and on to the Persian Gulf.[45] This conviction was naturally strengthened in December 1913 when the Germans sent one of their own Generals, Liman von Sanders, to a post in Constantinople which virtually put him in command of the Turkish army. Even the cautious members of the Council of Ministers were brought over by this step. Sazonov became persuaded that war with Germany was inevitable. He afterwards remarked in his memoirs: ' If anyone in Russia still doubted the real aims of German policy in the Near East, then the circumstances in which the mission [of Liman von Sanders] was conceived and carried out put an end to all uncertainties and ambiguities.'[46]

At the beginning of March 1914 a special conference was held, at Rodzyanko's home, of all Duma fractions from the Rights to the Kadets, to discuss the international situation and Russia's state

[45] GDSO, IV, 1, pt 3, cols 1079-92.   [46] Sazonov, *Vospominaniya*, pp 141-9.

of military preparedness. This was the prelude to a secret debate on credits for an increased military programme, which were passed by a huge majority, excluding the Kadets.[47]

On 10 May 1914 a major foreign policy debate took place in the Duma. Sazonov explained the difficulties Russian diplomacy had gone through in the previous year, and emphasised that his aim for the moment was to maintain peaceful relations with Germany; in this, he said, he was sorely hampered by the belligerent tone of the press, both in Russia and in Germany. Milyukov accepted the government's policy and also deplored the adventurist tone of press comment. He saw the raison d'être of the Balkan Alliance as the preservation of peace against the German *Drang nach Osten*, blamed Serbian irresponsibility for having destroyed the alliance and urged that it be restored as soon as possible. Bobrinsky attacked this attitude: it was impossible to preserve peace while Austria persecuted people of Russian culture whose only crime was to want to return to the Orthodox faith of their fathers. He was referring to a recent trial in Marmaros-Sziget of Ruthenian separatists in Hungary who had wanted to quit the Uniate church in favour of the Orthodox; he himself had appeared at the trial to plead for the defendants. Efremov, for the Progressists, argued that the real reason why the Balkan Alliance had broken down was that the Balkan states felt they could no longer rely on Russian promises. The Russian government could not indefinitely make concessions and agree to compromises, and must learn to rely on its own people. Only Markov 2 resisted the general mood and repeated Durnovo's arguments, insisting that there was no reason for a war between Russia and Germany, and that any such war would probably lead to a revolution. The Balkan Alliance, he added, had been temporary, inherently unstable and bound to break up whatever Russian diplomacy did.[48]

By the time of the Sarajevo crisis, then, Russian public opinion was thoroughly prepared. Only *Rech* assiduously urged efforts to localise the Austro-Serbian conflict. This line, as Milyukov says in his memoirs, rapidly became heretical, in the eyes of both official and public opinion, especially after the harsh Austrian note to

[47] Bestuzhev, ' Bor¹ba 1910-1914 ', pp 79-80; Chermenskii, ' Bor¹ba Klassov ', pp 439-44, 454.
[48] *GDSO*, IV, 2, pt 4, cols 336-89, 413-32; Markov's speech is translated in Golder, *Documents of Russian History*, pp 24-8.

Serbia of 10/23 July.[49] If, in the other European countries, the conviction that war was bound to come played a big part in actually causing it to do so, the same is no less true of Russia.

With the German declaration of war on Russia, even *Rech*'s tone changed, though the censor delayed its appearance until he was satisfied with its patriotism.[50] The papers were unanimous in calling for national unity, though their emphases differed. *Rech* pictured national unity in terms of the Duma:

Now that Russia for the first time enters a war with a representative assembly, it is natural that the Monarch's thoughts should first of all turn to the legislative institutions, as the nearest means of entering into union with his people . . . The State Duma must serve as the means of communication between the Tsar and his people for the whole extent of this terrible ordeal. Whatever fate may hold in store for us, the Duma must be ready to serve as the voice of the people's conscience.[51]

Novoe Vremya, on the other hand, took a straightforward Pan-Slav line, talked of ' the onslaught of the Germanic tribes against the Slavs ', and called for ' unity, strength of spirit, and a firm stance against the foe ' in a war ' for the very foundations of our fatherland '.[52]

At a special Duma session of 26 July, all the parties except the Social Democrats and the Labour group agreed on the overriding need for national unity, promised the government unswerving support and allowed the house to be prorogued. Milyukov, in a significant shift of his own position, even talked of the struggle to free ' Europe and Slavdom from Germanic domination ' and asserted that ' whatever our attitude to the internal policy of the government, our first duty is to keep our country whole and undivided '.[53]

Perhaps the hopes of the centre parties in the Duma were most clearly expressed by N. I. Astrov, at a Congress of Municipalities, on 14 September 1914, when he said: ' The war, by revealing all our internal strength, will give us the opportunity to defeat not only

---

[49] Milyukov, *Vospominaniya*, vol 2, pp 173-6.
[50] ibid, p 183; Gessen, ' V Dvukh Vekakh ', pp 325-7; Rodzyanko, ' Krushenie Imperii ', p 81.
[51] *Rech*[1], 20 July 1914.
[52] *NV*, 20 July 1914.
[53] *GDSO*, iv, 2, pt 6, 26 July 1914.

the external enemy, but will also open up joyful hopes for solving the problems of internal construction and reform.'[54]

The pledge of peace and unanimity with the government which the Duma gave on 26 July was thus a provisional one only. It contained the hidden threat, and perhaps expectation, that if the regime proved incapable of conducting the war competently, then others were ready, willing and able to take over.

Conclusion

Between 1906 and 1914, all political parties used the concept of ' people ' or ' nation ' to help them work out a theory for the new political situation. This concept was as important to them as those of ' revolution ', ' constitution ', or ' autocracy '. It was one of the guidelines essential to the understanding and conduct of politics in an era of transition from autocracy to pluralism.

For the Progressists, Kadets and some of the Octobrists, the concept took its meaning from the ' people's representative body ' (*narodnoe predstavitelstvo*), which they saw as the new and defining element in the political constellation of the Empire. In this view, the ' people ' was fighting to free itself from autocracy, and had been led by the political parties to a substantial measure of success, which must now be consolidated and broadened. For most of the Octobrists, and for the Moderate Rights/Nationalists, the ' people ' was a vaguer, at times semi-mystical entity, capable of definition in a Pan-Slav or more narrowly Russian nationalist sense. This ' people ' was in spirit close to its Monarch, ready to fight for him, and brought closer to him by the Duma: the Duma must therefore struggle against ' irresponsible ' court influences on behalf of firm and responsible government drawing its strength from the people. The Rights interpreted the ' people ' in a narrowly Russian sense, viewed them pessimistically as liable to revolutionary or Jewish seduction, and regarded the Duma's existence as dependent on the Emperor's will.

All these concepts raised profound questions concerning both personal identity and the locus of political power. By the outbreak of war, the ' dynastic ' concept of the ' people ' was confined to a very small, but influential, minority. The majority of public opinion lay in the spectrum between the Nationalists and the Kadets. The

[54] Chermenskii, ' Bor'ba Klassov ', p 465.

struggle between these two broad views was profound, and led in the end to mutual accusations of treason. The view of the Duma majority parties crystallised in the Progressive Bloc and dominated the policies of the Provincial Government, until all these concepts were rendered bankrupt by the peasants' and soldiers' movement of the summer and autumn of 1917.

9

General conclusions

The years 1907-14 were vital ones for the Russian monarchy. It was then that the most serious attempt was made to forge among the country's disunited élites a unity sufficient to sustain the existing political system. The challenge to the autocracy had come in 1905 in manifold and heterogeneous forms: workers' strikes, peasant outbursts and naval mutinies, as well as reform banquets, clandestine oppositional newspapers and meetings passing constitutional resolutions. These challenges were never focussed at any single point, which was why the 1905 revolution failed, but they did warn of the need for purposeful reform. In effect, Russia was going through several stages of her political development at once: the demands of her dissatisfied élites for political participation coincided with the demands of peasants and workers for a better material existence and a recognition of their human dignity. The ideologies involved in the struggle of 1905 ranged the whole scale from anarchism, Populism and Marxist socialism through the various shades of liberalism and moderate conserativism to monarchism. There was no consensus: each group had to fight for its life during 1905-6. These memories of violent conflict overshadowed the constitutional period with the sense that a further cataclysm might come at any time.

The constitution, then, was the child of disorder and confusion. It was ambiguous in the powers it accorded to the head of state, the government and the legislative chambers. Each political group saw different things in it, hoping and fearing usually too much from it. The socialists found it totally inadequate, employed by the ruling class merely as a subterfuge. The radical liberals grouped around the Kadet party also considered it insufficient, but accepted it as the first stage in the advance to a genuine parliamentary democracy. The moderate liberals around the Octobrist party saw it as a sufficient foundation, and were ready to work for the legislative fulfilment of its explicit promises. The right-wing groups interpreted it simply as a reinforcement of the existing state structure, not an essential modification of it. And the Emperor, who had hoped to pacify his people by means of the October Manifesto, tried to believe that he had not lost anything essential of his autocratic powers.

Out of the chaos of 1905-6, and out of the stark confrontation of the government with the first two Dumas, there did emerge a moderate alliance prepared (despite residual ambiguities) to work together in the interests of peaceful change. Guchkov and the Octobrist party wanted to work for social peace, reform and the full realisation of the new constitution; Stolypin's government wanted a reliable Duma majority to support the repression of revolution and the reform programme worked out in the bureaucracy under Witte. So they had an interest in the mutual reinforcement of each other, of the Duma and of the united Council of Ministers. They looked for social support above all from the nobility and from the employees and deputies of the zemstvos. The electoral law of 3 June 1907 was intended to provide the framework in which this support could be mobilised for the Duma.

Initially the focus of the co-operation between the government and the Octobrists was the agrarian reform. Its political significance as the keystone of an alliance, however, distorted its impact on the village. Its main point became the forestalling of compulsory expropriation of private land by encouraging the peasant to leave the commune and set up as an independent smallholder. Within these limits their co-operation was very successful.

But in no other area of reform was this success repeated. The interests of the nobles and the zemstvo men were often threatened by change, and where the Emperor and the government did not obviously stand together, they often tried to slow reform or prevent it altogether, working through the Right group in the State Council. In the Naval Staffs crisis of the spring of 1909 they defeated the Octobrists, at any rate symbolically, in their efforts to extend their influence in the military sphere. Stolypin's government was forced to strip some of the ambiguities from its declared position, and come down clearly on the side of autocracy in military affairs. The Duma's standing was weakened, and the working relationship between Stolypin's ministry and the Octobrists was undermined.

Some Octobrists left Guchkov's rather loose-limbed fraction at this point, but most of them were still prepared to work with

ERAL CONCLUSIONS

Stolypin in areas where they still had common aims. They combined in 1910 to pass legislation extending the powers of the Duma and the Council of Ministers in Finnish Affairs. The same 'constitutional nationalism' produced the agreement between Stolypin and the Octobrist leadership over the Western Zemstvo bill. But this bill was so complicated and partly injured so many interests that it did not prove difficult for the Rights in the State Council to defeat it. In overcoming this opposition, Stolypin used methods so blatantly unconstitutional as to destroy finally his relations with Guchkov and the Octobrists.

The diminution and splitting of the Octobrist fraction, and the breakdown of its relations with the government, brought the 3rd June system to a state of impotence. Almost all the other measures in the government's reform programme were emasculated or rejected outright – in the fields of factory life, education, religious toleration, local government and peasant courts. In the absence of a cohesive Duma majority and a resolute government, the nobility, the zemstvo men, the employers' organisations, the Holy Synod and the bishops were able to work through the right wing of the Duma, through the Rights in the State Council, and even through the Emperor himself, to frustrate reform legislation.

In face of these disappointments, the Octobrists split into three factions in 1913, while the Council of Ministers under Kokovtsev and Goremykin also divided into antagonistic groups, one of which, led by N. A. Maklakov, felt that legislation would be passed more speedily and repression of social disorder become more effective if the Duma was reduced to consultative status and the speeches of the deputies were censored.

As a result, the long-term consequences of the 3rd June system were different from what anyone had expected. Those who stood to profit from its disintegration, the opposition parties, were only groping towards unity by 1914, their rapprochement hindered by the entrenched personal and ideological barriers set up in 1905-6. But in their search for unity and an acceptable common programme to oppose to the muddlings of the government they raised important questions about the locus of power in an era when traditional autocracy is questioned. They sought their justification in the 'people' (moving close to the Octobrists on national and foreign policy issues), and elaborated a concept of Russian nationhood that would serve as a basis both for constitutional democracy and for Russia's foreign policy as a great power. In both internal and external affairs, they called for government 'responsible' to the people, as represented in the Duma. They opposed the defensive nationalism of the Right, inextricably linked to autocracy and the Orthodox church, they (in theory, at least) welcomed non-Russian peoples and cultures as part of one great multi-national empire, and they looked for a confident expansion of the influence of this empire among the Slav peoples of the Balkans and Austria-Hungary. This outlook was appealing enough to win support from all parties in the Duma except the extreme Rights and the socialists. As for the government, it tried to avoid rash involvements in the Balkans, but, when the crisis came in 1914, found itself espousing the ideals of the opposition (minus, at that time, Milyukov), rather than those of Durnovo and the conservatives who were so influential in home affairs.

But by 1914 mutual suspicion between the government and most of the Duma parties had become so intense that no working relationship was ever really re-established, in spite of the honeymoon mood at the outset of the war. Indeed, bitterness reached new heights before long with the legend of the 'dark forces' and hints of treachery in high places. The opposition came to see themselves as the bearers of the only true Russian patriotism: their thinking came to full fruition (after the initial stage of the Progressive Bloc) in the Provisional Government of 1917, whose foreign policy was based on the continued pursuit of the war with a renewed sense of national purpose.

The breakdown of the 3rd June system thus fatally weakened the functioning of the polity at Russia's entry into the war, and played a major part in bringing about the eventual collapse of the monarchy. Originally intended as a framework for social reform and political stability, the 3rd June system faced its greatest test in war. And here the suspicions dividing Russia's élites, not having been cured in peacetime, proved fatal and ultimately opened the way for revolution.

Appendix

A note on historiography and sources

Western historians of the constitutional period have so far given most of their attention to the first two Dumas, whose brief life and abrupt end dramatised the polarity of Russian politics. For this reason, they have described the functioning of the 3rd June system only in very general terms. Nevertheless, two main approaches are descernible.

One approach views the coup of 3 June 1907 as the 'Triumph of Reaction' (chapter-heading in M. T. Florinsky, *Russia: a History and an Interpretation*, New York 1960, vol 2, p 1200), in which the government created a 'docile and co-operative Duma' (p 1204), in order to return to bureaucratism, Great Russian nationalism and repression, while passing a minimum of reforms as slowly as possible. L. Kochan (*Russia in Revolution, 1890-1918*, London 1966, (p 104) likewise calls the events of June 1907 'The Fall of the Duma', whilst Alfred Levin (*The Second Duma*, New Haven 1940, pp 311, 352) characterises them as a 'resort to old bureaucratic methods' and compares Stolypin's general treatment of the Duma with earlier ministers' policies towards the zemstvos, as consisting in gradual hindrance and restriction. This approach has its origin in the contemporary Kadet view of events, which can be summed up in the much-quoted words of Milyukov:

There exist two Russias . . . Were I to label these two Russias, I should designate the one as the Russia of Leo Tolstoy, the great writer; the other as that of Pleve, the late Minister of the Interior. The former is the Russia of our 'intellectuals' and of the people; the latter is official Russia. One is the Russia of the future, as dreamed of by members of the liberal professions: the other is an anachronism, deeply rooted in the past, and defended in the present by an omnipotent bureaucracy. The one spells liberty, the other despotism. (From the preface to his published lectures; *Russia and its Crisis*, Chicago 1905.)

9

In this vision, 3 June 1907 meant the defeat of the people, the intelligentsia and liberty, and the triumph of bureaucracy and despotism.

The other main Western interpretation of the post-1907 Duma originated in the more pragmatic British liberalism of Sir Bernard Pares. He held that the Duma's continued existence was of itself a force inexorably bringing democracy to Russia's political life and gradually crowding the apparently triumphant reactionaries to the edge of the stage. Pares described Guchkov and the Octobrists as ' more akin [than the Kadets] to the ordinary instincts of English public life '. The Kadets, he maintained, ' had had their period and had failed hopelessly ', while the Third Duma had ' an admirable record ', ' was establishing itself as an indispensable part of the organisation of public life ', and ' was rapidly helping to fill up . . . the wide gap between the government and the public '. (*The Fall of the Russian Monarchy*, London 1939, pp 105-6, 118, 152-3.)

A similar view is presented in the writings of some émigré historians, rightly conscious of the considerable economic growth and cultural flowering of Tsarist Russia in its last years. Thus S. G. Pushkarev concludes his survey of nineteenth-century Russian history by asserting: 'And so, in all spheres of life – in state construction, in social organisation, economic activity and cultural creativity – Russia in the pre-war period was advancing fast and successfully, overcoming her backwardness and her defects. War and revolution broke off this ascending curve of development.' (*Rossiya v XIX veke, 1801-1914*, New York 1956, p 468.)

The view that Tsarist Russia had the potential for democratic development is presented with polemical sharpness in the writings of one Kadet, V. A. Maklakov. Like the other Kadets, he saw 3 June 1907 as a victory for reaction; on the other hand, unlike the other Kadets, he agrees with Pares in thinking that this victory was caused by the failure of the Kadet party in the first two Dumas. His work is devoted to analysing that failure. He diagnoses it as a continuation of the ' militant ' attitude of the pre-1905 period. when the Union of Liberation, uniting most liberals, was illegal and had to co-operate with the revolutionary parties. This attitude lost its relevance, he maintains, with the October Manifesto and the Fundamental Laws of April 1906, through which the government proved the sincerity of its intention to introduce a constitutional system. Stolypin's government he saw as an advocate of 'liberal reforms, but also strong government' (*Vtoraya Gosudar-stvennaya Duma,* Paris 1948, p 253). The Kadets' mistake was to refuse to try seriously to work with Stolypin: they thereby forced the government back on its own resources and compelled it to seek co-operation from the reactionary forces who dominated the Third and Fourth Dumas.

Maklakov's analysis (like Pares's) has the merit of emphasising the government's serious reforming intentions of 1905-7 and its consciousness of the need for public support. On the other hand he much overestimates the doctrinal devotion of Stolypin's govern-ment to constitutionalism. In essence, what he argues is that the Kadets should have tried the conciliatory policy which was actually adopted by the Octobrists; but he gives us no good reason for supposing that they would have had greater success. Nevertheless, Maklakov has had considerable influence on Western historical writing in the 1950s and 1960s, during which time it has been almost fashionable to accuse the Kadets of intransigence.

Of the two main currents in Western historiography, the first seems to me important in that it brings out the extremism and violence of Russian politics in the period, the second in that it emphasises the seriousness of the constitutional experiment in Russia, the contribution made to it by the electoral law of 3 June 1907, and the need for it felt by influential elements in both govern-ment and society. In my investigations, I have felt bound to reject certain aspects of both approaches as inadequate, but at the same time have been much influenced by both.

All Soviet historical writing on the period is based on the ideas of Lenin. His contemporary commentaries on the Duma were, perhaps fortunately, numerous and not always consistent, so that he can be quoted in support of somewhat different approaches. Broadly, however, the Leninist viewpoint, from which no Soviet historian can seriously depart, is that, through the state reforms of 1905-6, the feudal Tsarist monarchy was adapting itself to a bour-geois era, and henceforth, like Napoleons I and III in France or Bismarck in Germany, pursued a policy of 'manoeuvring' (*laviro-vanie*) between the two dominant classes, the landowners and the bourgeoisie. The centre of this policy was the 3rd June Duma (which provided a forum representing mainly the two ruling classes) and the agrarian reform (which aimed to strengthen the ruling classes

9*

by creating a new peasant property-owning class as a complement to them).

This conception has been most consistently developed in the writings of A. Ya. Avrekh, in his dissertations and articles (listed in the bibliography) and in his two published books, *Tsarizm i Tret'eiyunskaya Sistema* (M 1966) and *Stolypin i Tret'ya Duma* (M 1968). Avrekh concludes that the government, in its policy of ' manoeuvring ', deliberately created two majorities, a Right–Octobrist majority to support the government's nationalist and repressive policies, and an Octobrist–Kadet majority to pass the necessary minimum of bourgeois reforms. But even this tactic failed, because the country remained, after 1905-7, in what Avrekh calls a ' general revolutionary situation ', which made reform, while necessary, also dangerous. The two majorities were therefore unstable: they failed to agree among themselves about the extent and speed of reform, and from the second session of the Third Duma began to split among themselves, until the government could no longer rely on them and was exposed to the reactionary intrigues of the ' court camarilla ', the United Nobility and the right wing of the State Council.

This argument is cogent and is closely worked out in Avrekh's writings, It has the great merit of demonstrating at one and the same time (as no Western work has yet done) both the government's urgent desire for co-operation with certain sections of society in passing reforms, and also the depth of political polarisation which made such co-operation ultimately impossible. To that extent, my account has much in common with Avrekh's work, and has drawn from it.

However, Avrekh's presentation has some defects. His Leninist framework leads him to impute selfish class motives to all his actors, and indeed to adopt towards them a persistently sarcastic tone which can only be described as objectionable. He underestimates the importance of the zemstvos in Stolypin's political alliance, and hence also the Council for Affairs of Local Economy, which was their forum. At the same time he overestimates the element of conscious calculation on the part of all sides: in particular, his key theory of the consciously created ' two majorities ' presupposes wellnigh inhuman foresight on the government's part in drawing up the electoral law of 3 June, and also much overrates the importance of the Kadets in the Third Duma.

Other Soviet historians have contributed towards my understanding of the 3rd June system. E. D. Chermensky's *Burzhuaziya i Tsarizm v Revolyutsii 1905-7gg*, revised and in my view much improved in the edition of 1970, presents an account of the way in which it was set up. V. S. Dyakin (*Russkaya Burzhuaziya i Tsarizm v Gody Pervoi Mirovoi Voiny*, L 1967) provides an able summary of it in the first chapter, and then follows the story up to the February revolution. I. V. Bestuzhev, in one book (*Bor'ba v Rossii po Voprosam Vneshnei Politiki, 1906-10gg*, M 1961) and a number of articles, throws important light on the attitudes of parties and groups towards foreign policy questions and on the problem of the extent to which they were able to influence the government. Finally, V. Ya. Laverychev (*Po tu Storonu Barrikad: iz Istorii Bor'by Moskovskoi Burzhuazii s Revolyutsiei*, M 1967) contributes important information on the Moscow commercial bourgeoisie and on the foundation of the Progressist party.

The sources used in this study are acknowledged in their due place, in the footnotes to the text. But a little should be said about the special problems of the archival sources.

The most important political archives for the last years of Tsarist Russia are concentrated in the Moscow and Leningrad collections of the Central State Historical Archive. (At the time of my study trips, in the late 1960s, the Moscow collection was still under the name of Central State Archive of the October Revolution, *TsGAOR* for short, and I refer to it as such throughout this book.) During the last decade it has become possible for Western scholars to make use of these collections for the study of politics up to 1917, though documents of a military or diplomatic nature may still be withheld. However, the access granted to Western scholars is not quite so free as that enjoyed by their Soviet colleagues. It was not when I worked there the custom to allow Westerners (or perhaps any foreign scholars – I was not clear on this) to consult the detailed catalogues (*opisi*) which enumerate the individual items in each archive fund (*fond*). Instead one has to rely on the general published guides (sometimes quite seriously out of date, as there has been much reorganisation in the last few years in Soviet historical archives) and on the help of an archive-worker. It is my impression that I was expertly and conscientiously served, especially in Leningrad. However, one or two items were deliberately withheld from me, and it would be wrong for me to pretend that I gained the kind of knowledge which a historian normally likes to have of the archival resources available.

With that reservation, some archival materials were most useful to this study, and I append a brief list of the most consistently useful *fondy*.

(i) f 1276, Council of Ministers – contains the Journals in which the Council summed up its conclusions to submit to the Emperor; also early variants of bills, and protocols or summaries of interdepartmental discussions.

(ii) f 1278, State Duma – extended summaries of discussions in the Duma committees, which are usually not available elsewhere; also preliminary versions of bills.

(iii) f 115, Union of 17 October – contains a nearly complete though usually rather brief summary of all fraction meetings during the Third Duma; also papers relating to party organisation.

(iv) f 523, Kadet party – contains a wealth of material on party congresses, Central Committee and fraction meetings, conferences with local delegates, and on party organisation.

(v) f 102, Department of Police – contains illuminating reports on the activities of the opposition parties during the elections to the Fourth Duma and thereafter.

(vi) f 434, United Nobility – summaries of the meetings of the Permanent Council which conducted the affairs of the United Nobility.

(vii) f 1291, Zemskii Otdel (Ministry of the Interior) – material on the agrarian and local government reforms.

The personal *fondy* were by comparison very disappointing. A notable exception is that of I. S. Klyuzhev (f 669), secretary to the Octobrist fraction bureau; he and his wife kept a diary which records in some detail the dissensions in the fraction in 1907 and from 1910 to 1913.

List of Sources

1 UNPUBLISHED SOURCES

(i) Archives

Tsentral'nyi Gosudarstvennyi Arkhiv Oktyabr'skoi Revolyutsii (TsGAOR):

fond 63 (Moskovskoe Okhrannoe Otdelenie)
    102 (Departament politsii)
    115 (Soyuz 17-ogo Oktyabrya)
    434 (Sovet Ob''edinennogo Dvoryanstva)
    523 (Konstitutsionno-Demokraticheskaya Partiya)
    543 (Tsarsko-Sel'skii Aleksandrovskii Dvorets)
    555 (A.I.Guchkov)
    579 (P.N.Milyukov)
    595 (D.N.Trepov)
    601 (Nikolai II)
    629 (A.Tyrkova)
    810 (M.V.Chelnokov)
  1467 (Chrezvychainaya Sledstvennaya Komissiya Vremennogo Pravitel'stva)

Tsentral'nyi Gosudarstvennyi Istoricheskii Arkhiv v Leningrade (TsGIAL):

fond 408 (Komitet po Zemleustroitel'nym Delam)
    669 (I.S.Klyuzhev)
    869 (Yu.N.Milyutin)
    966 (V.N.Kokovtsev)
  1276 (Sovet Ministrov)
  1278 (Gosudarstvennaya Duma)
  1282 (Ministerstvo Vnutrennikh Del, Kantselyariya)
  1288 (Ministerstvo Vnutrennikh Del, Glavnoe Upravlenie po Delam Mestnogo Khozyaistva)
  1291 (Ministerstvo Vnutrennikh Del, Zemskii Otdel)
  1405 (Ministerstvo Yustitsii)
  1629 (I.Ya.Gurlyand)
  1662 (P.A.Stolypin)

(ii) Dissertations

Avrekh,A.Ya., ' Blok Pomeshchich'ikh i Burzhuaznykh Partii v 3-ei Dume: k Voprosu o Krakhe Stolypinskogo Bonapartizma ', candidate's dissertation, M 1954.
  ' Tret'ya Duma i Proval Stolypinskogo Bonapartizma ', doctoral dissertation, M 1967.

Chermenskii,E.D., ' Bor'ba Klassov i Partii v 4-oi Gosudarstvennoi Dume ', doctoral dissertation, M 1948.
Hutchinson,J.F., ' The Union of 17 October in Russian Politics, 1905-17 ', Ph.D. thesis, London 1966.
Piotrow,F.J., ' P.N.Milyukov and the Constitutional-Democratic Party ', D.Phil. thesis, Oxford 1962.
Simmonds,G.W., ' The Congress of Representatives of the Nobles' Associations, 1906-16: a Case-study in Russian Conservatism ', Ph.D. thesis, Columbia 1964.
Vaisberg,I.D., ' Sovet Ob''edinennogo Dvoryanstva i ego Vliyanie na Politiku Samoderzhaviya, 1906-14gg ', candidate's dissertation, M 1956.

2 BIBLIOGRAPHIES

Brusyanin,V.V., Ukazatel' Knig i Statei o Gosudarstvennoi Dume, M 1913.
Deev,A.S., Uzakatel' Knig i Broshyur o Gosudarstvennoi Dume, 1905-12gg, SPB 1913.
Ist. SSSR: Ukazatel' Sovetskoi Literatury za 1917-52gg (4 vols, including supplements), M 1958.
KA: Annotirovannyi Ukazatel' Soderzhaniya (edited by P.Ya.Zverev), M 1960.
Digest (vols 31-106), compiled and annotated by L.W.Eisele and A.A. Lobanov-Rostovsky, Michigan 1955.
Rubakin,N.A., Sredi Knig, 3 vols, M 1911-15.
Shapiro,D.M., A Select Bibliography of Works in English on Russian History, 1801-1917, Oxford 1962.
Shilov,A., Chto Chitat' po Istorii Russkogo Revolyutsionnogo Dvizheniya, Petrograd 1922.

3 NEWSPAPERS

Golos Moskvy   Rech'
Novoe Vremya   Utro Rossii

4 PUBLISHED DOCUMENTS

Doklady S.Yu. Vitte Nikolayu II, KA, vol 11, pp 144-58.
Golder,F.A. (ed), Documents of Russian History, 1914-17, New York 1927.
GDSO: 1-yi Sozyv, 2 vols, SPB 1906.
    2-oi Sozyv, 2 vols, SPB 1907.
    3-ii Sozyv, 5 Sessii (18 vols in all), SPB 1907-12.
    4-yi Sozyv, 2 Sessii (10 vols in all), SPB 1912-14.
    Prilozheniya, SPB 1907-14.
    Obzor Deyatel'nosti Komissii i Otdelov, SPB 1907-14.
    Ukazatel' (one for each session), SPB 1907-14.
GSSO: Sessii 1-9 , SPB 1906-14.
Interesnaya Nakhodka: ' Delo Kokovtseva ' (edited by A.L.Sidorov), Vop. Ist., 1964, no 2, pp 99-111, and no 4, pp 94-117.
Iz Arkhiva S. Yu. Vitte, KA, vol 11, pp 107-43.

Iz Istorii Podgotovki Tsarizma k Pervoi Mirovoi Voine, Istoricheskii Arkhiv, 1962, no 2, pp 120-55.

Kalinychev,F.I. (ed), *Gosudarstvennaya Duma v Rossii: Dokumenty i Materialy*, M 1957.

K Istorii Manifesta 6-ogoAvgusta, KA, vol 14, pp 262-70.

Lenskie Sobytiya 1912g: Dokumenty i Materialy, M 1925.

Lenskii Rasstrel 1912g, KA, vol 81, pp 153-206.

Manifest 17-ogo Oktyabrya, KA, vol 11, pp 39-106.

Mobilizatsiya Reaktsii v 1906g, KA, vol 32, pp 158-82.

Obzor Deyatel'nosti Gosudarstvennoi Dumy 3-ego Sozyva, SPB 1912.

Padenie Tsarskogo Rezhima: Stenograficheskie Otchety Doprosov i Pokazanii, dannykh v 1917g v Chrezvychainoi Sledstvennoi Komissii Vremennogo Pravitel'stva, Moscow–Leningrad 1925-7.

Petergofskoe Soveshchanie: o Proekte Gosudarstvennoi Dumy pod lichnym ego Imperatorskogo Velichestva predsedatel'stvom. Sekretnye Protokoly, Petrograd 1917.

Podkup ' Novogo Vremeni ' Tsarskim Pravitel'stvom, KA, vol 21, pp 223-6.

Semennikov,V.P. (ed), *Monarkhiya pered Krusheniem*, Moscow–Leningrad 1927.

Tsarskie Ministry o vseobshchem izbiratel'nom Prave, KA, vol 83, pp 224-5.

Tsarsko-Sel'skie Soveshchaniya 1905-6gg, Byloe, 1917, nos 3-6.

Veselovskii,B.B., Pichet,V.I., and Friche,V.M. (eds), *Agrarnyi Vopros v Sovete Ministrov v 1906g*, M 1924.

Zapiski A.S. Ermolova Nikolayu II v 1905g, KA, vol 8, pp 49-69.

5 BOOKS AND ARTICLES

For ease of reference all sources are listed in alphabetical order. In addition, on pp 273-4 they are categorised according to subject, the numbers cited there for each subject relating to the numbers in parentheses following the entries in the alphabetical list.

Abramson,V., *Osnovnye Nachala novogo Polozheniya o Vyborakh v Gosudarstvennuyu Dumu 3-ego iyunya 1907g*, Melitopol' 1907. (1)

Adamovich,G.V., *V.A.Maklakov, Politik,Yurist, Chelovek*, Paris 1959. (2)

Agrarnyi Vopros:Protokoly Zasedanii K.D. Agrarnoi Komissii 11-13 fevralya 1907g, SPB 1907. (3)

Albertini,L., *The Origins of the War of 1914*, 3 vols, Oxford 1952. (4)

Aldanov,M., ' P.N.Durnovo, Prophet of War and Revolution ', *Russian Review*, vol 2 (1942), pp 31-45. (5)

Aleksandrovskii,Yu.V., *Zakon 14 iyunya 1910g*, SPB 1911. (6)

Alyanchikov,N.N., *Russkie Politicheskie Partii*, Tver' 1907. (7)

Amburger,E., *Geschichte der Behördenorganisation Russlands von Peter dem Grossen bis 1917*, Leiden 1966. (8)

Anweiler,O., ' Die Russische Revolution von 1905 ',*JGO*, vol 3 (1955), pp 161-93. (9).

Arest Dumskoi ' Pyaterki ' v 1914g, KA, vol 64, pp 31-51. (10)

Aronson,G., *Rossiya nakanune Revolyutsii*, New York 1962. (11)

Astaf'ev,I.I., *Voennaya Trevoga v Pravyashchikh Krugakh Tsarskoi Rossii v Oktyabrye 1908g, Vestnik Moskovskogo Gosudarstvennogo Universiteta* (Istoricheskaya Seriya), 1965, no 3, pp 34-51. (12)

Astrov,N.I., *Vospominaniya*, Paris 1940. (13)

(ed), *Zakondatel'nye Proekty i Predlozheniya Partii Narodnoi Svobody, 1905-7gg*, SPB 1907. (14)

Avrekh,A.Ya., *Stolypin i Tret'ya Duma*, M 1968. (15)

Tsarizm i Tret'eiyunskaya Sistema, M 1966. (16)

'Agrarnyi Vopros v 3-ei Dume ', *Ist. Zap.*, vol 62, pp 26-83. (17)

' Lenskii Rasstrel i Krisis Tret'eiyunskoi Sistemy ', *Vop. Ist.*, 1962, no 4, pp 58-79. (18)

Stolypinskii Bonapartizm i Voprosy Voennoi Politiki v 3-ei Dume ', *Vop. Ist.*, 1956, no 11, pp 17-33. (19)

' Tret'eiyunskaya Monarkhiya i Obrazovanie Tret'edumskogo Pomeshchich'e-Burzhuaznogo Bloka ', *Vestnik Moskovskogo Gosudarstvennogo Universiteta* (Istoriko-Filologicheskaya Seriya), 1956, no 1, pp 3-70. (20)

' Tret'eiyunskaya Monarkhiya i Rabochii Vopros', *Ist. SSSR*, 1966, no 1, pp 42-69. (21)

' Tret'ya Duma i Nachalo Krizisa Tret'eiyunskoi Sistemy ', *Ist. Zap.*, vol 53, pp 50-109. (22)

' Vopros o Zapadnom Zemstve i Bankrotstvo Stolypina ', *Ist. Zap.*, vol 70, pp 61-112. (23)

Badaev,A., *Bol'sheviki v Gosudarstvennoi Dume*, Moscow–Leningrad 1929. (24)

Bakhirev,A.V., *Tret'ya Gosudarstvennaya Duma v Kartogrammakh*, SPB 1910. (25)

Balabanov,M., *Tsarskaya Rossiya v XX veke*, M 1927. (26)

Barandov,G., *Stolypinskaya Reaktsiya*, M 1938. (27)

Bark,P.L., ' Vospominaniya ', *Vozrozhdenie*, vols 43, 48 (1955), 157-70, 172-84 (1965-7). (28)

Bartoszewicz,J.de, ' L'Empire Russe ', *La Vie Politique dans les deux Mondes*, vol 2 (1908), pp 361-93. (29)

Bashmakov,A.A., *Poslednii Vityaz': Byvshii Predsedatel' Soveta Ministrov P.A.Stolypin*, SPB 1912. (30)

Bayan-Roslavlev, *Pyl': Sbornik Politicheskikh Statei, 1907-12*, M 1913. (31)

Belokonskii,I.P., *Zemskoe Dvizhenie*, M 1910. (32)

Berlin,P.A., *Russkaya Burzhuaziya v staroe i novoe Vremya*, M 1922. (33)

Bestuzhev,I.V., *Bor'ba v Rossii po Voprosam Vneshnei Politiki, 1906-10gg*, M 1961. (34)

' Bor'ba Klassov i Partii v Rossii po Voprosam Vneshnei Politiki nakanune Bosniiskogo Krizisa (1906-8gg)', *Ist. Zap.*, vol 64, pp 136-85. (35)

' Bor'ba v Pravyashchikh Krugakh Rossii po Voprosam Vneshnei Politiki vo vremya Bosniiskogo Krizisa ', *Istoricheskii Arkhiv*, 1962, no 5, pp 113-47. (36)

'Bor'ba v Rossii po Voprosam Vneshnei Politiki nakanune Pervoi Mirovoi Voiny 1910-1914gg ', *Ist. Zap.*, vol 75, pp 44-85. (37)

'Russian Foreign Policy, February-July 1914 ', *Journal of Contemporary History*, vol 1 (1966), no 2, pp 93-112. (38)

Bickel,O., *Russland und die Entstehung des Balkanbundes*, Königsberg 1933. (39)

Bilimovich,A.D., *Zemleustroitel'nye Zadachi i Zemleustroitel'noe Zakonodatel'stvo v Rossii*, Kiev 1907. (40)

Black,C.E. (ed), *The Transformation of Russian Society: Aspects of Social Change since 1861*, Cambridge, Mass., 1960. (41)

Blizhnii, *Gosudarstvennaya Duma i Gosudarstvennaya Oborona: obzor deyatel'nosti Gosudarstvennoi Dumy 3-ego sozyva 1908-9gg po gosudarstvennoi oborone*, SPB 1909. (42)

Bobrinskii,A.A., ' Dnevnik ', *KA*, vol 26, pp 127-150. (43)

Bogdanovich,A.V., *Tri Poslednikh Samoderzhtsa: Dnevnik (1880-1912)*, Moscow–Leningrad 1924. (44)

Bogolepov,A., ' Gosudarstvennaya Duma ', *Novyi Zhurnal*, vol 46 (1956), pp 199-219. (45)

Boiovich,M.M., *Chleny Gosudarstvennoi Dumy: Portrety i Biografii, 1-yi Sozyv (1906-11gg)*, M 1906. (46)

Chleny Gosudarstvennoi Dumy: Portrety i Biografii, 2-oi Sozyv (1907-12gg), M 1907. (47)

Chleny Gosudarstvennoi Dumy: Portrety i Biografii, 3-ii Sozyv (1907-12gg), M 1908. (48)

Chleny Gosudarstvennoi Dumy: Portrety i Biografii, 4-yi Sozyv (1912-17gg), M 1913. (49)

Bok,M.P., *Vospominaniya o moem Otse P.A.Stolypine*, New York 1953. (50)

' Stolypin in Saratov ', *Russian Review*, vol 12 (1953), pp 187-93. (51)

Bompard,M., *Mon Ambassade en Russie (1903-8)*, Paris 1937. (52)

Bovykin,V.I., *Ocherki Istorii Vneshnei Politiki Rossii: konets XIX veka – 1917g*, M 1960. (53)

Boyer,P., ' L'Empire Russe ', *La Vie Politique dans les deux Mondes*, vol 1 (1908), pp 367-95, 635-78. (54)

Bryanchaninov,A.N., *Mezhdudum'e: Sbornik Materialov dlya Kharakteristiki Politichiskogo Polozheniya pered Sozyvom 2-oi Dumy*, SPB 1907. (55)

Rospusk Gosudarstvennoi Dumy: Prichiny, Posledstviya, Pskov 1906. (56)

Buchanan,G., *My Mission to Russia and other Diplomatic Memories*, 2 vols, London 1923. (57)

Buryshkin,P.A., *Moskva Kupecheskaya*, New York 1954. (58)

Carlgren,W.M., *Iswolski und Aerenthal vor bosnischen Annexionskrise: Russische und Österreichisch-Ungarische Balkanpolitik*, Uppsala 1955. (59)

Charques,R., *The Twilight of Imperial Russia*, London 1958. (60)

Chasles,P., *Le Parlement Russe*, Paris 1910. (61)

' L'Empire Russe ', *La Vie Politique dans les deux Mondes* (a summary of political events in Russia, appearing annually from vol 3 (1909) to vol 7 (1914)).

Cherevanin, *Sovremennoe Polozhenie i Vozmozhnoe Budushchee: 3-ya Duma, Prichina ee Poyavleniya i ee Budushchee*. M 1908. (63)

258   THE RUSSIAN CONSTITUTIONAL EXPERIMENT

Chermenskii,E.D., *Burzhuaziya i Tsarizm v Revolyutsii 1905-7gg*, M 1939. (64)
Burzhuaziya i Tsarizm v Pervoi Russkoi Revolyutsii, 2nd edition, revised, with additions, M 1970. (65)
Fevral'skaya Burzhuazno-Democraticheskaya Revolyutsiya, M 1959. (66)
Istoriya SSSR: period Imperializma, 2nd, revised edition, M 1965. (67)
' Kadety nakanune Fevral'skoi Burzhuazno-Demokraticheskoi Revolyutsii ', *Istoricheskii Zhurnal*, 1941, no 3, pp 35-45. (68)
' Russkaya Burzhuaziya osen'yu 1905g ', *Vop. Ist.*, 1966, no 6, pp 56-72. (69)
' Vybory v 4-uyu Gosudarstvennuyu Dumu ', *Vop. Ist.*, 1947, no 4, pp 21-40. (70)
' Zemsko-Liberal'noe Dvizhenie nakanune Revolyutsii 1905-7gg ', Ist. *SSSR*, 1965, no 5, pp 41-60. (71)
Chernovskii,A. and Viktorov,V.P. (eds), *Soyuz Russkogo Naroda*, Moscow–Leningrad 1929. (72)
Chernyshev,I.V., *Agrarno-Krest'yanskaya Politika Rossii za 150 let*, Petrograd 1918. (73)
Krest'yane ob Obshchine nakanune 9 noyabrya 1906g, SPB 1912. (74)
Krest'yanskoe Pravo i Obshchina pered Gosudarstvennoi Dumoi, SPB 1907. (75)
Chernyshev–Bezobrazov, *Kratkii Obzor Deyatel'nosti Upolnomochennykh Dvoryanskikh Obshchestv*, SPB 1909. (76)
Chetverikov,S.I., *Bezvozvratno Ushedshaya Rossiya*, Berlin n.d. (77)
Chistyakov,P.S., *K predstoyashchim Vyboram v 4-uyu Gosudarstvennuyu Dumu*, SPB 1912. (78)
Chmielewski,E., *The Polish Question in the Russian State Duma*, Knoxville 1970. (79)
' Stolypin and the Russian Ministerial Crisis of 1909 ', *California Slavic Studies*, vol 4 (1967), pp 1-38. (80)
' Stolypin's Last Crisis ', *California Slavic Studies*, vol 3 (1964), pp 95-126. (81)
Chuprov,A.A., ' The Break-Up of the Village Community in Russia ', *Economic Journal*, vol 22 (1912), pp 173-97. (82)
Conroy,M.S., ' Stolypin's Attitude towards Local Self-Government ', *SEER*, vol 46 (1968), pp 446-61. (83)
Crisp,O., ' The Russian Liberals and the 1906 Anglo-French Loan to Russia ', *SEER*, vol 39 (1961), pp 117-29. (84)
Curtiss,J.S., *Church and State in Russia: the Last Years of the Empire, 1900-17*, New York 1940. (85)
Danilov,Yu.N., *Velikii Knyaz' Nikolai Nikolaevich*, Paris 1930. (86)
Deyatel'nost' Soveta i Kratkie Svedeniya o S''ezdakh Predstavitelei Promyshlennosti i Torgovli za 1908g, SPB 1908 (issued each year up to 1913, with similar titles). (87)
Dmovskii,R., *Germaniya, Rossiya i Pol'skii Vopros*, SPB 1909. (88)
Dnevnik A.A. Polovtseva, KA, vol 3, pp 75-172, and vol 4, pp 63-128. (89)
Dnevnik Velikogo Knyazya Andreya Vladimirovicha, L 1925. (90)
Dobrotvor,N.M., *Rabochie Deputaty v 3-ei Gosudarstvennoi Dume*, Gor'kii 1957. (91)

' O Vyborakh v 3-yu Gosudarstvennuyu Dumu po Rabochei Kurii ', *Vop. Ist.*, 1955, no 1, pp 95-101. (92)

Dopros Kolchaka, Moscow–Leningrad 1925. (93)

Dorosh,H., *Russian Constitutionalism*, New York 1944. (94)

Dubrovskii,S.M., *Stolypinskaya Zemel'naya Reforma*, revised edition, M 1963. (95)

Dyakin,V.S., *Russkaya Burzhuaziya i Tsarizm v Gody Pervoi Mirovoi Voiny*, Leningrad 1967. (96)

Dymsha,L., *Kholmskii Vopros*, SPB 1910. (97)

Efremov,I., *Russkie Narodnye Predstaviteli v Anglii i Frantsii Letom 1909g*, SPB 1911. (98)

Efremov,P.N., *Vneshnyaya Politika Rossii, 1907-14*, M 1961. (99)

El'chaninov,A.G., *Tsarstvovanie Gosudarya Imperatora Nikolaya Aleksandrovicha*, SPB 1913. (100)

Elkin,B., 'Attempts to revive Freemasonry in Russia ', *SEER*, vol 44 (1966), pp 454-72. (101)

Entsiklopedicheskii Slovar' (published Granat and Co.), vol 17 (brief biographies of all members of the first three Dumas), and vol 23 (brief biographies of all members of the State Council, 1801-1914). (102)

Episkop Evlogii (Volynskii), *Put' moei Zhizni*, Paris 1947. (103)

Eropkin,A.V., *Chto Delala i chto Sdelala Tret'ya Gosudarstvennaya Duma? (Otvet Kadetam)*, SPB 1912. (104)

Eroshkin,N.P., *Ocherki Istorii Gosudarstvennykh Uchrezhdenii Dorevolyutsionnoi Rossii*, 2nd, revised, edition, M 1968. (105)

Fischel,A., *Der Panslawismus bis zum Weltkrieg*, Stuttgart 1919. (106)

Fischer,F., *Germany's Aims in the First World War*, London 1967 (translated from the German). (107)

Fischer,G., *Russian Liberalism: from Gentry to Intelligentsia*, Cambridge, Mass., 1958. (108)

' The Russian Intelligentsia and Liberalism ', *Harvard Slavic Studies*, vol 4 (1957), pp 317-36. (109)

Florinsky,M. T., *The End of the Russian Empire*, New York 1961 edition. (110)

' The Russian Mobilisation of 1914 ', *Political Science Quarterly*, vol 42 (1927), pp 203-27. (111)

Fraktsiya Narodnoi Svobody v period 15 okt 1908 – 2 iyunya 1909, SPB 1909 (similar titles were issued annually up to 1914, also 1916). (112)

Fraktsiya Progressistov v 4-oi Gosudarstvennoi Dume: Sessiya 1, 1912-3gg, SPB 1913 (no more issued). (113)

Frank,S., *Biografiya P.B. Struve*. New York 1956. (114)

Galai,S., ' The Impact of War on the Russian Liberals in 1904-5 ', *Government and Opposition*, vol 1 (1965), pp 85-109. (115)

Gan.L., ' Ubiistvo Stolypina ', *Istoricheskii Vestnik*, vol 135, pp 960-97, and vol 136, pp 192-215. (116)

Gerasimov,A., *Der Kampf gegen die erste russische Revolution*, Leipzig 1934. (117)

Ger¹e,V., *Pervaya Gosudarstvennaya Duma*, M 1906. (118)
   Vtoraya Gosudarstvennaya Duma, M 1907. (119)
   Vtoroe Raskreproshchenie: Obshchie Preniya po Ukazu 9-ogo noyabrya 1906g v Gosudarstvennoi Dume i v Gosudarstvennom Sovete, M 1911. (120)
   Znachenie Tret¹ei Gosudarstvennoi Dumy v Istorii Rossii, SPB 1912. (121)
Gertsenshtein,M.Ya., *Agrarnyi Vopros v Programmakh Razlichnykh Partii*, M 1906. (122)
   Zemel¹naya Reforma v Programme Partii Narodnoi Svobody, M 1906. (123)
Gessen,I.V., ' V Dvukh Vekakh ', *Arkhiv Russkoi Revolyutsii*, vol 22, Berlin 1937. (124)
Gilliard,F., *Thirteen Years at the Russian Court*, London 1921. (125)
Gindin,A.F., ' O nekotorykh Osobennostyakh ekonomicheskoi i sotsial¹noi struktury Russkogo Kapitalizma v nachale xx veka ', *Ist. SSSR*, 1956, no 3, pp 48-66. (126)
   ' Russkaya Burzhuaziya v Period Kapitalizma, ee Razvitie i Osobennosti ', *Ist. SSSR*, 1963, no 2, pp 57-80, and no 3, pp 37-60. (127)
Goldenweiser,A., ' Paul Milyukov, Historian and Statesman ', *Russian Review*, vol 16 (1957), pp 3-14. (128)
   ' The Russian Duma ', *Political Science Quarterly*, vol 29 (1914), pp 408-22. (129)
Golovanov,V.I., *Zemel¹nyi Vopros vo Vtoroi Gosudarstvennoi Dume*, SPB 1907. (130)
Golovin,F.A., ' Vospominaniya ', *KA*, vol 19, pp 110-49, vol 58, pp 140-9; continued in *Istoricheskii Arkhiv*, 1959, no 4, pp 136-65; no 5, pp 128-54; no 6, pp 56-81. (131)
Goremykin,M.M., *Agrarnyi Vopros: nekotorye dannye k Obsuzhdeniyu ego v Gosudarstvennoi Dume*, SPB 1907. (132)
Gorn.V., ' Spasiteli Rossii (etyud politicheskoi statistiki) ', *Sovremennyi Mir*, 1908, no 1, pt 2, pp 1-34. (133)
Gorn,V., Mech¹,V. and Cherevanin,N., *Bor¹ba Obshchestvennykh Sil v Russkoi Revolyutsii*, 3 vols, M 1907. (134)
Gribovskii,V.M., *Gosudarstvennoe Ustroistvo i Upravlenie Rossiiskoi Imperii*, Odessa 1912. (135)
Grunt,A., ' Progressivnyi Blok ', *Vop. Ist.*, 1945, nos 3-4, pp 108-17. (136)
Grunt,A.Ya., and Firstova,V.N., *Rossiya v Epokhu Imperializma, 1907-17gg*, M 1960. (137)
Guchkov,A.I., ' Iz Avtobiografii ', *Poslednie Novosti*, 9 August 1936 and subsequent issues. (138)
A.I.Guchkov v 3-ei Gosudarstvennoi Dume (Sbornik rechei), SPB 1912. (139)
Gurko,V.I., *Features and Figures of the Past: Government and Opinion in the Reign of Nicholas II*, Stanford 1939. (140)
Gushka,A.O., *Predstavitel¹nye Organizatsii Torgovo-Promyshlennogo Klassa v Rossii*, SPB 1912. (141)
Haimson,L., ' Social Stability in Urban Russia, 1905-1917 ', *SR*, vol 23 (1964), pp 619-42, and vol 24 (1965), pp 1-22 (this article is followed by a discussion in subsequent articles, to which other scholars contributed). (142)

Harcave,S., *First Blood: the Russian Revolution of 1905*, London 1965. (143)

Hare,R., *Portraits of Russian Personalities between Reform and Revolution*, Oxford 1959. (144)

Harper,S.N., *The New Electoral Law for the Russian Empire*, Chicago 1908. (145)

Helmreich,E.C., *The Diplomacy of the Balkan Wars, 1912-13*, Cambridge, Mass., 1938. (146)

Hodgson,J.H., ' Finland's Position in the Russian Empire, 1905-10 ', *Journal of Central European Affairs*, vol 20 (1960), pp 158-73. (147)

Hoetzsch,C., *Russland: eine Einführung auf Grund seiner Geschichte von 1904 bis 1912*, Berlin 1913. (148)

Hosking,G.A., ' P.A.Stolypin and the Octobrists ', *SEER*, vol 47 (1969), pp 137-60. (149)

Ivanovich,V., *Rossiiskie Partii, Soyuzy i Ligi*, SPB 1906. (150)

Iz Bumag D.F. Trepova, KA, vols 11-12, pp 448-66. (151)

Iz Perepiski P.A. Stolypina c Nikolaem Romanovym, KA, vol 30, pp 80-8. (152)

Izgoev,A.S., *P.A.Stolypin*, M 1912. (153)

' P.A.Stolypin ', *Russkaya Mysl'*, vol 28 (1907), no 12, pp 129-52. (154)

' Zatvory Spushcheny ', *Russkaya Mysl'*, vol 30 (1909), no 4, pp 178-93. (155)

Izvolsky,A.P., *Memoirs*, London 1920. (156)

Jablonowski,H., ' Die russischen Rechtsparteien, 1905-1917 ', *Russlandstudien: Denkschrift für Otto Hoetzsch*, Stuttgart 1957. (157)

' Die Stellungnahme der russischen Parteien zur Aussenpolitik der Regierung von der russisch-englischen Verständigung bis zum ersten Weltkrieg ', *Forschungen zur Osteuropäischen Geschichte*, 1957, pp 60-92. (158)

Jutikkala,E., *A History of Finland*, London 1962. (159)

K Istorii Agrarnoi Reformy Stolypina, KA, vol 17, pp 81-90. (160)

K Istorii Aresta i Suda nad S.D. Fraktsiei 2-oi Gosudarstvennoi Dumy, KA, vol 16, pp 76-117. (161)

V.K., ' I.G. Shcheglovitov: iz Vospominanii ', *Byloe*, no 30 (1925), pp 146-50. (162)

Kadety v 1905-6gg, KA, vol 46, pp 38-68. (163)

Kalinychev,F.I., ' Novye Materialy o Bol'shevistskoi Fraktsii v 4-oi Gosudarstvennoi Dume ', *Vop. Ist.*, 1960, no 2, pp 130-6. (164)

Kaminka,A.I., and Nabokov,V.D., *Vtoraya Gosudarstvennaya Duma*, SPB 1907. (165)

Karpov,N.I., Agrarnaya Politika Stolypina, L 1925. (166)

Karpovich,M., ' Two Types of Russian Liberalism : Maklakov and Milyukov ', in E.Simmonds (ed), *Continuity and Change in Russian and Soviet Thought*, Cambridge, Mass., 1955, pp 129-43. (167)

Katkov,G., *Russia 1917: the February Revolution*, London 1967. (168)

Kaufman,A.A., *Agrarnyi Vopros v Rossii*, M 1908. (169)

' Duma 3-ego iyunya i Ukaz 9-ogo noyabrya ', *Russkaya Mysl'*, vol 30 (1909), no 4, pp 119-57. (170)

Keep,J.L.H., ' Russian Social-Democracy and the First State Duma ', *SEER*, vol 34 (1956), pp 180-99. (171)

Kerensky,A.F., *The Crucifixion of Liberty*, London 1934. (172)

Izdaleka: Sbornik Statei (1920-21), Paris 1922. (173)

The Kerensky Memoirs: Russia and History's Turning-point, London 1966. (174)

Khrushchov,A., *Andrei Ivanovich Shingarev: ego zhizn¹ i deyatel'nost¹*, M 1918. (175)

King,V., ' The Liberal Movement in Russia, 1904-5 ', *SEER*, vol 14 (1935), pp 124-37. (176)

Kizevetter,A., *Na Rubezhe Dvukh Stoletii*, Prague 1929. (177)

Napadki na Partiyu ' Narodnoi Svobody ' i Vozrazheniya na nikh, M 1907. (178)

Klyachko,L.I., *Povesti Proshlogo: Vremenshchiki Konstitutsii*, L 1929. (179)

Kochan,L., *Russia in Revolution, 1890-1918*, London 1966. (180)

Kohn,H., *Panslavism, its History and Ideology*, 2nd, revised edition, New York 1960. (181)

Kokoshkine,F.F.. *Le Conseil des Ministres de Russie et les Affaires Finlandaises*, Helsingfors 1909. (182)

Kokovtsev,V.N., *Iz Moego Proshlogo*, 2 vols, Paris 1933. (183)

Koni,A., *Na zhiznennom Puti*, SPB 1914. (184)

Konstantinopol¹ i Prolivy, KA, vol 6, pp 48-76, and vol 7, pp 32-54. (185)

Korablev,P.N., *Slav¹yanskii S¹¹ezd v Prage 1908g*, SPB 1908. (186)

Korbut,M., *Rabochee Zakonodatel'stvo 3-ei Gosudarstvennoi Dumy*, Kazan¹ 1935. (187)

Korostowetz,W., *Graf Witte, der Steuermann in der Not*, Berlin 1929. (188)

Kotlyarevskii,S.A., *Yuridicheskie Predposylki Russkikh Osnovnykh Zakonov*, M 1912. (189)

Kovalevskii,M.M., *Chem Rossiya obyazana Soyuzu Ob¹¹edinennogo Dvoryanstva?* M 1914. (190)

' Finlyandskii Vopros ', *Vestnik Evropy*, vol 45 (1910), no 1, pp 253-77. (191)

' Sotsial'noe Zakonodatel'stvo Gosudarstvennoi Dumy 3-ego Sozyva ', *Vestnik Evropy*, vol 47 (1912), no 1, pp 202-17. (192)

' Sud¹ba Obshchinnogo Vladeniya v nashei Verkhnei Palate ', *Vestnik Evropy*, vol 45 (1910), no 6, pp 58-81. (193)

' The Upper House in Russia ', *Russian Review*, vol 1 (1912), no 2, pp 60-70. (194)

' Vospominaniya ', *Ist. SSSR*, 1969, no 4, pp 59-79, and no 5, pp 76-100. (195)

' Zemstvo v shesti Guberniyakh Zapadnogo Kraya ', *Vestnik Evropy*, vol 46 (1911), no 6, pp 243-59. (196)

Kramář,K., *Die Russische Krisis*, Munich 1925. (197)

Krasil'nikov,N., *Petr Arkad'evich Stolypin i ego Deyatel'nost¹ v pervoi, vtoroi i tret'ei Gosudarstvennoi Dume*, SPB 1912. (198)

Krechetov,P., *Petr Arkad'evich Stolypin: ego Zhizn¹ i Deyatel'nost¹*, Riga 1910. (199)

Kryzhanovskii,S.E., *Vospominaniya, iz Bumag S.E. Kryzhanovskogo, poslednego Gosudarstvennogo Sekretarya Rossiiskoi Imperii*, Berlin n.d. (200)

Kucherov,S., *Courts, Lawyers and Trials under the last three Tsars*, New York 1953. (201)

Kuplevaskii,N.O., *Istoricheskii Ocherk Preobrazovaniya Gosudarstvennogo Stroya v Tsarstvovanie Nikolaya II*, SPB 1912. (202)

Kurlov,P.G., *Gibel' Imperatorskoi Rossii*, Berlin 1923. (203)

Kuz'min-Karavaev,V.D., *Iz Epokhi Osvoboditel'nogo Dvizheniya*, SPB 1907. (204)

Langer,W.L., ' Russia, the the Straits Question and the Origins of the Balkan League, 1908-12 ', *Political Science Quarterly*, vol 43 (1928), pp 321-63. (205)

Laverychev,V.Ya., *Po tu Storonu Barrikad:iz Istorii Bor'by Moskovskoi Burzhuazii s Revolyutsiei*, M 1967. (206)

' Moskovskie Promyshlenniki v Gody Pervoi Russkoi Revolyutsii ', *Vestnik Moskovskogo Gosudarstvennogo Universiteta (Istoricheskaya Seriya)*, 1964, no 3, pp 37-53. (207).

Lavrinovich,Yu., *Itogi Rossiiskoi Konstitutsii*, SPB 1907. (208)

Lazarevskii,N.I., *Lektsii po Russkomu Gosudarstvennomu Pravu*, SPB 1910. (209)

Russkoe Gosudarstvennoe Pravo, Tom 1: Konstitutsionnoe Pravo, SPB 1913. (210)

Zakonodatel'nye Akty Perekhodnogo Vremeni, 1904-6gg, SPB 1907. (211)

Zakony o Vyborakh v Gosudarstvennuyu Dumu, SPB 1906. (212)

Lenin,V.I., *Polnoe Sobranie Sochinenii*, 5th edition, 55 vols, M 1958-65. (213)

Leontowitsch,V., *Geschichte des Liberalismus in Russland*, Frankfurt-am-Main 1958. (214)

Leroy-Beaulieu,A., *L'Empire des Tsars et les Russes*, 3rd edition, 3 vols, Paris 1893. (215)

The Letters of Tsar Nicholas and Empress Marie, edited by E.J.Bing, London 1937. (216)

Levin,A., *The Reactionary Tradition in the Election Campaign to the Third Duma*, Oklahoma State University publication : Arts and Sciences Studies: Social Studies Series, no 8, Stillwater. Oklahoma, 1963. (217)

The Second Duma, New Haven 1940. (218)

' 3 June 1907, Action and Reaction ', *Essays in Russian History* (a Collection dedicated to George Vernadsky), edited by A.D.Ferguson and A.Levin, Connecticut 1964, pp 231-74. (219)

' Peter Arkad'evich Stolypin: a Political Re-appraisal ', *JMH*, vol 37 (1965), pp 445-63. (220)

' Russian Bureaucratic Opinion in the Wake of the 1905 Revolution ', *JGO*, vol 11 (1963), pp 1-12. (221)

' The Russian Voter in the Elections to the Third Duma ', *SR*, vol 21 (1962), pp 660-77. (222)

' The Shornikova Affair ', *SEER*, vol 21 (1943), pp 1-18. (223)

' The 5th Social Democratic Congress and the Duma ', *JMH*, vol 11 (1939), pp 484-508. (224)

Levinson,M.M., *Gosudarstvennyi Sovet*, Petrograd 1915. (225)

Levitsky,S.L., ' Interpellations according to the Russian Constitution of 1906 ', *Etudes Slaves et Est-Européennes*, vol 1 (1956-7), pp 220-31. (226)

' Legal Consequences of Interpellations in the Russian Duma ', *Etudes Slaves et Est-Européennes*, vol 5 (1961-2), pp 228-40. (227

' Legislative Initiative in the Russian Duma, *ASEER*, vol 15 (1956), pp 313-24. (228)

Lindeman,K., *Obozrenie Deyatel'nosti Tsentral'nogo Komiteta Soyuza 17-ogo oktyabrya v 1910-11gg*, M 1911. (229)

Livshin,Ya.I., ' " Predstavitel'nye " Organizatsii Krupnoi Burzhuazii v Rossii v kontse xix veka i nachale xx veka ', *Ist. SSSR*, 1959, no 2, pp 95-117. (230)

Logachev,V.V., *Sbornik Rechei P.A. Stolypina (1906-11)*, SPB 1911. (231)

Lokot',T.V., *Opravdanie Natsionalizma*, Kiev 1910. (232)

Politicheskie Partii i Gruppy v Gosudarstvennoi Dume, M 1907. (233)

Louis,G., *Les Carnets de Georges Louis*, 2 vols, Paris 1926. (234)

Lyubosh,S.B., *Russkii Fashist: Vladimir Purishkevich*, n.p. 1925. (235)

McNeal,R.H. (ed), *Russia in Transition, 1905-14*, New York 1970. (236)

Maevskii, V.A., *Borets za Blago Rossii: k Stoletiyu so Dnya Rozhdeniya P.A.Stolypina*, Madrid 1962. (237)

Maiskii,B.Yu., ' Stolypinshchina i Konets Stolypina ', *Vop. Ist.*, 1966, no 1, pp 134-44, and no 2, pp 123-40. (238)

Maklakov,V.A., *Iz Vospominanii*, New York 1954. (239)

Pervaya Gosudarstvennaya Duma, Paris 1939. (240)

Vlast' i Obshchestvennost' na Zakate Staroi Rossii, 3 vols, Paris 1936. (241)

Vtoraya Gosudarstvennaya Duma, Paris 1948. (242)

' Iz Proshlogo ', *Sovremennye Zapiski*, nos 38, 40-60 (1929-36). (243)

' Local Justice in Russia ', *Russian Review*, vol 2 (1913), no 4, pp 127-46. (244)

Maklakov,V.A., and Pergament,O.Ya., *Nakaz Gosudarstvennoi Dumy*, SPB 1907. (245)

Mandelstam,A., *La Politique Russe d'Accès à la Mediterranée au XX Siècle*, Paris 1935. (246)

Manuilov,A., 'Agrarian Reform in Russia ', *Russian Review*, vol 1 (1912), no 4, pp 131-49. (247)

Marchand,R., *Les Grands Problèmes de la Politique Intérieure Russe*, Paris 1912. (248)

Maslov,P.P., *Agrarnyi Vopros v Rossii*, 4th edition, 2 vols, SPB 1908. (249)

Massie,R.K., *Nicholas and Alexandra*, London 1968. (250)

May,A.J., *The Hapsburg Monarchy, 1867-1914*, Cambridge, Mass., 1960. (251)

Maynard,J., *Russia in Flux*, London 1943. (252)

Mazour,A.G., *Finland between East and West*, New York 1956. (253)

Mechelin,L.H.S., *Raznoglasiya po Russko-Finlyandskim Voprosam: Kriticheskii Obzor*, SPB 1908. (254)

' 1809-1909 ', *Vestnik Evropy*, vol 44 (1909), no 4, pp 606-20. (255)

Mel'gunov,S.P., *Vospominaniya i Dnevniki*, vol 1, Paris 1964. (256)

Menashe, L. ' " A Liberal with Spurs " : Alexander Guchkov, a Russian Bourgeois in Politics ', *Russian Review*, vol 26 (1967), pp 38-53. (257)

Meyendorff,A., *The Background of the Russian Revolution*, New York 1928. (258)

LIST OF SOURCES 265

'The Working of the Russian Constitution, *Russian Review*, vol 1 (1912), no 2, pp 27-37. (259)

Miege,J. *Russland und die Bosnische Annexionskrise*, Cologne 1933. (260)

Miketov,Ya., *Chto Sdelalo Narodnoe Predstavitel'stvo 3-ego Sozyva*, SPB 1912. (261)

Mikhailov,V.E., *Chto Sdelala 3-ya Gosudarstvennaya Duma dlya Promyshlennosti i Torgovli?* SPB 1912. (262)

Miller,M.S., *The Economic Development of Russia, 1905-14*, London 1926. (263)

Milligan,S., 'The Petrograd Bolsheviks and Social Insurance, 1914-17', *Soviet Studies*, vol 20 (1968-9), pp 369-74. (264)

Milyukov,P.N., *Balkanskii Krizis i Politika A.P. Izvol'skogo*, SPB 1910. (265)

God Bor'by: Publitsisticheskaya Khronika (1905-6), SPB 1907. (266)

Natsional'nyi Vopros:Proiskhozhdenie Natsional'nosti i Natsional'nye Voprosy v Rossii, Prague 1925. (267)

Tri Popytki: k Istorii Russkogo Lzhekonstitutsionalizma, Paris 1921. (268)

Vospominaniya (1859-1917), 2 vols, New York 1955. (269)

'Dnevnik P.N. Milyukova', *KA*, vols 54-5, pp 3-48. (271)

'The Case of the Second Duma', *Contemporary Review*, vol 92 (1907), pp 457-67. (270)

'Politicheskie Partii v Gosudarstvennoi Dume za 5 let', *Ezhegodnik Gazety Rech'*, 1912, pp 77-96. (272)

'Rokovye Gody', *Russkie Zapiski*, vols 3-19. (273)

'Sud nad Kadetskim Liberalizmom', *Sovremennye Zapiski*, vol 41 (1930), pp 348-71. (274)

Milyukov,P., Seignebos,C. and Eisenmann,L., *Histoire de Russie*, 3 vols, Paris 1932-3. (275)

Ministerstvo Vnutrennikh Del, *Vybory v Gosudarstvennuyu Dumu 3-Ego Sozyva: Statisticheskii Otchet Osobogo Deloproizvodstva*, SPB 1911. (276)

Minsky,E.L., *The National Question in the Russian Duma*, published by the Jewish Labour League, 1915. (277)

Mironenko,K.N., 'Manifest 17-ogo oktyabrya 1905g', *Uchenye Zapiski Leningradskogo Gosudarstvennogo Universiteta (Seriya Yuridicheskikh Nauk)*, vol 10 (1958), pp 158-79.

'Sovet Ministrov po Ukazu 19-ogo oktyabrya 1905g, *Uchenye Zapiski Leningradskogo Gosudarstvennogo Universiteta* (Seriya Yuridicheskikh Nauk), vol 1 (1948), pp 348-70. (279)

Moseley,P.E., 'Russian Policy in 1911-12', *JMH*, vol 12 (1940), pp 69-86. (280)

Mosolov,A.A., *Pri Dvore Imperatora*, Riga 1937. (281)

Mosse,W.E., 'Stolypin's Villages', *SEER*, vol 43 (1964-5), pp 257-74. (282)

Mukhanov,A.A., and Nabokov,V.D. (eds), *Pervaya Gosudarstvennaya Duma*, 3 vols, SPB 1907. (283)

Natsionalisty v 3-ei Gosudarstvennoi Dume, SPB 1912. (284)

Naumov,A.N., *Iz Utselevshikh Vospominanii*, 2 vols, New York 1954-5. (285)

Neklyudoff,A., *Diplomatic Reminiscences*, London 1920. (286)

Nelegal'naya Rabota Bol'shevistskoi Fraktsii 4-oi Gosudarstvennoi Dumy, *KA*, vol 77, pp 61-90. (287)

Nicolaevsky,B., *Azeff: the Russian Judas*, London 1934. (288)

Nikolai II, *Dnevnik (1890-1906gg)*, Berlin 1923. (289)

Nikolai Romanov ob Ubiistve Stolypina, KA, vol 35, pp 209-11. (290)

Nikol'skii,B., ' Dnevnik ', *KA*, vol 63, pp 55-97. (291)

Nikonovich,F., *Iz Dnevnika Chlena Gosudarstvennoi Dumy ot Vitebskoi Gubernii*, Vitebsk 1912. (292)

Nisselovich,L.N., *Evreiskii Vopros v 3-ei Gosudarstvennoi Dume*, SPB 1908. (293)

Nol'de,B.E., *Dalekoe i Blizkoe*, Paris 1930. (294)

Ocherki Russkogo Gosudarstvennogo Prava, SPB 1911. (295)

Oberländer,E. and others (eds), *Russia enters the Twentieth Century*, London 1971. (296)

Obninskii,V.P., *Novyi Stroi*, 2 vols, M 1909. (297)

Obshchestvennoe Dvizhenie v Rossii v Nachale XX veka (edited by L. Martov, P.Maslov and A.Potresov), 4 vols, SPB 1909-11. (298)

Okreits,S., 'Audientsiya u P.A. Stolypina i Katastrofa 12-ogo avgusta ', *Istoricheskii Vestnik*, vol 131, pp 864-79. (299)

Ol'denburg,S.S., *Tsartsvovanie Imperatora Nikolaya II*, 3 vols, Belgrade and Munich 1939-48. (300)

Ol'shanskii,N.N., *Chetvertyi Sozyv Gosudarstvennoi Dumy: Portrety, Biografii, Avtografii*, M 1913. (301)

Tretii Sozyv Gosudarstvennoi Dumy:Portrety, Biografii, Avtografii, M 1910. (302)

Ososov,A., *Zemel'nyi Vopros v 3-ei Gosudarstvennoi Dume*, SPB 1912. (303)

Owen,L.A., *The Russian Peasant Movement, 1906-17*, London 1937. (304)

Oznobishin,A.A., *Vospominaniya Chlena 4-oi Gosudarstvennoi Dumy*, Paris 1927. (305)

Paléologue,M., *La Russie des Tsars pendant la Guerre*, 3 vols, Paris 1921-3. (306)

Palme,O., *Die Russische Verfassung*, Berlin 1910. (307)

Pares,B., *The Fall of the Russian Monarchy*, London 1939. (308)

My Russian Memoirs, London 1931. (309)

Russia and Reform, London 1907. (310)

'Alexander Guchkov ', *SEER*, vol 15 (1936), pp 121-34. (311)

' Conversations with Mr Stolypin ', *Russian Review*, vol 2 (1913), no 2, pp 101-10. (312)

' The New Land Settlement in Russia ', *Russian Review*, vol 1 (1912), no 1, pp 56-74. (313)

' The Peterhof Conference ', *Russian Review*, vol 2 (1913), no 4, pp 87-120. (314)

' The Second Duma ', *SEER*, vol 2 (1923), pp 36-55. (315)

Pavlovsky,G.P., *Agricultural Russia on the Eve of the Revolution*, London 1930. (316)

Pazhitnov,K., *Gorodskoe i Zemskoe Samoupravlenie*, SPB 1913. (317)

' " Novyi Kurs " Politiki po Rabochemu Voprosu ', *Vestnik Evropy*, vol 44 (1909), no 3, pp 218-50. (318)

Perepiska N.A. Romanova i P.A. Stolypina, KA, vol 5, pp 102-28. (319)

Perepiska Nikolaya i Aleksandry Romanovykh, Byloe, vol 23 (1924), pp 243-82. (320)

Perepiska Vil'gel'ma II i Nikolaya II, Petrograd 1923. (321)

Pervaya Balkanskaya Voina, KA, vol 15, pp 1-29, and vol 16, pp 3-24. (322)

Petrunkevich,I.I., ' Iz Zapisok obshchestvennogo Deyatelya : Vospominaniya ', *Arkhiv Russkoi Revolyutsii*, vol 21, Berlin 1934. (323)

Pikhno,D.I., *Predstaviteli Zapadnoi Rusi v Gosudarstvennom Sovete*, Kiev 1909. (324)

Pipes,R., *The Formation of the Soviet Union: Communism and Nationalism, 1917-23*, Cambridge, Mass., 1954. (325)

Struve: Liberal on the Left, Cambridge, Mass., 1970 (first volume of an uncompleted biography). (326)

' Max Weber and Russia ', *World Politics*, vol 7 (1955), pp 371-401. (327)

Pis'mo Balasheva k Stolypinu, KA, vol 9, pp 291-4. (328)

Polenov,A.D., *Ob''yasnenie k Programme Soyuza 17-ogo oktyabrya po Krest'yanskomu Voprosu*, M 1907. (329)

Polezhaev,P., *Za shest' let, 1906-12*, SPB 1912. (330)

Polivanov,A.A., *Iz Dnevnikov i Vospominanii po Dolzhnosti Voennogo Ministra i ego Pomoshchnika (1907-16)*, M 1924. (331)

Polner,T.I., *Zhiznennyi Put' Knyazya G.E. L'vova*, Paris 1932. (332)

Polnoe Sobranie Zakonov Rossiiskoi Imperii, Seriya 3-ya, SPB 1885-1916. (333)

Popov,A., ' Diplomaticheskaya Podgotovka Balkanskoi Voiny 1912g ', *KA*, vol 8, pp 3-48; vol 9, pp 3-31; vol 15, pp 1-29. (334)

Posnikov,A.S., 'Agrarnyi Vopros v 3-ei Dume ', *Vestnik Evropy*, 1909, no 1, pp 233-48; 1910, no 1, pp 285-97; 1910, no 9, pp 239-47; 1911, no 2, pp 71-91. (335)

' Politika Razrusheniya v Agrarnom Voprose ', *Vestnik Evropy*, 1908, no 5, pp 243-67. (336)

Preyer,A.D., *Die Russische Agrarreform*, Jena 1914. (337)

Prokopovich,S.M., *Agrarnyi Krizis i Meropriyatiya Pravitel'stva*, M 1912. (338)

Purishkevich,V.M., *Dnevnik Chlena Gosudarstvennoi Dumy V.M. Purishkevicha*, Riga 1924. (339)

Pushkarev,S.G., *Rossiya v XIX veke, 1801-1914*, New York 1956. (340)

Pyatnitskii,N., ' P.A.Stolypin ', *Vozrozhdenie*, vol 117 (1961), pp 52-61. (341)

Radkey,O., *The Elections to the Russian Constituent Assembly of 1917*, Cambridge, Mass., 1950. (342)

Raeff,M., ' The Russian Autocracy and its Officials ', *Harvard Slavic Studies*, Vol 4 (1957), pp 77-91. (343)

' Some Reflections on Russian Liberalism ', *Russian Review*, vol 18 (1959), pp 218-30. (344)

Raukh,G.O., ' Vospominaniya ', *KA*, vol 43, pp 55-91. (346)

Rediger,A.F., ' Iz Zapisok ', *KA*, vol 45, pp 86-111, and vol 60, pp 92-133. (347)

Rein,G.E., *Iz Perezhitogo: Ocherk glavneishikh politicheskikh Techenii v Rossii za poslednie Gody Tsarstvovaniya Nikolaya II*, 2 vols, Berlin 1935. (348)

Rennet,F., ' The Campaign against the Duma ', *Russian Review*, vol 2 (1913), no 3, pp 137-41. (349)

Rennet,F. and Pares,B., ' Onlookers at the Duma ', *Russian Review*, vol 1 (1912), no 3, pp 80-96. (350)

Riha,T., *A Russian European: Paul Milyukov in Russian Politics*, Notre Dame 1969. (351)

' Milyukov and the Progressive Bloc in 1915: a Study in Last-Chance Politics ', *JMH*, vol 32 (1960), pp 16-24. (352)

' Rech¹, Portrait of a Russian Newspaper ', *SR*, vol 22 (1963), pp 663-82. (353)

Robinson,G.T., *Rural Russia under the Old Regime*, New York 1932. (354)

Rodichev,F.I., ' The Liberal Movement in Russia, 1855-1917 ', *SEER*, vol 2 (1923), pp 1-13, 249-62. (355)

Rodzyanko,M.V., ' Gosudarstvennaya Duma i Fevral¹skaya Revolyutsiya 1917g ', *Arkhiv Russkoi Revolyutsii*, vol 6, Berlin 1922. (356)

' Krushenie Imperii: Zapiski Predsedatelya Russkoi Gosudarstvennoi Dumy ', *Arkhiv Russkoi Revolyutsii*, vol 17, Berlin 1926. (357)

' The Third Duma ', *Russian Review*, vol 1 (1912), no 3, pp 11-13. (358)

Rogger,H., ' The Beilis Case: Anti-Semitism and Politics in the Reign of Nicholas II ', *SR*, vol 25 (1966), pp 615-29. (359)

' The Formation of the Russian Right, 1900-1906 ', *California Slavic Studies*, vol 3 (1964), pp 66-94. (360)

' Russia in 1914 ', *Journal of Contemporary History*, vol 1 (1966), no 4, pp 95-119. (361)

' Was there a Russian Fascism? The Union of the Russian People ', *JMH*, vol 36 (1964), pp 398-415. (362)

Roosa,R.A., ' Russian Industrialists look to the Future: Thoughts on Economic Development, 1906-17 ', *Essays in Russian and Soviet History in honour of Geroid Tanquary Robinson*, edited by J.S.Curtiss, Leiden 1963, pp 198-218. (363)

Ropp,A.N., *Chto Sdelala 3-ya Gosudarstvennaya Duma dlya Narodnogo Obrazovaniya?* SPB 1912. (364)

Rozental¹,N.N., *Istoricheskii Ocherk Partii Narodnoi Svobody*, Petrograd 1917. (365)

The Russo-Finnish Conflict (the Russian case as stated by representatives of the Russian Government), London 1910. (366)

Salomon,R., 'Aus den letzten Jahren des russischen Kaisertums ', *Jahrbücher für Kultur und Geschichte der Slaven*, vol 2 (1926), pt 1, pp 9-18. (367)

Samuel,M., *Blood Accusation*, New York 1966. (368)

Savich,G.G., *Novyi Gosudarstvennyi Stroi Rossii*, SPB 1907. (369)

Savickij,N.A., ' P.A.Stolypine ', *Le Monde Slave*, November 1933, pp 227-63; December 1933, pp 360-83; December 1934, pp 378-403; April 1935, pp 41-61; March 1936, pp 341-81. (370)

Sazonov,S.D., *Vospominaniya*, Paris 1927. (371)

Schapiro,L., ' The Vekhi Group and the Mystique of Revolution ', *SEER*, vol 34 (1955), pp 56-76. (372)

Scheibert,P., ' Uber den Liberalismus in Russland ', *JGO*, vol 7 (1959), pp 34-48. (373)

Sef,S.E., *Burzhuaziya v 1905g*, M 1927. (374)

Seletskii,V.N., ' Obrazovanie Partii Progressistov ', *Vestnik Moskovskogo Gosudarstvennogo Universiteta* (Istoricheskaya Seriya), 1970, no 5, pp 33-48. (375)

Semennikov,V.P., *Nikolai II i Velikie Knyaz'ya*, Moscow–Leningrad 1925. (376)

Semenov,N., ' Svetloi Pamyati P.A. Stolypina ', *Vozrozhdenie*, vol 118 (1961), pp 79-100. (377)

Seraphim,E., ' Zar Nikolaus und Graf Witte : eine historisch-politische Studie ', *Historische Zeitschrift*, no 161 (1940), pp 277-308. (378)

Sergeevskii,N.D., *Zaprosy po Finlyandskomu Upravleniyu v Gosudarstvennoi Dume*, SPB 1908. (379)

Seton-Watson,H., *The Decline of Imperial Russia*, London 1952. (380)
The Russian Empire, 1801-1917, Oxford 1967. (381)

S''ezd Progressistov: 11, 12 i 13 noyabrya 1912g, SPB 1913. (382)

Shakovskoi,D., ' Soyuz Osvobozhdeniya ', *Zarnitsy*, 1909, Sbornik 2. (383)

Shakhovskoi,V.N., *Sic Transit Gloria Mundi, Paris* 1952. (384)

Shatsillo,K.F., *Russkii Imperializm i Razvitie Flota*, M 1968. (385)

Shelokhaev,V.V., 'Agrarnaya Programma Kadetov v Pervoi Russkoi Revolyutsii ', *Ist. Zap.*, vol 86, pp 172-230. (386)

Shidlovskii,S.I., *Vospominaniya*, 2 vols, Berlin n.d. (387)
' Imperial Duma and Land Settlement ', *Russian Review*, vol 1 (1912), no 1, pp 18-26. (388)

Shingarev,A.I., *Melkaya Zemskaya Edinitsa*, M 1917. (389)

Shipov,D.N., *Vospominaniya i Dumy o Perezhitom*, M 1918. (390)

Shtil'man,G., *Vneparlamentskoe Zakonodatel'stvo v Konstitutsionnoi Rossii (Stat'ya 87 Osnovnykh Zakonov)*, SPB 1908. (391)

Shul'gin,V.V., *Dni*, L 1927 edition. (392)
Vybornoe Zemstvo v Zapadnom Krae, Kiev 1909. (393)
' Glavy iz knigi " Gody " ', *Ist. SSSR*, 1966, no 6, pp 65-91, and 1967, no 1, pp 123-59. (394)

Shvanebakh,I.Kh., ' Zapiski Sanovnika ', *Golos Minuvshego*, 1918, nos 1-3, pp 115-38. (395)

Shvarts,S.M., *Sotsial'noe Strakhovanie v Rossii v 1917-1919gg*, New York 1968. (396)

Sidel'nikov,S.M., *Obrazovanie i Deyatel'nost' Pervoi Gosudarstvennoi Dumy*, M 1962. (397)

Sidorov,A.L., (ed), *Ocherki Istorii SSSR (1907-17gg)*, M 1954. (398)

Simonova,M.S., 'Agrarnaya Politika Samoderzhaviya v 1905g ', *Ist. Zap.*, vol 81, pp 199-215. (399)
' Bor'ba Techenii v Pravitel'stvennom Lagere po Voprosam Agrarnoi Politiki v kontse XIX veka ', *Ist. SSSR*, 1963, no 1, pp 65-82. (440)
' Politika Tsarizma v Krest'yanskom Voprose nakanune Revolyutsii 1905-7gg ', *Ist. Zap.*, vol 75, pp 212-42. (401)

Skriptsyn,V.A., *Bogatyr' mysli, slova i dela: posvyashchaetsya pamyati P.A. Stolypina*, n.p. 1911. (402)

Slepkov,A.N., *Klassovye Protivorechiya v 1-oi Gosudarstvennoi Dume*, Petrograd 1923. (403)

Sliozberg,G.B., *Dorevolyutsionnyi Stroi Rossii*, Paris 1933. (404)

Slonimskii,L.Z., *Konstitutsiya Rossiiskoi Imperii*, SPB 1908. (405)

' Nashi Monarkhisty i ikh Programmy ', *Vestnik Evropy*, vol 42 (1907), no 5, pp 255-72. (406)

Smirnoff,S., ' P.N.Milyukov: Essai de Biographie et Aperçu de son Activité ', *Le Monde Slave*, 1929, no 3, pp 354-72. (407)

Smirnov,A., *Kak proshli Vybory vo 2-uyu Gosudarstvennuyu Dumu*, SPB 1907. (408)

Smith,C.J., *The Russian Struggle for Power, 1914-17: a Study of Russian Foreign Policy during the First World War*, New York 1956. (409)

' Milyukov and the Russian National Question ', *Harvard Slavic Studies*, vol 4 (1957), pp 395-419. (410)

' The Russian Third State Duma : an Analytical Profile ', *Russian Review*, vol 17 (1958), pp 201-10. (411)

Sommer,W., *Die Geschichte Finlands*, Munich 1938. (412)

Soyuz 17-ogo oktyabrya v 1906g, KA, vol 35, pp 151-75, and vol 36, pp 84-121. (413)

Spiridovich,A.I., *Les dernières Années de la Cour de Tsarskoïé Sélo*, 2 vols, Paris 1928. (414)

Stakhovich,A., ' Kholmskii Vopros ', *Russkaya Mysl¹*, vol 32 (1911), no 2, pp 74-95, and no 3, pp 87-105. (415)

Stal¹nyi,V., *Kadety: Partiya Narodnoi Svobody*, Khar¹kov 1929. (416)

Stavrou,T.G., (ed), *Russia under the Last Tsar*, Minneapolis 1969. (417)

Stepanskii,A.D., ' Politicheskie Gruppirovki v Gosudarstvennom Sovete, 1906-7gg ', *Ist. SSSR*, 1965, no 4, pp 49-64. (418)

' Reforma Gosudarstvennogo Soveta v 1906g ', *Trudy Moskovskogo Gosudarstvennogo Istoriko-Arkhivnogo Instituta*, vol 20 (1965), pp 179-211. (419)

P.A.Stolypin i Frantsuzskaya Pressa, KA, vol 32, pp 209-11. (420)

P.A.Stolypin i Smertnaya Kazn¹ v 1908g, KA, vol 19, pp 215-21. (421)

P.A.Stolypin i Sveaborgskoe Vosstanie, KA, vol 49, pp 144-48. (422)

Stolypin,P. and Krivoshein,A., *Poezdka v Sibir¹ i Povolzh¹e*, SPB 1911. (423)

Stolypine,A., *L'Homme du dernier Tsar, Stolypine*, Paris 1931. (424)

P.A.Stolypin, Paris 1927. (425)

Strakhovsky,L.I., ' The Statesmanship of Peter Stolypin : a Re-appraisal ', *SEER*, vol 37 (1959), pp 348-70. (426)

' Stolypin and the Second Duma ', *Canadian Slavonic Papers*, no 6 (1964), pp 3-18. (427)

Struve,P.B., *Idei i Politika v sovremennoi Rossii*, M 1906. (428)

Patriotica: Sbornik statei za 5 let, SPB 1911. (429)

' Velikaya Rossiya: iz Rasmyshlenii o probleme Russkogo Mogushchestva ', *Russkaya Mysl¹*, vol 28 (1908), no 1, pp 143-57. (430)

Suchomlinow,W.A., *Erinnerungen*, Berlin 1924. (431)

Suvorin,A.S., *Dnevnik*, Moscow–Petrograd 1923. (432)

Syromyatnikov,S., ' Reminiscences of Stolypin ', *Russian Review*, vol 1 (1912), no 2, pp 71-88. (433)

Szeftel,M., ' The Form of the Government of the Russian Empire prior to the Constitutional Reforms of 1905-6 ', *Essays in Russian and Soviet History in honour of Geroid Tanquary Robinson*, edited by J.S.Curtiss, Leiden 1963, pp 105-19. (434)

' Personal Inviolability in the Legislation of the Russian Absolute Monarchy ', *ASEER*, vol 17 (1958), pp 1-24. (435)

Tagantsev,N.S., *Perezhitoe*, Petrograd 1919. (436)

Tager,A.S., *The Decay of Czarism: the Beilis Trial*, Philadelphia 1935. (437)

Tarle,E.V., ' Germanskaya Orientatsiya i P.N. Durnovo v 1914g ', *Byloe*, no 19 (1922), pp 161-76. (438)

Taube,M.A., *La Politique Russe d'Avant-Guerre et la Fin de l'Empire des Tsars*, Paris 1928. (439)

Tcharykov,N.V., *Glimpses of High Politics*, London 1931. (440)

Thaden,E.C., *Conservative Nationalism in 19th Century Russia*, Seattle 1964. (441)

Russia and the Balkan Alliance, 1911-12, Pennsylvania 1965. (442)

Tikhomirov,L., ' Iz Dnevnika ', *KA*, vol 72, pp 120-59. (443)

' Vospominaniya ', *KA*, vol 61, pp 82-128. (444)

Tikhonov,T.I., *Zemstvo v Rossii i na Okrainakh*, SPB 1907. (445)

Tomsinskii,S.G., *Bor'ba Klassov i Partii vo 2-oi Gosudarstvennoi Dume*, M 1924. (446)

Törngren,J.A., *L'Evolution de la Russie pendant les annees 1904-7*, Paris 1914 (translated from the Swedish). (447)

Den Tredje Duman, Stockholm 1912. (448)

Treadgold,D.W., *The Great Siberian Migration*, Princeton 1957. (449)

' The Constitutional Democrats and the Russian Liberal Tradition ', *ASEER*, vol 10 (1951), pp 85-94. (450)

' Was Stolypin in Favour of Kulaks?', *ASEER*,vol 14 (1955), pp 1-14. (451)

Tret'ya Gosudarstvennaya Duma: Materialy dlya Otsenki ee Deyatel'nosti, SPB 1912. (452)

Trudy 1-ogo S''ezda Upolnomochennykh Dvoryanskikh Obshchestv, SPB 1906 (similar titles for all congresses up to the ninth in 1913). (453)

Tsvetkov,A., *Mezhdu dvumya Revolyutsiyami*, M 1957. (454)

Tsytovich,N.M., *Sel'skoe Obshchestvo kak Organ Mestnogo Upravleniya*, Kiev 1911. (455)

Turner,L.C.F., ' The Russian Mobilisation of 1914 ', *Journal of Contemporary History*, vol 3 (1968), pp 65-88. (456)

Tverskoi,P.A., ' K Istoricheskim Materialam o pokoinom P.A. Stolypine ', *Vestnik Evropy*, vol 47 (1912), no 4, pp 183-201. (457)

Tyrkova-Vil'yams,A., *Na Putyakh k Svobode*, New York 1952. (458)

' The Cadet Party ', *Russian Review*, vol 12 (1953), pp 173-86. (459)

' Russian Liberalism ', *Russian Review*, vol 10 (1951), pp 3-14. (460)

Tyumenev,A.I., *Ot Revolyutsii k Revolyutsii*, L 1925. (461)

Tyutryumov,I.M., *Zakon 14 iyunya 1910g*, SPB 1911. (462)

Urusov,S.D., *Memoirs of a Russian Governor*, London 1908. (463)

E.V., *Gosudarstvennaya Deyatel'nost' P.A. Stolypina*, 3 vols, SPB 1909-11. (464)

Vasilevskii,E., *Ideinaya Bor'ba vokrug Stolypinskoi Agrarnoi Reformy*, M 1960. (465)

Vekhi: *Sbornik statei o Russkoi Intelligentsii*, M 1909. (466)

Velikaya Rossiya: *Sbornik statei po Voennym i Obshchestvennym Voprosam*, published by V.P.Ryabushinskii, M 1910. (467)

Velikhov,L., *Sravnitel'naya Tablitsa Russkikh Politicheskikh Partii*, SPB 1906. (468)

Veselovskii,B.B., *Istoriya Zemstva za sorok let*, 4 vols, SPB 1909. (469)

Vinaver,M.M., *Nedavnee: Portrety i Memuary*, Paris 1926. (470)

Vinogradov,P., *Self-Government in Russia*, London 1915. (471)

Vitte,S.Yu., *Samoderzhavie i Zemstvo*, SPB 1908 edition. (472)
Vospominaniya, 3 vols, M 1960 edition. (473)
Zapiska po Krest'yanskomu Delu, SPB 1905. (474)

Vladimirov,A., ' Burzhuaziya mezhdu dvumya Revolyutsiyami ', *Problemy Marksizma*, 1931, nos 8-9. (475)

Vodovozov,V.V., *Kak proizvodyatsya Vybory v Gosudarstvennuyu Dumu po Zakonu 3-ego iyunya 1907g*, SPB 1907. (476)
Sbornik Programm Politicheskikh Partii v Rossii, 5 vols, SPB 1905-6. (477)

Voeikov,V., *S Tsarem i bez Tsarya*, Helsinki 1936. (478)

Voitinskii,V.S., ' Delo S.D. Fraktsii 2-oi Gosudarstvennoi Dumy i Voennaya Organizatsiya ', *Letopisi Revolyutsii*, vol 1, pp 99-125. (479)

Volin,L., *A Century of Russian Agriculture: from Alexander II to Khrushchev*, Cambridge, Mass., 1970. (480)
' Land Tenure and Land Reform in Modern Russia ', *Agricultural History*, vol 27, pp 48-55. (481)

von Dietze,G., *Stolypinsche Agrarreform und Feldgemeinschaft*, Leipzig 1920. (482)

von Laue,T.H., ' The Chances for Liberal Constitutionalism in Russia ', *SR*, vol 24 (1965), pp 34-46. (483)
' Of the Crises in the Russian Polity ', *Essays on Russian and Soviet History in Honour of Geroid Tanquary Robinson*, edited by J.S.Curtiss, Leiden 1963, pp 303-22. (484)
Die Revolution von aussen als erste Phase der russischen Revolution von 1917 ', *JGO*, vol 4 (1956), pp 138-58. (485)

Vorovskii,V., ' Pered Tret'ei Dumoi ', *Sochineniya*, M 1933, vol 3, pp 253-314. (486)

Vyazigin,A.S., *Gololobovskii Intsident: Stranichka is Istorii Nashikh Politicheskikh Partii*, Khar'kov 1909. (487)
V Tumane Smutnykh Dnei, Khar'kov 1908. (488)

Walkin,J., *The Rise of Democracy in Pre-revolutionary Russia*, London 1963. (489)
' Government Controls over the Press in Russia, 1905-14 ', *Russian Review*, vol 13 (1954), pp 203-9. (490)

Walsh,W.B., ' The Composition of the Dumas ', *Russian Review*, vol 8 (1949), pp 111-16. (491)
' Political Parties in the Russian Dumas ', *JMH*, vol 22 (1950), pp 144-50. (492)

Weber,M., ' Russlands Ubergang zum Scheinkonstitutionalismus ', *Archiv für Sozialwissenschaft und Sozialpolitik*, vol 23, pp 165-401. (493)
' Zur Lage der Bürgerlichen Demokratie in Russland ', *Archiv für Sozialwissenschaft und Sozialpolitik*, vol 22, pp 234-353. (494)
Wieth-Knudsen,K.A., *Bauernfragen und Agrarreform in Russland*, Munich 1913. (495)
Wolters,M., *Aussenpolitische Fragen vor der Vierten Duma. Ein Beitrag zur Geschichte des russischen Parteiwesens in der konstitutionellen Monarchie, insbesondere der Stellung zur Aussenpolitik während des ersten Weltkrieges*, Hamburg 1969. (496)
Wuorinen,J.H., *A History of Finland*, New York 1965. (497)
The Rise of Nationalism in Finland, New York 1931. (498)
Yaney,G.L., ' The Concept of the Stolypin Land Reform ', *SR*, vol 23 (1964), pp 215-93. (499)
' Some Aspects of the Imperial Russian Government on the eve of the First World War ', *SEER*, vol 43 (1964), pp 68-90. (500)
Yurskii,G., *Pravye v 3-ei Gosudarstvennoi Dume*, Kharʹkov 1912. (501)
Zaionchkovskii,A.M., ' Vokrug Anneksii Bosnii i Gertsegoviny ', *KA*, vol 10, pp 41-53. (502)
Zalezhskii,V.N., *Monarkhisty*, Kharʹkov 1930. (503)
Zalieskii,V.F., *Chto takoe Soyuz Russkogo Narodo?*, Kazanʹ 1907. (504)
Zaslavskii,D.O., *Rytsarʹ Chernoi Sotni V.V. Shulʹgin*, L 1925. (505)
Zeman,Z.A.B., *The Break-Up of the Habsburg Empire*, London 1961. (506)
Zenʹkovskii,A., *Pravda o Stolypine*, New York 1956. (507)
Znosko-Borovskii,A.A., *Polozhenie o Zemleustroistve*, SPB 1912. (508)
Zvegintsev,A., ' The Duma and Imperial Defence ', *Russian Review*, vol 1 (1912), no 3, pp 49-63. (509)
Zyryanov,P.N., ' Tretʹya Duma i Vopros o Reforme Mestnogo Suda i Volostnogo Upravleniya ', *Ist. SSSR*, 1969, no 6, pp 45-62. (510)

6 BOOKS AND ARTICLES CATEGORISED BY SUBJECT

(i) *Biographies, memoirs, letters, etc.*: 2, 5, 13, 28, 43, 44, 46-9, 52, 57, 77, 86, 89, 90, 102, 103, 114, 117, 124, 125, 128, 131, 138, 140, 151, 156, 162, 172, 174, 175, 177, 183, 184, 188, 195, 200, 203, 216, 234, 235, 239, 243, 250, 256, 257, 266, 268, 269, 271, 273, 281, 285, 286, 289, 291, 292, 294, 301, 302, 305, 306, 311, 320, 321, 323, 326, 331, 332, 339, 345, 347, 348, 351, 356, 357, 371, 376, 378, 384, 387, 390, 392, 394, 395, 407, 414, 431, 432, 436, 443, 444, 458, 463, 470, 473, 478, 505.

(ii) *Stolypin*: 30, 50, 51, 83, 116, 152, 153, 154, 198, 199, 220, 231, 237, 238, 290, 299, 312, 319, 341, 370, 377, 402, 420-2, 424, 425, 426, 427, 433, 457, 464, 507.

(iii) *On the work of the individual Dumas*: 15, 16, 18-23, 25, 42, 55, 56, 63, 70, 78, 80, 81, 91, 92, 104, 118, 119, 121, 133, 139, 149, 161, 165, 171, 187, 192,

Index